Forces Sweethearts

Forces Sweethearts

Service Romances in World War II

ERIC TAYLOR

ROBERT HALE · LONDON

ISBN 0 7090 4196 9

Robert Hale Limited
Clerkenwell House
Clerkenwell Green
London EC1R 0HT

Photoset in North Wales by
Derek Doyle & Associates, Mold, Clwyd.
Printed in Great Britain by
St Edmundsbury Press, Bury St Edmunds, Suffolk
and bound by WBC Bookbinders Ltd.

Contents

Illustrations

Between pages 48 and 49

Between pages 144 and 145

PICTURE CREDITS

Imperial War Museum: 1, 6, 9, 39, 44. Ian Carmichael: 25–6.

Acknowledgements

The information for this book came mostly from servicemen and women whose lives were touched by love in the Second World War. I must here express my sincere gratitude to them for submitting patiently to in-depth interviews and allowing me to ransack their memories during the last two years. Some of these people prefer not to be named, and I have respected their wishes; others have generously allowed me to recount their very personal experiences and have often helped me greatly by supplementing information from interviews with treasured written accounts in the form of diaries, letters, newspaper clippings and personal documentation.

It has not been possible to include all the personal accounts communicated to me but they have all been most valuable in providing colourful context and depth to the other experiences which have been dovetailed into the jigsaw picture of wartime love in its many and varied forms.

To all of these ex-servicemen and women I express again the sincere thanks I have already given privately: Nancy Adams, E.L. Anderson, Mabel Baguley, Ken Barker, Rosemary Barker, Brenda Beeston, Bernice Belfall, Marjorie Bennett, Dorothy Bond, Joy Bone, Sybil Brazell, Pat Bridger, Stuart Brown, Audrey Brownlow, Margaret Bruce, Sadie Burroughs, Jean Campbell, Margaret Camarda, Harry Carling, Ian Carmichael, Louisa Carr, Dennis Castle, Marion Charter, Joan Chatterton, Margaret Clark, Vera Cole, Barbara Collins, Reginald Cooke, Sonia Cooper, T. Cooper, Maureen Cope, Catherine Culbert, Martin Culbert, Margaret Dippnall, Ada Donellan, Myrtle Double, Joan Dunhill, Jean Edge, Edna Ruscoe Ellison, Margaret Ellsby, Derrick Etches, M. Flowers, Dorothy Gledstone, Steve Guinell, Jenny Hamilton, Ronald Hankinson, Joan Hemingway, Terry Hersey, Diana Hess, Ena Hold, B. Homer, Ann Ivy, Monica Jackson, Terry Jackson, Pat James, Peter Jeffrey, Peter Johnson, Helen Jones, Joy King, Jean Kingdon, Ann Kinmond, Eileen Kisby, Betty Koch, Ernest Kohler, Janet Kovac, Diane Lee, Helena Lee, Peggy Linington, H. Lowndes, Stewart McCallum, Edward McAlwain, Sheila McCall, Lena McGaffey, Colin McGregor, Yvonne McIntosh, Jenny McKenzie,

Dorothy Mahoney, Mary Maycock, Ken Marchant, Daniel Militello, Peggy Woolley Millard, Kitty Moore, Ruth Negus, D.M. Nicholson, Ruth Nixon, Violet O'Brien, L. Oiseau, Mary Osborne, Ronald Page, Stanley Palmer, P.M. Parker, Jean Petrie, Ghislaine Perard, Jean Rawles, D.R. Reeves, Rene Robbins, Joyce Rowland, Ada Ryder, Gwen Saull, June Seaton, Dennis Shrives, Margaret Shunkies, Hope Smeaton, Jo Smith, Hilary Stanger Leathes, Kathleen Strom, Catherine Roberts Swauger, Cathie Henderson Taylor, Margaret Taylor, P. Turner, Sylvia Turner, Winifred Vallese, Irma Whiting, Sylvia Whiting, Kathleen Parker Williams, Pamela Winfield, Dora Winter, Pearl D. Witts, Peggy Wooley, Joyce Wright, Marguerite Yates.

I should like to record my gratitude also to all those officials of the Ministry of Defence who have given me of their time, and in particular the Earl of Arran; R.M. Gibbon Conditions of Service Division; and Mervyn Wynne-Jones of the Press Office. I am grateful also for the friendly and efficient assistance of the staff of the Public Record Office, the Imperial War Museum, the National Newspaper Library at Colindale, and the Reference Libraries of Leeds and York for the research facilities they provided.

For access to American 'sweethearts' mentioned in the book I owe a special debt of gratitude to my friend and researcher *par excellence*, Hy Schorr of New York; to Pat Morgan, editor of *Together Again* and Janet Kovac, president of the Transatlantic Brides and Parents Association.

Over the period of two years taken to research and write the book, I have received wise advice and encouragement from my friend, military historian Charles Whiting, for which I am most grateful. I give sincere thanks to Sheila Surgener for her invaluable assistance with research, constructive critical comment and meticulous checking of drafts.

Last, but not least, I owe a considerable debt of gratitude to Ann Milner, who, by burning the midnight oil, produced an immaculate typescript for the publisher with a week to spare before the deadline.

What became increasingly clear as the war went on was that those men and women now separated were not fighting for some abstract idea of patriotism but for the day when they would be together with their sweethearts and wives again.

Senior Army welfare officer

Night Out

Tonight I'd've been out with Suzy,
A kiss and a cuddle for sure.
Back seat at the Ritz,
She's not choosy.
But tonight I'm over the Ruhr.

At the Ritz I'm her Errol Flynn,
Though at first she'd play coy and pure.
But now I've soared to a bigger sin,
In a turret over the Ruhr.

Suzy is soft and warm to hold,
Sighing love that's a cert to endure.
Back of this Lanc I'm alone and cold,
In the mad sky over the Ruhr.
And strangely I hear my Suzy say,
'The boy I loved he just flew away.'

Roy Baum
(By permission of the
Salamander Oasis Trust)

Author's Note

A pathetic letter recently appeared in the *Liverpool Echo* newspaper. It was from a Belgian woman who must now be in her early sixties, and she was appealing for news of a certain Mr Albert Crossland who, she believed, was a doctor in the Liverpool area. To make identification perhaps more positive, the lady added that the man's sister was a concert pianist. The Belgian woman had been Albert Crossland's sweetheart in 1944 and would very much like to meet him again.

It was a story of a 'might-have-been' or, if you like, of what a different life story Albert Crossland might have had if he had married his Belgian sweetheart, who had never forgotten him and still wanted to meet him again forty-five years later.

I know Albert Crossland. He did not reply to the letter – at least, I do not think he did. And so, I suppose, the Belgian woman is still waiting and occasionally recalling those far-off days when she was young and in love with a Royal Army Medical Corps corporal who daydreamed of becoming a doctor and talked about his younger sister, a brilliant pianist for her age.

He did not become a doctor. He became something far less romantic, a plumber. His sister became the organist in a Methodist chapel. But if he had married the Belgian girl …?

The story left me wondering about all the other service romances, not just the 'might-have-beens' but also the romances of men and women who had the courage to make up their minds and take love as it came in that most hostile of environments, war, and despite all the difficulties put in their way.

I too enlisted the help of the press and appealed to ex-servicemen and women of the Second World War for their stories, and they came in their hundreds, by letter, tapes, telephone and personal interviews. My research led me to write this book, which presents a moving selection of the love stories of a cross-section of service sweethearts, from the highest to the humblest in uniform.

For me, as a writer who experienced that war in uniform too, the collating of all those stories was an emotional experience I have been most privileged to have had.

Eric Taylor
York
December 1989

1   Wish Me Luck
As You Wave Me Goodbye ...

Girls from the South and Lassies from the North,
Sisters and sweethearts bustle back and forth.
> Alice Coates, 'The Monstrous Regiment'
> from *Chaos in the Night*, Catherine Reilly

It was coming! By the summer of 1939 no one had any real doubt about that. One day soon they would all wake up to hear the newspaper boys shouting, 'WAR DECLARED!'

It seemed a long time since that previous September evening when a tired, elderly gentleman, Prime Minister Neville Chamberlain, had stepped out of his plane at London's Heston airport, umbrella hooked over one arm, waving his little piece of paper and proclaiming: 'Peace in our time!'

Soon everyone realized that the 1938 Munich Agreement had given Europe no more than a respite, and in the months that followed, tension increased dramatically. The world, and especially sweethearts and wives, waited in suspense for Hitler's next move, and as the year 1938 drew to a close, everyone was left with a general sense of foreboding. It was to grow with each successive month.

In the United States, too, the fearful spectre of war loomed ominously. The goodwill visit of Britain's king and queen that year had done little to allay the fears of ordinary men and women that once again Americans would be dragged into another European conflict. Well-known jockey Daniel Militello, then riding winners all over the States, felt an uneasy qualm about the inexorable advance of Fate. It was a Fate that would put him in the front line, fighting for his country and then in a longer confrontation fighting to bring back his German sweetheart. But for a few months more, for him and everyone in the States, life went on more or less as usual.

In Britain, though, mobilization for war had already begun. Women were being appealed to from all quarters to fill the place of men who had been drafted into the armed forces. The newly formed women's Auxiliary Territorial Service even sent loudspeaker vans round the streets calling for volunteers. Jean Kingdon answered the call at

Winchester. At first she lived at home and travelled daily to the barracks by bus and tram! 'It was so exciting,' she recalls. But she would have been even more excited had she been able to look into the future and see how her service romances would lead to travel beyond her wildest dreams, and to nightmares behind the Iron Curtain, in Czechoslovakia. But then, early in 1939, the very pace of world events was exciting enough for this latest recruit to the ATS, for war was coming.

Margaret Dippnall saw this clearly enough on 20 March 1939. She remembers the date well, for the events of that day were to lead to romance in the Western Desert which would affect the whole of her life thereafter.

> I was wandering through the shopping streets of Hull. It was my half day off and I had little else to do when I spotted a big notice in a shop window. It read: 'The ATS wants more women like you. You'll wear a proud uniform. You'll get a close-up of the war.' Why not?, I thought, and walked straight in.
>
> 'What trade would you like to join?' asked the sergeant.
>
> 'What are you short of?' I replied.
>
> The answer was cooks, and so a cook I became, although I must say I hadn't done much in that line. I suppose what prompted me to join the ATS then was that I hadn't many friends. We had moved from Chatham to Hull and I really had not had the opportunity of making friends with anyone. I thought, 'Here's a chance to broaden my outlook on life and make some friends.' I soon found this to be true when I started training at Walton Barracks. It was great fun!

Though training was fun, it was thorough and taken far more seriously than hitherto. Five days before Margaret joined up and barely six months after the Munich 'peace in our time' agreement, Hitler had brushed aside his promises and occupied the whole of Czechoslovakia. He knew that Britain had not yet rearmed enough to go to war for some little-known mid-European country. He guessed correctly too that France, which also had a friendship pact with Czechoslovakia, would not fight alone. And so, without firing a shot, Hitler captured the valuable Skoda armament factory, the largest in Europe, and almost the whole of the Czechoslovakian Army, 1½ million strong. But not quite all. Thousands of Czech soldiers were destined to come to Britain, to fight with the Allies and to take home British brides such as the new ATS recruit, Jean Kingdon.

It was after the Czechoslovakian crisis that the Italian dictator, Mussolini, sent his troops into Albania. Now the world saw the German–Italian axis in its true colours.

It was about this time that America's ambassador in London, Joseph Kennedy, secretly informed President Roosevelt that a European war might easily break out within a few months, and he began to make arrangements to send his family back home to the comparative safety of the States.[1] There could also have been another reason for packing his family off so soon. His daughter Kathleen had fallen in love with an officer of the Coldstream Guards. He must have been the most eligible bachelor in Britain. He was handsome, fit and the eldest son of the wealthiest family in the country – William Hartington, heir to the Duke of Devonshire's estates. But he was an Anglican, Kathleen a devout Roman Catholic. Both families disapproved of the relationship and hoped it would never lead to anything serious. They were to be proved wrong.

Meanwhile, Kathleen went home, and the usual programme of social events in London went on without her presence. It was 'The Season' – and this year the gaiety was intensified, as if the threat of war brought its own stimulus. The uncertainty of the future drove many sweethearts into hurried marriages.

Typical of the whirlwind courtships and marriages then was that of Randolph Churchill, son of the wartime Prime Minister, and Lady Pamela Digby.[2]

Shortly after the war broke out, Randolph, then a 28-year-old lieutenant in the 4th Hussars, came to London on twenty-four hours' leave. As he pushed his way through the revolving door of the Ritz Hotel, an old friend, Lady Mary Dunn, whirled round the other side. 'Can you have dinner?' he shouted. 'I've got twenty-four hours in town and nothing to do ...' Mary replied firmly that she couldn't, as she was dining elsewhere. 'However, I know someone who might,' she added, 'and I can tell you where to ring her. She's called Pamela Digby, who has just arrived from Dorset and I'm sure you'll like each other.' Randolph snatched the proffered number and rushed to the phone box.

The voice of a young woman answered his call. Randolph asked who she was. She hesitantly replied that she was Pamela Digby. Randolph explained how he had been given her telephone number by Mary Dunn, who had said also that she might like to have dinner with him. And then, almost as an afterthought, he asked the direct question, 'What do you look like?'

Most women of Pamela's age would have been taken aback by such a question but she replied calmly enough, 'Red-headed and rather fat, but Mummy says that puppy fat disappears.' That was enough for Randolph, who asked, 'Will you come out with me to dinner?'

Three days later their engagement was announced. Three weeks later they were married. Their courtship from blind date to altar had lasted less than a month.

Why so much haste? His friends wondered, asked and received various answers. According to Pamela, it was Winston Churchill who urged them to marry immediately, whilst her own family thought they ought to wait. Randolph's explanation was different. Rather ungallantly, he gave it to American writer John Gunther.[3] It was that he must have a son and heir as soon as possible, since he was convinced he would soon be killed in action. The same feeling, that time was running out, affected countless young servicemen.

Fighter pilot Peter Townsend (who hit the headlines in the 1950s through his relationship with Princess Margaret) explained his whirlwind courtship and marriage to his first wife, Rosemary, in these terms: 'Rosemary lived with her parents hard by our airfield at Hunsdon in Hertfordshire. She was twenty, tall and lovely, never more so than that evening we met at a local country house. I could not wait to make her my wife, for life in those dangerous days seemed a brief precious thing. So, true to that wartime phenomenon, the urge to reproduce, we rushed hand in hand to the altar. At the ancient church at Much Hadham, we vowed – alas all too hastily – to be one another's for ever. Exactly nine months later our first child was born.'[4]

And former Wren Joan Dunhill, stationed on the Clyde, remembers how, 'Sailors home after a hazardous Atlantic run were ready to fall for every Wren they danced with. In those days, when you never knew if they would survive, it was all too easy to be swept off your feet to a wedding, with everyone wearing their tiddly suit [best suit] and trying to make the best of a wartime wedding breakfast.'

There was another convincing reason for quick weddings. If you didn't snap up your girl when you had the chance, somebody else might when you were posted abroad. Former Prime Minister Edward Heath has revealed that he was close to marrying a doctor's daughter during the war, but he was sent overseas and she married somebody else.[5]

Harry Lewis, a small, dark and handsome saxophonist playing with the Ambrose Orchestra at London's Park Lane Hotel, also shared the view of many young couples then that there was little point in long courtships and engagements. He knew that he would soon be in uniform, and he was very fond of the new vocalist he always sat alongside in the coach as they travelled the country doing the round of theatres and ballrooms as a break from hotel work. And so it was that one evening, whilst playing at the Brighton Hippodrome, he turned to the pretty young singer he so much admired and simply asked her to marry him. To his relief, she agreed. He was not to know then that within a few months of his donning the uniform of the Royal Air Force the attractive and talented young woman who had so readily accepted his proposal of marriage would be the sweetheart of so many more young servicemen. She would be heading for fame and fortune, establishing herself well and truly as 'The Forces' Sweetheart'.

That young singer was, of course, Vera Lynn. She too felt, that winter of 1939, that there was no point in putting things off. She wrote later:

'We would have preferred to get married within about three months of getting engaged, after all this was wartime, and who knew what sort of future we could expect?'[6] She tells what the immediate future did hold for her fiancé. It had become obvious to everyone in the Ambrose Dance Orchestra that soon every able-bodied man would be called up for military service and that it would probably be better if they took the initiative and chose their form of employment.

'It dawned on several members of the band that if they went in individually they would have no control over where they were sent, whereas if a group of them volunteered, as musicians, they at least stood a chance of remaining together as the nucleus of a working band,' recalled Vera Lynn later.

Consequently eight members of the band, including Harry, went to the RAF recruits depot at Uxbridge and presented themselves ready for enlistment. They were accepted, received the traditional 'king's shilling' (actually 5 shillings at that time) and then, having gone through all the formalities, turned to leave.

'Where do you think you're going?' the sergeant asked them.

The musicians, thinking perhaps that they would later be receiving instructions, explained that they were working that evening in a dance band in London. The sergeant soon disillusioned them: 'You're not. You've had your knife, fork and spoon and the king's shilling, you're all in the RAF now. In!'

Fortunately for these rather naïve young men, the commanding officer was obliging enough to sort things out in a way which pleased everyone. He gave them a week's leave to finish their engagement with Ambrose. 'At one go,' wrote Vera Lynn later, 'Ambrose had lost half his musicians and I had acquired a fiancé in uniform.'

It was a summer for dreaming. A glorious one, almost as if nature were doing its best to compensate for what was to come. Lidos and swimming-pools swarmed with life. In office and factory bronzed faces, reddened chests and mahogany-coloured hands suggested holidays in the tropics rather than in Britain. Those who were old enough might have remembered the similarly marvellous summer of 1914: then, too, people were given a last chance to enjoy themselves and at the end of the day walk hand-in-hand in the glow of a warm evening.

But as the summer drew to an end, an atmosphere of indescribable tension developed. Events moved rapidly towards a climax when, in August, Hitler signed his non-aggression pact with the Soviet Union. He had now secured his eastern frontier, avoiding his greatest fear – fighting a war on two fronts. Britain then knew for certain that war was inevitable. Even the pacific Neville Chamberlain was convinced: 'We are now confronted with the imminent peril of war,' he said.

People began to take heed and prepare for the worst.

ATS volunteer Catherine Culbert and her Territorial Army husband got to work on their house: 'We painted the skylights black, cleared out the rubbish from the cellar and bought three old beds from the secondhand shop to put down there ready for air raids in the night. On all the windows we put strips of sticking-paper to protect ourselves from blast blowing the glass in on us. We bought paste, thick black paper, drawing-pins and yards of black sateen cloth for blacking out the windows. Somehow we never gave a thought to the fact that we might not be living in the house if war came.'

On the last Sunday evening in August, a young BBC news-reader, Robert Dougall, was given a strange assignment. The head of overseas talks came to him and said, 'Bob, this is a terrible thing to do to you, but we want you to put out a last minute appeal to the Germans. It will be at eleven o'clock. You will be speaking as an anonymous Englishman.'[7]

The script for this broadcast was not yet written. Consultations were still going on at the Foreign Office. Then the script had to be translated into German. With only three minutes to spare before the broadcast, Robert Dougall received the first page of the script. He recalls: 'The red light came on and it was up to me. It was an intensely dramatic script and most of the pages were fed to me at the microphone, so I had to get it right first time. God knows I put my heart into it.

'We all felt this might just make the difference. At least it was leaving the Germans in no doubt that Britain had finally taken her stand and that if Hitler went into Poland it would be war.'

On 1 September 1939 Hitler's army marched into Poland, his aircraft crushing almost all resistance. Two days later the British government delivered its ultimatum, telling Hitler to withdraw from Polish territory by 11 a.m., otherwise a state of war would exist between Germany and Britain.

The Second World War had begun.

Or had it? After that first false air raid warning minutes after Chamberlain's 11 a.m. speech, nothing happened. Fighter pilots of 605 Squadron at Tangmere, their aircraft ready and armed, were perplexed. Peter Townsend recalls, 'We lay down in the grass beside our Hurricanes, waiting for the English sky to blacken, as Goering had promised it would, with hordes of his bombers. But only flakey white clouds sailed across the English sky, our sky. The larks trilled their energetic songs, and human voices came floating intermittently across the warm air. Never had I known such peace; it was unthinkable that we were at war.'

An even more peaceful scene was to be found where 609 Fighter Squadron was stationed on a small airfield almost hidden in the lush, undulating Scottish countryside at Drem, close to North Berwick.

There a rather bizarre, childish game was in progress. A curly-brown-haired girl stood facing a hangar wall, her back towards a small group of boys intent on approaching without being 'caught' on the move whenever she turned suddenly – the age-old game of 'Grandmother's Footsteps'. The girl was 16-year-old Jean Edge; the boys, two or three years older, were fighter pilots.

In that golden September weather it was a marvellous day for silly games, for laughter and for love. No thoughts of war or death troubled the minds of these young fliers or the girl. It was great to be alive and in love.

'I was in love with them all,' recalls Jean today. 'My father was an honorary member of the officers' mess, and when the commanding officer had a squadron dinner night, we were invited, and as there was only one married officer in the unit, his wife would sit at one end of the table and I would sit at the other. The chaps moved two places round after each course, so that we all met. Needless to say, I adored them all.'

They were not to know, nor was Jean, that within a few months they would be flying into the shooting war, into the black pall of smoke brooding over the beaches of Dunkirk, into the flash of enemy anti-aircraft guns and the puffs of flak staining the May sky. And of all the fresh, smiling faces Jean loved, only four would return. One of these would be the love of her life. But at Drem, in that September sunshine, all seemed quiet and peaceful.

However, even in Berwickshire people were already on the move. Telegrams had called Army reservists and territorials to the colours. Stuart Brown, an 18-year-old reporter on the *Berwick Advertiser*, was forced to come out of the closet. He had joined the territorials without telling his parents and had hidden his uniform in the reporters' office cupboard. When the mobilization order came, he barely had time to say goodbye to his family and girlfriend before reporting to Berwick Drill Hall.

'I had enlisted,' he said, 'not so much from a sense of patriotism but from the awareness that, at eighteen, national service was looming inescapably and I preferred serving with people I knew ... I was extremely self-conscious of the ancient uniform with its brass-buttoned tunic, soft cap and drainpipe trousers designed for puttees ... I felt embarrassment rather than pride when wearing it and sneaked out to our weekly parades by the quietest streets so that I would meet as few people as possible.'

On 1 September 1939 he was flushed out into the open to report to the headquarters of the Royal Northumberland Fusiliers at Berwick Drill Hall. The war, for Fusilier Brown, had now begun. Fortunately for him, he had no idea just how short his particular war would be.

The mobilization orders for reservists and territorials, though not altogether unexpected, came as a shock to many men. They had enjoyed escaping from family responsibilities and chores for weeks and weekends away on training camps. For townbound men especially, venturing out into the countryside under canvas and in uniform had been the highlight of their lives. And, of course, there was always the possibility of 'having a bit of a fling'. But leaving their loved-ones for an indefinite period of time was a different matter altogether. It was even worse when the wife was also a part-time soldier in the ATS!

Such was the predicament of Catherine and Martin Culbert. Martin was at work in a Newcastle woodyard when the telegram boy with his black bell-boy hat and belted pouch arrived on his red bike to deliver the cryptic message for Martin to report to his barracks.

> I was flabbergasted. I was on my own at the time. You know I had to read that telegram through time and time again to see the date I had to be there. The day after tomorrow! I remember I just gazed down at that plank of wood I was about to cut and didn't know what to do next. There was so little time and so much to do. I had a pencilled list in my pocket, but it all seemed so unimportant now – the garden gate to repair, the house insurance to renew, the rates to pay, and so on. And then there came another horrifying thought that made me tighten up inside so I could hardly breathe. I suddenly realized that, if I had got my call-up papers, what about my wife, Catherine? Would she too be called up? You see, she had joined the auxiliary women's army, the ATS. It had not mattered before if we ever happened to be away on camps at the same time, because my 6-year-old daughter, Jennifer, went next door to her gran's. I felt sick at the thought of it all.

Martin Culbert lost no time in taking leave of his boss and rushed homewards. He packed his small kit, toilet essentials and even a few packets of camomile tea, which he took for his catarrh. Very soon he was making his way along with thousands of others to the railway station. A week later his wife, Catherine, was reporting for duty at her ATS training centre. Jennifer was parked 'for the duration' with her grandmother.

Catherine felt pleased and excited to be walking into the long wooden hut with thirty-five other women for her first pep talk and the 'taking down of particulars'.

On that Monday morning, all the world and his dog seemed to be on the move. In Britain 3½ million people – one in every fourteen of the population – were travelling somewhere.

Soldiers of the regular Army, some 250,000 of them, had already set off for France, by night, from railway-siding sheds and several ports. No bands played them off. No flags waved. The reservists and territorials were reporting to barracks, and thousands of callow conscripts in their cumbersome boots and stiff, ill-fitting khaki battledress uniforms were joining them. Women, most of them still in civilian clothes, were forming three ranks and marching off to the recruitment depot clothing store.

The nation was off to war – a war that would change everyone's life for ever, a war that would be the most destructive in human history. And, moreover, it would be a war, unlike any before, that would separate so many families, husbands and wives, brothers and sisters, and sweethearts.

The first effects of that war were to be seen at railway stations all over Britain as loved-ones said goodbye to each other – some for the last time, others going off to meet a new love altogether.

It must be recognized that not everyone saw the outbreak of war as a personal catastrophe. Many saw it as a way of solving their immediate problems.

Walter Bygraves, the 17-year-old son of battling Tom Smith of Bermondsey, was starting his new job as a carpenter and tea-boy on a building site in the summer of 1939 when he fell off a ladder.[8] He made up his mind that there was no future for him in building, went for a medical examination and three days later received his papers to report to RAF Cardington.

On the first evening new recruits, still in civvies, were sitting in the NAAFI canteen when a sergeant walked on to the stage and blew a short blast on a whistle. He gave instructions about parades they would have to attend the next day and then asked if any of the new arrivals could do a turn to entertain the others. A chap who had sung Gilbert and Sullivan put up his hand, and Walter, with a pint of NAAFI beer inside him, said he could do an impersonation of Max Miller. On to the stage he went, did his party piece and got a great reception. The next day, the new boys in the barrack room, who did not yet know anyone's name, naturally christened Walter 'Max', because of his impression of Max Miller the night before.

So 'Max' Bygraves was born.

After that first stage performance, Max Bygraves started singing with the station band, and one day, when he was walking past the mess hall, a pretty young WAAF called out, 'Were you the chap singing "If I had my way" with the band last night?' She wanted to know the words, and would he write them down for her ... Thus a romance which would last for many decades began. It was all as easy as falling off a ladder.

Another young man who was to become a household name in the entertainment world was wondering what to do at that time.[9] In that summer of 1939 Jimmy Young was living in temporary accommodation, opposite the barracks in Newport. He then had no academic qualifications to speak of, he was not technically minded and there were few jobs open to him. He could see too, as many young men then could, that he had no real prospects in civil life anyway, for soon he would be called up. So, he said to himself, 'Join the Army, Jim.'

No sooner said than done. He packed his kit in an attaché case, walked across the road into the guard-room and said he wanted to join the Army. A friendly sergeant asked him if he had eaten breakfast. He hadn't. 'Well, you'd better come and have some then,' said the sergeant.

Jimmy related how he joined a table of khaki-clad squaddies tucking into two eggs, bacon, toast, and 'enough tea to float a battleship'. After that he returned to the guard-room to sign the forms of attestation. Here his honesty was his undoing. He gave his age as seventeen. The sergeant stood up. 'Sorry, son,' he said, 'You've got to be eighteen to join this army. Hope you enjoyed your breakfast. Good morning!'

Disappointed, Jimmy walked down the hill, turned into the RAF recruiting office, gave his age as eighteen and filled in the forms. No bacon and eggs this time, but for the moment he had solved the problem of what to do with his life. The war was only a few hours old when he was on a train puffing its way to the RAF station at Padgate.

Elsewhere in the bustle of those first few days of the war, Barbara Collins, neat and trim in her new ATS uniform, stood at the platform barrier of Nottingham's railway station watching the milling throng, an aimless swirl of blue, navy blue and khaki. Her eyes were misted, but she was not crying. For the 19-year-old girl, it was all very thrilling to be in a crowd on this second morning of wartime Britain. It was almost like being in a film, unreal and yet real enough when she forced herself to think of what was happening at that very moment. For the first time in her life – but not for the last – she felt rather like a tragic actress. Perhaps she ought to be crying? A guilty thought streaked across her conscience. Was it only Anglo-Saxons who were ashamed of tears and taught from early childhood to hold them back?

She looked hard at the crowd now surging away from her down the platform. Somewhere amongst them was her husband of three weeks, Peter Collins ('Tich' to his joking friends), a pilot officer navigator. He should not be difficult to spot. He was tall and thin and never seemed to walk but to bounce along; a smiling, fair-haired, cherubic schoolboy who looked too young to have anything to do with war at all.

Peter was the only child of parents who had saved every penny to keep him at the local grammar school until he was eighteen. It was at school that he had 'caught the flying bug', when an old boy had come back to talk to the fifth and sixth forms about life in the RAF. From that moment on, all Peter Collins wanted to do was to fly. Thus, in the summer of 1937, with Higher School Certificate exams behind him, he had virtually walked straight out of school and into the Air Force. In every stage of his training he shone, putting one hundred per cent effort into it, finally passing out with glowing reports as a pilot officer navigator.

Peter Collins was not a demonstrative man and did not say much about how he felt. Barbara knew she was falling in love – she would have been half-witted not to know. And it was a very special kind of love, for she knew that here was a man whom she would have to share with his other love – flying.

For six weeks they spent every available day or evening of spare time together: cycling, swimming and walking. It was during one of those walks, along Miller's Dale in Derbyshire, one warm weekend in July '39 that Peter stopped suddenly to admire the view. He turned and said: 'Let's get married.'

A month later they were back on the same rocky track, on honeymoon from their hotel in Bakewell.

There had been time for only one more long weekend together before war broke out. Now Peter was bouncing off down the platform as if he were going on another picnic. And as Barbara stood watching her husband disappear in the crowd, the shattering prospect of what it all meant hit her: indefinite separation.

She had wanted to give him one last long hug and kiss before he passed through the ticket barrier, but officers did not indulge in emotional scenes in public. And it certainly would not have been the proper behaviour for an 'officer and gentleman' to be seen cuddling a woman of the 'Other Ranks'! Why, that would almost amount to 'conduct prejudicial to good order and military discipline'. In the class-ridden British society of that time the orders governing 'officers and other ranks consorting in public' were deliberately vaguely defined so as not to invite criticism from the press, but in practice the customs of the service were rigidly applied by commanding officers. (Except, as we shall shortly see, when the officers' mess waitress was the commanding officer's wife!) So Barbara stayed where she was, at the ticket barrier, hoping to have the opportunity at least for one last wave.

Throngs of women in the uniform of the ATS, WRNS and WAAF were pushing their way through the station crowd now, on to grime-coated platforms, attracting stares from a public not yet used to seeing women in military uniforms. On that September morning the servicewomen looked the model of elegant decorum, neat little curls tucked round their service caps, buttons brightly polished, uniform pressed stylishly. True, some had their skirts just a fraction short of regulation length, and most of them, contrary to regulations, had used a touch of lipstick so that in their blue and khaki uniforms they had lost none of their femininity. Indeed, to many onlookers, the tightly fitting tunic had its own special kind of appeal.

Suddenly Barbara's arm shot high in the air. She had spotted Peter, his body pushing halfway out of a carriage window as he waved frantically. She tried to look cheerful and smile as she waved back but found her eyes full of tears. From further up the platform there came a billowing of steam, porters shouted officiously and slammed doors. And then slowly, ponderously slowly, as if overloaded, and with much fussing of steam and smoke, the long train pulled out of the station.

For a few moments Barbara stayed where she was, staring, wondering. She bit her lip, striving for composure.

A small group of Royal Marines, pushing a railway trolley piled high with kitbags, approached the barrier. They looked very young, fit and perhaps a trifle over-confident and nervously high-spirited, like actors afflicted with stage fright but determined to hide their feelings. Their clean-cut faces were smiling as they sang discordantly:

The Royal Marines are going away
They won't be back for many a day.
They've put all the girls in the family way
To fight for England's glory.

'Mind your body, lady,' said one of the marines, winking at her.

'I *am* minding it,' she told him, causing a laugh among others standing by the woman ticket-collector.

Barbara was surprised at her own quick-witted response. It was not like her at all. As she walked slowly through the station main hall, her words echoed in her head, and she wondered how well, in this new wartime world, she would be able to 'mind her body'.

However, after serving six months in the part-time ATS she had learned to stop asking herself hypothetical questions. The future now was far too uncertain for that. Her civilian life was over. Now it was back to barracks. But it would not be long before she found just how significant had been the morning's experience of waving goodbye to her husband.

At RAF Scampton Peter Collins and his friend Stewart McCallum barely had time to dump their kit and have a wash before being called to briefing.

The station commander's address was short and to the point. The squadrons were to launch the first attack of the war; the target, the German fleet. Destination, Wilhelmshaven.

The station commander then asked that special attention be paid to what he had to say next. It was a directive straight from Air Ministry: 'The greatest care is to be taken not to injure the civilian population. The intention is to destroy the German fleet. *There is no alternative target.*'

It was not emphasized in quite the same way that the German fleet in the Heligoland Bight was so heavily protected by 'flak' ships and fighters that it would soon be known to all Bomber Command as 'the hornet's nest'.

The aircraft were tested, bombs loaded. Crews were dressed and about to get on the trucks taking them to dispersal points when a message came from 'Operations': 'Take-off delayed.' So these young lads – some looked scarcely old enough to shave – lay down in the sun again, sweltering, smoking more heavily, saying little now but thinking perhaps of the loved-ones they were leaving behind. And it was during this extra time that Peter Collins came to an 'arrangement' with his pal, Stewart. They scribbled addresses on bits of paper. Just in case ...

At last the message came. A few women of the WAAF came out of the map room to say goodbye and 'See you tonight!'

Audrey Brownlow remembered: 'That first time was so unreal. It was like saying goodbye to a patient in hospital who is not really expected to recover except by some miracle.'

One by one the bombers took off in a stream of dust. The sound of their engines grew into a shuddering roar that gripped the earth with a vibration felt by all who were watching, until gradually the noise faded into a distant murmur and the normal sounds of a late summer's afternoon could be heard again.

At eleven o'clock the next day, Barbara Collins went into the NAAFI canteen early. It was there you could buy anything a soldier might need, from bootlaces to Brasso, bangers-and-mash, mugs of tea, chips and 'wads' – the NAAFI version of a rock bun with raspberry jam inside. She had managed to get hold of a *Daily Mail* to browse through while drinking her mug of tea. Her eye was caught by a headline: 'THE RAF RAID KIEL CANAL'. It was an exciting report: 'Pilots and crews of the aircraft which took part in the successful attack on the German naval bases of Wilhelmshaven and Brunbuttel, at the entrance to the Kiel Canal, returned to their bases in fine fettle. They were proud to have been chosen to strike the first blow at the German war machine.'

Barbara felt a flush of pride. Perhaps some of Peter's friends were there, she mused. Her eyes skimmed rapidly along the lines of print: 'Weather conditions entirely adverse ... attack pressed home with greatest vigour ... heavy rain ... visibility poor ... they flew low to make sure of hitting their targets ... naval craft and port batteries kept up intense anti-aircraft fire and our bombers were attacked by German fighters ... some of our aircraft failed to return ... '

There was a rough, quick scraping sound of chairs being flung back; the amateur pianist, who picked out a tune with his right hand and hit anywhere with his left, stopped vamping; boots stamped as men adjusted the fold of their battledress trousers neatly over their blancoed gaiters. It was time for drill. Practice for the whole unit ready for a general's inspection.

For the next forty minutes Barbara Collins advanced in review order, in open order, she retired in close order, she advanced in column of route, she saluted to the right and to the front. She stamped and turned to the right and marked time until the muscles running along her shin felt as if they were on fire. Usually, in a curious kind of way, she enjoyed the drill, for she was good at it. She was the 'right marker'. But this morning she was not altogether as smart as usual. She was obscurely worried at the back of her brain. And to the rhythm of the hobnailed boots on the tarmac parade ground there came an echo of the last few innocent-sounding words of the news report: 'Some of our aircraft failed to return.'

Wednesday afternoon always was sports afternoon in the Army and in the Air Force. The war was not allowed to interfere with that routine. Everyone on Barbara's unit was 'encouraged' to take part in some form of physical recreation or alternatively go on a cross-country run or route march. Barbara chose to play badminton.

She was on court in the big gymnasium when she saw the small, rotund figure of the ATS orderly room sergeant approaching purposefully. She never walked as women did: she strutted and hardly ever stopped her strutting without stomping her feet as if coming to attention to address an officer. Her face was red as the setting sun. She stomped on the sideline of the court to attract the players' attention, and called Barbara over.

'You have a visitor to see you. Come to the company office right away.'

Barbara did not even pause to pick up her khaki pullover but trotted off in her plimsolls towards the cluster of wooden huts which housed the company offices. They lay in a slight depression, and as Barbara ran down the pathway, she could see into the orderly room. She had a fleeting glimpse of an Air Force blue cap and jacket. It brought a flicker of joy. She dashed to the door and stepped into the room. The RAF officer turned, and he caught the flash of surprise in her eyes. For a moment they stood looking at each other. It was not Peter.

'Stewart?' she said.

Stewart McCallum had planned what he had to say. He stood up, took a deep breath and cleared his throat nervously. He took another breath to speak and then didn't but instead walked towards Barbara, raising his arms so that his hands held the outside of her shoulders as if holding her in position. She knew at once, as if by instinct, what he had to say. She noted the tremulous quality of his voice. Her spirits sank as his rehearsed words came tumbling out.

'Barbara, there is only one way of saying this. Peter's aircraft went missing on Monday's raid on Kiel. We don't know yet what happened exactly. We might get to know more later, but I wanted to let you know before you got the official telegram from the Air Ministry. We, Peter and I, agreed that ...' Stewart's voice faltered. He felt like a clockwork toy slowly running down. An ATS officer brought a chair from the corner of the room and then retired into an outer office. Barbara sank slowly down on to the hard seat.

'Missing?' she asked.

'Missing. No one saw his aircraft hit or go down. Visibility was awful.'

For a few moments they sat together, hardly speaking, sipping from the mugs of hot tea which a clerk had placed quietly on the grey blanket which covered the table. Barbara shivered in her thin PT vest and hugged herself.

'I'll have to go and change,' she said. 'Let me know if ...' She wiped her eyes, smoothed her hair and walked woodenly to the door.

'I'll keep in close touch,' said Stewart, as the door closed.

Outside the hut, Barbara hunched her shoulders against the cool September breeze and hurried along the concrete pathway, a sensation of fainting weakness trickling through her body. 'Missing.' 'Missing.' 'Missing.' What had happened to Peter? Would she ever see him again? All she wanted to do now was to reach the seclusion of her own empty barrack room. She opened the Nissen hut door and was immediately thankful for the fuggy, smoky warmth coming from the crackling, old-fashioned stove. She flopped heavily on to her narrow bed and buried her face in the pillow. Grief overwhelmed her. Every bone in her body felt weighted down by the most dreadful fatigue, a fatigue that was leaden and stupefying. Poor Peter! He was too young to die. She began to weep, tears streaming down her face unchecked. And as she lay, in a trance-like state, one last memory of Peter returned poignantly. It was a picture of his happy, excited and so lovable face beaming from the carriage window as he waved his last goodbye.

Missing? Dead? It could not be possible. Yet somewhere in the recesses of her mind, in her innermost soul, she knew the worst. But now all she could do was wait.

2 'After You've Gone ...'

The decisive struggle is now upon us. Let no one be mistaken.
It is the issue of life or death for us all.
King George VI's call to his people
24 May 1940

Now wives and sweethearts all over Britain – and some in the United
States – were waiting for news. For although the British Expeditionary
Force in France was small, there was not, it seemed, a family in the
United Kingdom which did not look with fearful anxiety towards
France, where the fighting raged and some loved-one stood between life
and death. They waited for letters which did not come. They waited for
news in the papers. They waited for the BBC's wireless bulletins. But all
they got was news that was vague and contradictory.

They listened to the wireless as they had never listened before – the
nine o'clock news in most households became an institution almost as
sacrosanct as family prayers had once been.

They even listened in the United States. Kathleen Kennedy, the
younger sister of future US President Jack, was worried as she sat in her
Bronxville home knitting a scarf for her much-loved Billy Cavendish,
the young Lord Hartington, who was with the Coldstream Guards in the
BEF. Desperate for news, she wrote to her father, the American
ambassador in London, saying that she had not heard for some time but
that earlier she had received some gloomy letters, written at the Maginot
Line.

'Daddy, *I must know* exactly what has happened to them all. Is Bill all
right?'[1]

Kathleen was most unlikely to receive a reply that would satisfy her
anxiety. At that time no one was saying what was happening to the
British Army in France and Belgium. It was all so terribly depressing. In
fact, Lieutenant Billy Cavendish's Guards battalion was then fighting a
desperate defensive battle on the River Dyle along the Belgian border.
Gallantly they repulsed the most determined attacks but still had to fall
back behind the French frontier. From that point onwards it was a
matter of battling to maintain the shrinking perimeter of the beaches
around Dunkirk, from which they hoped to escape. Such an action was

not without a terrible cost. Two battalions of the Coldstream Guards would lose 444 officers and men killed and wounded before they would finally be taken off those beaches as one of the last units to leave. But the public could not yet be told of the plight in which the BEF found themselves.

On this occasion, Billy Cavendish would get home unscathed to strengthen the bond with Kathleen Kennedy. But not for long.

The same question that Kathleen had put to her father was being asked of one another by wives and sweethearts all over Britain. What *was* happening to their menfolk in France? No one seemed able to tell them. Dreadful rumours went round, sped on their way to some extent by German propaganda broadcasts by American-born, Irish renegade William Joyce, alias 'Lord Haw Haw'. His grating, arrogant, nasal voice with its affected aristocratic accent – 'Jairmany calling, Jairmany calling' – sent shivers of rage and fear down the spines of listeners. Though for the British he was an object of absolute odium, thousands still tuned to his broadcasts from Hamburg every night. It is not surprising that, ill-informed by the British media, they did listen, for they were so anxious and hungry for news, from whatever the source.

On 26 May, though, Britain knew for certain that something awful was happening, for the Archbishop of Canterbury let the cat out of the bag. It was during the usual BBC Sunday evening church service, broadcast to the nation. On this occasion it came from Westminster Abbey and was attended by His Majesty King George VI and a host of other dignitaries, including the new Prime Minister, Winston Churchill.

In the middle of that service the congregation and listeners throughout Britain got a nasty shock. They heard the archbishop pause in his address and then say, in a voice tremulous with emotion, 'Let us now pray for our soldiers in dire peril in France.'

'Dire peril'? That day the BBC news bulletin had merely said: 'British troops have made a strategic withdrawal to previously prepared positions according to plan.' What on earth *was* happening?

The truth was that some 400,000 Allied troops lay pinned against the coast of Flanders near the French port of Dunkirk, hoping for some miracle that would get them safely back home.

The truth was that the British Army in France was beaten, exhausted and sick of fighting, sick of being let down by reluctant allies and sick of their own incompetent generals and of the politicians who had sent them into battle poorly equipped and badly trained.

The truth was that the government, the BBC and newspapers were not giving those anxious sweethearts and wives in Britain the real picture of the war. New legislation had provided the Home Secretary with powers to suppress any newspaper which systematically published matter 'calculated to foment opposition to the progress of the war'.

News editors had their hands tied; they were 'officially guided' by the Ministry of Information, which fed them untruths.

It was hard for those wives and sweethearts who waited. But would it have been any easier if they had known the truth about the chaotic Allied retreat and the catastrophe which loomed ever nearer?

When, in September 1939, the British Expeditionary Force had been sent to France it was more as a gesture of Allied solidarity than as an efficient fighting force. Indeed, General Montgomery in the hindsight of his memoirs was to write: 'The British Army was totally unfit to fight a first class war on the continent of Europe ... In the years preceding the war, no large scale exercises of troops had been held in England for some time. In fact the regular army was unfit to take part in a realistic exercise.'[2] Nevertheless, the troops had gone off to war and settled into their front-line positions in a holiday mood and full of confidence. They had been told by War Minister Hore-Belisha that they were far better equipped than the Germans, whose weaponry was held up to ridicule. And in any case the Allied troops were safe behind the impregnable French Maginot Line fortifications. Or so the newspapers assured the British public.

Wives and sweethearts, it soon seemed, had far more to worry about than what the German Army might do to their menfolk. What were the French and Belgian women doing to them? The men had been over there for months, waiting and amusing themselves. It was 'the Phoney War' or, as the newspapers called it, 'the Bore War'.

Boring it might have been for wives and sweethearts left on their own, coping with the family at home, but it was not particularly boring for the officers and men of Lord Gort's British Expeditionary Force. Tedious at times maybe, especially in the never-ending daytime routine of digging slit trenches and building pillboxes, but at night and at weekends it was a different matter altogether. There was plenty of scope for leisure and luxury living.

Major Reg Cooke, then a sergeant-major in the Northamptonshire Regiment, recalled later: 'You had to be careful not just about what you ate but where you ate and whom you ate with. There were some bars and hotels where women almost threw themselves at you, as if you were a long-lost lover returned from the front, or Clark Gable and Cary Grant rolled into one. We were always a bit suspicious about their amorous advances, feeling these women were likely to be either fifth columnists or paid German agents gathering information. The pillow-talk technique.'

(The term 'fifth columnist' had originated in the Spanish Civil War, when General Mola, advancing on Madrid in 1937 with four columns of rebel troops, claimed that the Francoist supporters within the city were his 'fifth column', ready to undermine the defence from the rear. The

German version of this was that, when advancing into a country with a German-speaking minority (as in the Ardennes, parts of Czechoslovakia and Poland), their forces could rely for help upon Nazi sympathizers among the population. British troops retreating through France found this to be all too true, and French women were always suspect.)

One such woman with seductive charm was remembered by Colonel Ewan Butler and Major Selby Bradford: 'She was a woman with a saturnine face and neat black dress behind the cash desk at the Hotel Moderne in Arras. On the morning of 10 May 1940, she was arrested, tried before a brief court martial, taken out of the courtroom and shot in the moat of the ancient fortress. She was no Mata Hari but paid the same price for treachery as her most celebrated predecessor for purveying information to the German Secret Service.'[3]

Everyone had to be on guard against such women. There were warning notices in most bars, for soldiers to be on guard against talking too freely to women who asked questions.

The possibility of beautiful spies lying in wait for them in bars did nothing to deter British troops from patronizing *estaminets* around Lille and Tourcoing during the Phoney War period. They enjoyed making friends with the local girls and making merry with the local wine, which they liked because, as one of them said, 'It was cheaper and made you drunk quicker than the watery beer back home.' The bars made fortunes, but the local young men were not at all pleased. They resented the patronage of British troops in the same way as some British later resented the American troops, because the foreigners could afford to lure their women away from them. And they used this as propaganda to stir up trouble between the French and the British.[4]

Despite this antagonism of local young men, the plain fact was that soldiers far from home often felt the need for female company, and many of the girls they met in the *estaminets* did become the sweethearts – and then the wives – of servicemen. Language difficulties were soon overcome – as with most problems, love would find a way.

One of the first of these marriages was between Staff Sergeant Gordon Stanley of General Headquarters Signals, stationed at Arras, and Jeanne Michez. After the wedding, in February 1940, Staff Sergeant Stanley was granted a 'sleeping-out' pass. From then on, he was in the felicitous and much-envied situation of living a life of peacetime domesticity.[5]

And so for eight months the British Army lived well and grew soft. As one medical officer reported: 'The three major sicknesses ailing this Army were gastric ulcers, scabies and venereal disease: the result of strange food, strange beds and stranger women.'[6]

One soldier not afflicted in any of these ways was Private Bill Hersey, a storeman of the East Surrey Regiment.[7] Not for him the high life and womanizing. He was happy enough with his favourite diet of fried egg and chips, getting merry on 10 francs' worth of plonk and singing the rousing barrack-room songs. He was a lean, devil-may-care sort of chap, with hair lightened by the hot sun of India, where he had last been stationed, as a regular soldier. His skin was nut-brown and tinged russet-red across his cheekbones from long exposure to the elements. He exuded the virility of ruddy health and had a cleft in his strongly moulded chin – indicative of a stubborn streak. And when he laughed, his whole face seemed to light up.

It was into one of those smaller *estaminets*, the Café L'Epi d'Or, that he rushed for first aid one day. He had been cooking a piece of steak over a makeshift petrol stove which had flared up and burned his hand badly.

'You attend to him, Augusta,' said Papa Six, the *patron*, to his daughter. 'After all, you are the expert now.' She had been attending first aid classes.

Augusta took one look at Bill's inflamed hand, held it over the bar sink and poured ninety per cent neat alcohol over it. Bill jumped as though a thousand volts had been pushed through his body. But he gave his hand back to the girl. He liked the look of her.

So it was that day after day Bill went back to the little Café L'Epi d'Or for treatment and to have the dressing changed. He sat on the bar stool whilst Augusta demonstrated her newly acquired first aid proficiency. He gazed in wonderment, noting every detail of her luxuriant black hair, which was pulled back smoothly and tied with a red polka-dot bow that nestled in the nape of her neck. Her cheeks dimpled when she smiled, and that was often. She had large, bright green eyes set below curling black lashes – captivating eyes, and Bill was caught. Head over heels in love.

All that was in December 1939. For the next few weeks Bill Hersey courted Augusta with all the charm he could muster in his limited French vocabulary. Strangers though they were at first, they took to one another, and a kind of understanding sprang up between them, a sort of compatibility, so that they were curiously at ease with each other. At times, because of the language problem, they would sit together in silence, yet it was a harmonious silence. Brief as their acquaintance was, their intimacy grew rapidly, and from the loving expressions which flooded their faces it was apparent to everyone that here was a couple really in love.

It was not a time for long courtships. Many of Bill's friends had married girls they had known for only a short time before their embarkation leave. That was the accepted way then, and Bill was well aware of the trend. But he was moved towards marriage by reasons different from those of his friends who had married hastily. His turbulent life in the regular army, with many postings, had left him with a strong desire for a life and a home of his own.

But it was not going to be easy.

First there were Augusta's fears to consider. She went through all kinds of emotions about leaving her native land, her friends and family, her close relatives in the village. That had not been easy for her to accept. But the love she had for Bill was far greater, far stronger, than any of those other ties. She knew there would be problems with the priests: she was a Roman Catholic, he a Protestant. There would be problems too with her father, and of course there would be problems with the Army, which positively discouraged men from becoming emotionally involved and taking on the responsibilities of a wife and family. The Army preferred to have aggressive, unattached young men in its ranks.

Neither Bill nor Augusta was going to be put off. One cold February evening, they went to see her father, Papa Paul Six. They did not have to speculate on how they would be received. They knew. Bill went armed with a dictionary and a rock-steady determination. Augusta was the woman he had chosen to start a new, settled life with.

Face to face with the father in the room behind the bar, Bill opened his pocket dictionary and pointed to one word: 'Marriage'. Simply, in the few words of French he had mastered, he then said: '*Votre fille Augusta.*'

Papa Six's eyes opened wide in surprise. A disturbed and disapproving look flashed onto his face, and then he exploded and thumped the table violently to emphasize each word: '*Non! Non! Non! Mille fois non!*' – 'A thousand times no!'

Unwavering in his determination, Bill waited for the man's anger to subside. Calmly he pointed again to the word 'Marriage'.

Papa Six turned to face his daughter. 'He drinks too much cognac,' he shouted.

Augusta's mouth tightened into the resolute line which her father had long recognized. His daughter was blessed with an implacable will, and it overcame any misgivings which she or anyone else might have. In this matter of marriage to Bill, she was determined not to be thwarted. 'Bill will stop drinking,' she said. She then presented all her arguments and expressed in no uncertain terms her determination to go through with the marriage despite anything her father might say or do. After all, she was twenty-one.

It was not a very long meeting. Papa Six knew when he was beaten, especially when Augusta's mother weighed in on her side. At last he conceded defeat, petulantly but positively: 'All right, get married then. But you'll have to sort it out with the Church.'

Now Bill had landed himself with a real problem. Getting married meant obtaining permission from his commanding officer and arranging for all the civil processes. The local priests were not at all helpful. They raised objections. It would take time. And, as everyone now knew, there was no time to spare.

Bill Hersey went to see his company commander, Captain Harry Smith, in whom he had a lot of faith. It was not misplaced. Captain Smith knew how to fight fire with fire. He went personally to see the brigade RC padre and persuaded him to intervene on Bill Hersey's behalf with the local Catholic priests, so that they would drop the objections they were raising. He did. After that there were no administrative delays at all. On 17 April 1940 Bill and Augusta were married.

Three weeks later, on 10 May 1940, the real problem came for BEF soldiers with French wives. After eight long months of waiting, the Second World War began in deadly earnest. Now, as an avalanche of steel and fire rapidly approached the Allied positions, what were men such as Bill Hersey and Gordon Stanley to do?

The day had dawned brightly and Staff Sergeant Stanley had left home much earlier than usual, for there had been a great increase in signals traffic the night before, and so he put in an earlier appearance at his office in Arras. Consequently he was one of the first to know that 'the balloon had gone up' – the German attack was in force. He had time, therefore, before his unit was rushed hurriedly forward into Belgium, to send a message to his wife, Jeanne, telling her to go back as quickly as she could to her mother's *estaminet* in the nearby village of Servins. 'Wait there for me and I'll come back for you when all this is finished,' he wrote.

Jeanne did exactly that. Naturally she was somewhat alarmed then but secure in the knowledge that her mother would welcome her back with open arms. Of course, she was not to know then that this present German attack would drive so many civilians out of their houses to their deaths on the roadside.

On that same 10 May, Bill Hersey just had time to say a brief 'goodbye' to Augusta. He hugged her tightly, smiled somewhat shakily and assured her he would soon come back and take her to Britain when it was all over. Then he was off. His brigade sped sixty miles eastwards into Belgium. They took up defensive positions on the River Dyle, which ran right across the country, cutting it into halves, and so formed a natural defensive position. Then came news from further south: the main German attack was in fact not going to be through Belgium, as in the 1914–18 war, but through the Ardennes, and it soon became clear that the Allied system of defence was altogether wrong. The German General von Rundstedt was thrusting through the hilly Ardennes with forty-four infantry and seven Panzer divisions. The British and Belgian troops to the north were being cut off; their vital supply lines were about to be severed. Soon they would have no ammunition, no food, no means of retreating to the coastal ports.

There was only one course of action the BEF could take: retreat. Bill Hersey and his pals were mystified. They had only just arrived, dug in and repelled a German attack. They were not doing at all badly. Yet they were being ordered to retire!

Retreat was difficult. Roads to the west were jammed with refugee traffic. It was a pitiful stream of humanity that Bill Hersey looked upon. The more fortunate had cars, others had prams heaped with a few possessions, rickety carts, traps, carriages very obviously dug out from some forgotten corner of a stable-yard, wheelbarrows, anything that had wheels. Behind these vehicles came the people, their faces for the most part quite blank with horror. Fear was abroad at all levels, suspicion and distrust were rampant. Riflemen plagued by treacherous fifth columnists had very itchy trigger-fingers. Every man felt he could no longer tell friend from foe. The situation got worse when tales were told of a German SS unit shooting British prisoners of war. British troops were in a mood to retaliate. And they did. No one was safe.

Bill Hersey now began to worry about Augusta. How was she going to manage in all this chaos?

Staff Sergeant Gordon Stanley was at Signals Headquarters, where messages were received from the front covering the withdrawal, and from which orders were transmitted to those units. He too was anxious about his wife. He took matters into his own hands, 'borrowed' a staff car and drove to the *estaminet* in Servins where his wife was staying with her mother. 'The Germans are coming,' he told her. 'We must leave right away!' Jeanne pushed a few clothes into a bag, along with two bottles of rum which her mother had thoughtfully brought, 'in case of emergencies', and within the hour they were off. Jeanne, incongruously dressed in a broad-brimmed blue hat, blue coat and matching blue dress, almost as if she were going to catch a holiday train to Paris, said a hasty farewell to her mother.

They drove away at a good speed, but as soon as they reached the main road they had to slow to a crawl, as they encountered more and more refugees. On one occasion they had to stop because Jeanne's big hat blew off and sailed out of the window. Gordon Stanley, still the perfect gentleman, got out and ran back for it.

That was the wrong moment to be caught at the halt. The first dive-bomber was attacking. For the next two days the Stanleys seemed to spend half their time leaping into ditches, as low-flying aircraft came strafing down the road, and scrambling back into the car again before someone else took it over. By then, the broad-brimmed hat had literally gone with the wind.

After several nerve-racking days and nights of travelling, continually harassed by low-level dive-bombers, Jeanne and Gordon pulled into the small French town of Bailleul and threw themselves upon the mercy of an elderly French woman, Madame Jonkerick. She had seen it all before, twenty years ago, and was sympathetic. No one could have been more compassionate: she fed them well, gave them a warm, soft bed to sleep in for the night and in the morning insisted they eat a good cooked breakfast before venturing out again.

It could have been the contrast between that peaceful night's haven and the hounding by day from the Stukas that brought Gordon to making a decision. He was putting his wife at risk. He turned the car round and drove back to Madame Jonkerick's house. She was not surprised to see them and willingly agreed to Gordon's request for Jeanne to stay there until the roads were clear and she could return safely to her home in Servins.

That afternoon Sergeant Stanley said goodbye to his young wife. His eyes never left her face, as if he were trying to take a mental photograph of all he saw and at the same time give greater assurance to the woman he loved that he really meant what he was about to say: '*I shall come back for you. It will be a month or two. But as soon as I can.*'

Gordon Stanley was an honourable man. He kept his promise, and he did come back. As soon as he could. Not in two months though. It took him five years.

It was at this time, in mid-May 1940, that Bill Hersey had a nightmare vision of his wife's being forced from her house on to roads choked with troops and civilians. Fortunately, the route of retreat which his own brigade was following led towards her café at Tourcoing. He too came to a decision. He must find a way to take her with him.

'Excuse me, sir, my wife's in Tourcoing. How can I get her back to England?'

Captain Smith was not one to be trammelled with red tape at this stage of the war. He gave Bill a short answer: 'Go and get her.'

Bill Hersey, wings on his feet at the thought of seeing Augusta, dashed to the stores where the bikes were kept. The unit was now only two miles from the Café L'Epi d'Or. He jumped on his bike and pedalled as if all the witches and warlocks of the world were after him, speeding through the cobbled, curfewed streets without a thought for military traffic. He was worried in case his unit might move off before he got back with Augusta.

It was 11.30 at night when he hammered on the café door, calling out Augusta's name and his own. The girl herself opened the door.

'Quick! Pack a bag, we're leaving,' he said.

Augusta turned and ran. She woke her mother, dressed and shoved a few essentials into a small bag. At the time Bill was calling, 'Hurry,

hurry, hurry!' And as if to emphasize the need for speed, the unmistakable 'burp burp' of German machine-gun fire could be heard getting nearer with each passing minute. Finally Augusta looked in her purse and left half her money with her mother. Father had not returned yet from a trip to Bordeaux, where he had gone to find a safe place for the family outside the battle zone. Augusta then brought her own bike from a back room, and together they were off, racing as fast as they could to Bill's unit. His fears had been well founded. The unit trucks were already on the move, but Captain Smith was still there.

'Here she is, sir. Now what?'

'Get her kitted up, battledress, trousers, cap, the lot,' he said. 'Then put her in my truck. She can travel with my batman.'

At La Panne, on the coast, Bill's unit and Augusta joined a long queue near the jetty. After an age of waiting they reached the head of the queue. A whaler loomed up from the darkness. They toppled in. Then for an hour they bobbed about, a mile out to sea, waiting to get alongside a destroyer. Augusta was feeling ill, she was exhausted, and it took the last ounce of her energy to climb up the scrambling-net onto the deck. There she collapsed. Bill and another soldier helped her down to the mess deck and made her as comfortable as possible under a table, packed around with soldiers, some of whom were only partly dressed and all in the last stages of exhaustion. Augusta's helmet fell off as she lay back, and her long black hair, previously hidden, fell down. But no one cared enough to comment. They were on their way home. That was all that mattered now.

The word must have got to the ship's captain's ears, however, for when, later that night, the destroyer was edging its way slowly alongside the Admiralty Pier at Dover and the embarkation officer on the quayside could be heard shouting: 'How many aboard?', the captain caused quite a stir as he boomed through his loudspeaker: '599 men *and one woman*.'

They disembarked to a hero's welcome – although they had suffered a tremendous defeat: British Tommies and French *poilus*, the walking wounded and the blood-stained stretcher cases. A miracle was concluding: 338,226 men and more than one woman were being snatched from the claws of the German Army.

As trainloads of weary, dishevelled men pulled into the stations of Waterloo, Victoria and London Bridge, mothers, wives and sweethearts stood clustered hour by hour at the end of the platforms. They scanned each tired face as bedraggled soldiers tumbled out of the carriages and shuffled through the barriers. Many were the tearful reunions, but all too many were the lonely, unrewarded vigils, for 48,000 men had been left in France – dead or prisoners.

Bill and Augusta could not travel together. At the last moment military police hustled Bill onto a troop train bound for a London reception centre. He just had time to scribble his mother's address on a piece of paper and hand it to Augusta before they were separated.

Now there she was, on the quay at Dover, unable to speak a word of English and wondering how on earth she would ever get to the little village of Addlestone in Surrey. She told herself to be patient: once this had been endured, she would be with Bill, and the happy family life they had planned together would begin. It was this hope – that most wonderful of all human feelings – that gave her strength and made every hour of weariness and waiting irrelevant.

Eventually, helped by women in green hats and green sweaters, the WVS, and by the frequent displaying of her marriage certificate, she was put on a train. Throughout the journey she was puzzled by one thing: all the cheering and the flag-waving. These funny English! If this was the way they took a defeat, how would they celebrate a victory? Would she ever be able to understand them? Would she ever be happy in this strange land – which Bill had called her 'Promised Land'? Gradually, though, as the train steamed through the Kent countryside and she looked out of the window at the passing woods, the lush orchards, the neat little farms and the patchwork quilt of green fields where men worked getting in the yellow hay, all fears evaporated. It was a lovely place in which to live. She looked forward then with confidence to building a happy future with Bill, of having a home and the children they had so often talked about.

3 'As Time Goes By'

In times when smiling eyes and lips tell lies,
And only dead men tell no tales, no tales
Casting their last disguise,
Love alone avails.'

John Pudney, 'When Bullets Prove'[1]

The British Army had been saved to fight another day, but France was down and out, the battle for the continent lost. And over forty thousand young men were left over there as prisoners of war. Amongst them was young Stuart Brown, who had joined the Terriers in Berwick and landed in France with the 51st Highland Division on All Fools' Day, 1 April 1940. Now he faced nearly five years as a prisoner of war, and during that time he would lose one sweetheart but win a wife.

Back home in Britain, whilst sweethearts, wives and mothers grieved for the dead and for those prisoners in Germany, the rest of the country settled down to carry on the fight somehow. Churchill assured everyone of this. In a speech announcing the safe return of the British Expeditionary Force, he said: 'We shall go on to the end. We shall defend our island, whatever the cost.'

The cost of that defence was already high. Not only had the Army been mauled but the Air Force too. Fighter Pilot Peter Townsend recalled: 'With one chance of survival in five – not counting the burnt and the wounded – only a handful could come through.'[2] Despite these odds, women dismissed the risk of being widowed within weeks or left with a maimed and disfigured husband, and married their loved-ones whilst they could. That took another kind of courage.

Jean Edge was one of thousands who took the risk: 'At Dunkirk, 609 Squadron was decimated; only four of all the boys I had known at Drem came back. Paul was one of them, and my father said I'd better marry him whilst I still had the chance and before the Battle of Britain began. And so we were married on 7 August 1940, just before the main German attack was launched.'

It had not gone unnoticed that, in the speech about the coming Battle of Britain, Churchill had said: 'We shall carry on the struggle until, in

God's good time, the New World, with all its power and might, steps forth to rescue and liberate the old.'

The New World was already responding. From the United States, despite the Neutrality Acts which forbade US nationals from taking part in foreign wars, the first steady stream of adventurous men was on its way. They were mainly pilots or those eager to train as pilots, who had watched Britain bracing itself for invasion and could no longer stand aloof. Undeterred by threats of being fined $20,000, of serving ten years in prison or even of losing their US citizenship, they were determined to fly and fight in a war which was not their own and to play a full part in the fight against the threatened tyranny of National Socialism.

'What we came for was partly that we couldn't take the Nazis and all that Adolf stands for, partly we couldn't bear to be left out in case we were missing something we'd regret and partly we came for a lark,' said Chris Martin shortly after his arrival in Britain.[3] Sadly, his 'lark' ended in 1944, when he was killed over Friedrichshaven on Lake Constance. But he had already given more than his ration of guts in the fight against the evil of the Hitler regime.

Disguised as travellers, consultants and tourists, these young American fliers had first to cross into Canada and then embark on ships bound for Britain, to join the Royal Air Force Eagle Squadrons. At times they had to lie. They lied about their ages if they were too young, about their educational qualifications and about their pilot training; they 'padded' their flying log books to increase their hours of flying experience; all to ensure acceptance and enrolment. And for what?

Simply for a cause in which they believed. Certainly not for a future in flying. They knew well enough that they were likely to die in air combat – in fact, a third of them did. But they were young men eager to accept the challenge, and they adopted a 'devil-may-care' attitude of 'If it's to be a short life, make it a merry one.' These were men who led the way into a battle in which their homeland would eventually join. They were the Eagle Squadrons – a veritable vanguard of eagles.

To the British they were the lovable 'Yanks', the first of the Yanks to fight the German–Italian Axis, the first to have British sweethearts, the first to have British brides. And the first batch of them arrived at Southampton in the last week of August 1940.

Women in Britain saw them as glamorous symbols of young American courage, skill and dedication. Authorities saw them also in that light, but as a wild bunch too, with little respect for authority. It was perhaps a flaw that was to make the first of the British sweethearts one of the first GI brides and a widow within a few days.

The unfortunate bride was Penny Craven, of the cigarette firm Craven 'A'.[4] She had fallen in love with Eagle pilot Andy Mamehof shortly after he arrived in Britain. Without doubt he was an attractive

young man of irresistible charm. Not only was he tall, dark and
handsome but his chubby face, with a broad, close-cropped moustache,
creased so readily into an engaging smile.

Andy managed to clock fifty valuable operational flying hours before
France collapsed, then he and others had to flee south to Spain and
from there took a boat to Britain. He was welcomed with open arms and
posted to an operational squadron, No. 71, based at Church Fenton,
about eight miles south of York, in September 1940. He was in time to
gain more operational experience in the Battle of Britain.

During the next few months, however, there was still time for Andy
and his colleagues to set a few female hearts a-fluttering. And one was
rather special, Penny Craven. All was going well until Andy got a posting
which meant moving down to Fowlmere, a Fighter Command station
south of Cambridge. In those days, as we have seen already, postings
often sparked off decision-making. Penny and Andy decided to get
married.

The ceremony was to be held at Epping parish church, a matter of
sixty miles south of Andy's station at Fowlmere. But arrangements hit a
snag. All aircrew at Fowlmere were put on 'stand-by'. They could not
leave the station, for they had to be on constant readiness for take-off in
case of a German raid.

Andy and the best man, Vic Bono, had permission to carry on with the
wedding arrangements as planned. It was then that Vic Bono had a
brainwave. So that Andy's colleagues would not miss the wedding
entirely, he thought up a plan that would give the happy couple a
memorable send-off ...

Everything went according to plan. While the wedding reception was
in progress at a local inn, two Hurricanes roared over; as the guests
rushed out, the squadron came thundering in at zero height. 'Never
before had planes flown so low,' recalled the best man, Vic Bono. 'It was
market day in the town. Livestock went berserk, pigs, sheep, poultry
scattered to the four corners of the town. The market-place was
wrecked.'

Protests poured into Fighter Command headquarters. The patience
of senior officers there was already strained to the limit by reports from
other quarters about the Eagle Squadron. 'These reckless young men
don't expect to live out the war and don't give a damn. They're out for
every possible thrill and that usually centres on flying and women!' said
one report.

Yet another report told how one pilot, brandishing a revolver, had
burst into his commanding officer's room in the middle of the night
shouting: 'You've got my Popsy in your bed!' Prudently, with some
restraint, the commanding officer replied: 'Positively not, Sir. You may
look for yourself.'

Another commanding officer, an elderly group captain at Hartlesham, had been making a late-night tour of inspection when he saw an airwoman jump out of his senior pilot's ground-floor window. The irate station commander was not going to stand for any more of this flouting of station standing orders. He banged loudly on the door, intent on having a confrontation with the miscreant. As he did so, another WAAF emerged from the window. The fighter pilot was demoted.

Riotous behaviour could not be tolerated. Fighter Command chose the occasion of the Epping 'beat-up' fly-past to post 133 Squadron from Fowlmere to Northern Ireland, for 'further instruction'.

Unfortunately another kind of storm was brewing just then. A climatic one. High, buffeting winds and torrential rain lashed the airfields of Britain. It was not weather for flying across the Irish Sea, and in any case, Andy Mamehof was about to go on his honeymoon. Nevertheless, the Air Ministry was adamant. The *whole* of 133 Squadron was to report forthwith for further flying training at Egglington, Northern Ireland. And that was that!

So it was that on 8 October 1941, in atrocious weather for flying, fifteen pilots squelched through glutinous mud to their Hurricanes. Water sluiced over the short runway as they took off from Fowlmere. They reached their first fuelling stop at Sealand, near Chester, in less than an hour. The airfield there was just as water-logged and slippery. As soon as they had refuelled, they took off again. Now a gale was gusting. Only six pilots made it to the next planned stop at Andreas in the Isle of Man; three made emergency landings at other airfields, two turned back to Sealand, the other four perished. Amongst them was the bridegroom, Andy Mamehof.

Penny Craven was stunned. She became just another of those sad statistics amongst the thousands of sweethearts who never had the chance to love their husbands properly as a wife.

Coming to terms with the death of a husband, sweetheart or brother was something men and women coped with in a curiously wartime way. Margaret Sherman's experience typified that of others: 'I was in the ATS when I lost my brother, an RAF pilot killed just after his nineteenth birthday. I said at first it was unbearable, but it got better. You never forgot, or lost the pain in your heart, but as time went on you remembered all the happy things – not just that he was killed, and in a way you were glad that his memory could never die, and you were very proud, and the pride wrapped itself around the loneliness and that made it easier.'[5]

Servicemen submerged their feelings in their own peculiar way – particularly the aircrew, as Eagle pilot George Sperry once said: 'Several thousand miles from home, feeling we had a rather questionable future, we indulged in unbridled celebrations and uninhibited acts that gave others the impression that we thought that we owned the whole of England. We saw so many friends die that we developed a defence mechanism against betrayal of emotion and refused to sentimentalize friendship and parting and death. To many, therefore, we seemed to be without loyalty or deep feeling. We trained for air warfare in England during a time of great tension and war nerves, when liquor, carousing and wenching provided an escape from the grim realities.'[6]

One cannot help wondering whether the sweethearts of those young men now look back and realize what a tremendous task they were taking on and what support they really were giving to those men, many of whom had given up hope of ever surviving the war. For let there be no mistake about this: only those who have experienced such horror and fear as they took day after day can know that to give up hope was the only effective way of coming to terms with fear and of sustaining the courage needed for carrying on.

A pilot and medical officer, Wing Commander Roland Winfield DSO, DFC, who flew ninety-eight operational sorties against the enemy with American and RAF squadrons, came to this conclusion: 'It is hope that plagues one's mind, saps one's energy, distracts one's concentration and impairs one's skill. Hope that although operating is dangerous and highly lethal, one will nevertheless return from the next flight.'

US Air Force Lieutenant Chris Martin said almost the same thing: 'It's hope that causes all the trouble – hope that you won't get the chop tonight. What we ought to be thinking about is that death is nothing compared to the time spent in helping to fight the enemy. The moment that hope of personal survival was replaced by pride in doing your job as well as you could was the moment when peace of mind returned.'[7]

In all this mental turmoil, wives and sweethearts had a vital part to play, but in many ways the odds were stacked against the women. Why? Because operational flying made such exacting demands on a man that it provided the bride or sweetheart with a succession of situations that were often incomprehensible to them. Those women who managed to stick it out and keep the bonds of a loving relationship intact were sometimes able to give useful advice to sweethearts with less experience. Somehow they all had to develop that quality of patience that is born of insight and understanding of the problems faced by men confronting the possibility of sudden death every day. This was asking a lot, as Dr Roland Winfield wrote: 'So many of these emotional relationships either took the heart out of the man or left him with a desperately hurt and unhappy wife or sweetheart.'

There was another difficult situation that women had to face too: rivals for their love – the love of flying and the love of sharing danger with good comrades. 'Something grows within the hearts of those who share danger and fear that others never know. It is an understanding and companionship that is stronger and greater than, but different from, that shared by parent and child, brother and sister, and even husband and wife,' wrote Dr Winfield.

The sheer delight and love of flying were particularly strong with fighter pilots. 'We saw things differently. We actually felt a race apart from other aircrew. It affected our attitude to girls. We just didn't want to get involved. We didn't want to be troubled with emotional entanglements we couldn't handle,' said former fighter pilot Steve Guinnell.

Fighter Ace Johnnie Johnson, DSO, DFC, felt that way until he met a beautiful 19-year-old called Paula: 'From time to time our girl friends came to stay in nearby pubs and hotels for the weekend or whenever we held a dance in the mess. For me these were light-hearted affairs and not taken seriously. Anything of that nature, we were firmly resolved, must wait until after the war. But one night at a party in Norwich I met the beautiful Paula Ingate and we began to see a lot of each other. She worked in the Norwich operations room of the Auxiliary Fire Service, and after a month or so we became engaged. I did not possess sufficient spare cash to buy a decent engagement ring, so she managed without one until long after we were married.'[8]

Living with the anxiety for a loved-one in battle on the sea, on land or in the air was something with which so many thousands of sweethearts and wives had to cope, but a far greater problem arose when the man returned home terribly maimed and disfigured.

On 10 May 1940, somewhere in the Belgian Ardennes, an RAF Fairy Battle bomber glided down towards the green fields.[9] Its engine spluttered, flames streamed backwards from the engine, but the pilot, well in control, landed the old aircraft safely in the centre of a field. The fire in the engine, no longer fanned, died down. Suddenly it flared up, fiercely engulfing the pilot's cockpit, flames streaking thirty feet into the air. The air gunner and observer scrambled out of the rear cockpit near the tail, climbed on to the wing and dragged out the pilot, who had become stiffened in the sitting position, a human torch. They pulled him to the ground, rolled him in the long, lush grass to put out the flames and carried him away to safety.

So began the long and painful process through which the burnt and mutilated body of Squadron Leader Bill Simpson was nursed back to life.

For eighteen months, in seven French hospitals, he lay helpless, emaciated and near death. But by 1941 he had recovered sufficiently to be repatriated, by way of Spain and Portugal, to Britain. His legs were stiff and scarred from below each knee up to the groin, his eyelids burnt off, along with the left nostril of his nose. His mouth, cheeks and forehead were ribbed with keloid scars. But worst of all were his hands. No fingers remained on his left hand; badly burnt, they had rotted and then been torn off when dressings were changed. On his right hand only a few stumps remained, but he had not yet been able to move them.

He recalls those first few days back in Britain: 'The outlook for the future seemed very black. I was entirely dependent on other people. I could not even feed myself. At times it seemed to me that I had lost everything – my health, my youth, my career.'

William Simpson was one of thousands of wounded men with sweethearts and wives to face. The women had waved goodbye to fit young men with smartly cropped hair and cheerful, handsome faces, stepping jauntily off to a war that was not of their making. Back to these women were given deformed strangers, badly disfigured, with patchy, lop-sided features created by plastic surgery from bits and pieces taken from various parts of the body, and with hands that would never again caress their bodies in the same way.

The situation presented men with a dilemma, as Bill Simpson recalls: 'What is a man to do when he feels the desire to bestow all the inner floods of affection and love cooped up in his nature on his wife? What is he to do if he is disfigured and maimed and in part helpless? Can he really ask any girl to accept life with him which will involve embarrassment and much self-sacrifice for her? Will he ever find a girl who can love him physically and mentally to the extent he desires and needs, irrespective of his ugliness?'

Yet women worked wonders after the surgeons had finished rebuilding their patients' bodies.

At first it was the nurses who played an important role. 'There is no doubt in my mind that a pretty nurse is a tremendous inspiration to a disfigured patient, particularly in the first few self-conscious months when each glimpse of his reflection in a mirror gives him hell, and often causes him acute embarrassment.'

ATS Corporal Vera Cole and some of her friends found how helpful was the company of women to these young men trying to make their way back into the community:

We were invited to a social evening at the convalescent home, and our instructions were to treat the men as if there was nothing wrong with them. To us they had to be normal fellows enjoying a dance with us.

I well recall the first time we went to the hospital. The door was of glass, and it opened on to a small lobby which in turn opened on to a round hall with a coloured floor and many high glass windows. There, clad in their Air Force uniforms, stood these young men. Remember we were very young, and whilst I was perhaps just a little older than the other girls, my first reaction was to run, because I could not believe the plight of these young men. But I remembered my brother, who had been blown up in the Western Desert and was now suffering from first-degree burns there, and I recalled how my brother-in-law had been shot down in his bomber, badly burnt, and was at that time in a dirty prisoner-of-war camp in Germany. So I gritted my teeth and walked straight up to one of them and began to talk. The other girls followed my example. Soon the scarred hands and faces faded into the background.

If someone like Vera Cole, unrelated to these men, could feel that way, one can imagine the thoughts of a wife or sweetheart approaching the bedside of a loved-one.

This is how it was for the wife of Tom Gleave. His face, hands, arms and legs were badly burnt when a German cannon shell hit the fuel tank of his Hurricane fighter over London in 1940. 'The cockpit,' he recalled, 'was like the centre of a blow lamp nozzle when I baled out.'[10]

After his period of treatment and an emergency operation at Orpington, the nursing sister told him that his wife had arrived at the hospital and would be coming in to see him.

I was well enough to worry about Beryl seeing me as I was. My hands, forehead and legs were encased in dried tannic acid. My face, which felt the size of the proverbial melon, was treated in the same way and I peered through slits in the mask.

I heard her footsteps approaching the bed and then saw my wife standing gazing at me. She flushed a little and said, 'What on earth have you been doing with yourself, darling?'

'Had a row with a German,' I replied.

She tried to smile and sat down by my side. It was not until I saw my face in a mirror weeks later that I realized how brave she had been.

Brave they were indeed. At the beginning of the war it was thought that the best thing to do with badly disfigured servicemen was to tuck them quietly away in a country institution where they would never be seen again and would be spared having to face the world. But very soon this policy was reversed. Meeting people, particularly women, helped men to recover more quickly and take their place in society again.

Pat Bridger, an ATS driver, often drove mutilated men to the limbs-fitting centre at Roehampton and took them for lunch at the Railway Inn near Barnes: 'We had no medical attendant with us, so I had to attend to their needs, cut up their food and collect their cash for the bill. But nine times out of ten some member of the public had already paid the bill. It was always a cheerful occasion, and joking about physical difficulties seemed to help a lot.'

Once they got over their initial shock, women took most of the problems in their stride. Quickly they learnt to see the man behind the expressionless red mask and to make contact with the real character

Morning

A last embrace. The guard has blown his whistle. A soldier
outside the open door of his compartment remains on the
platform for a final kiss. The white line at the edge of the
platform is a guide for travellers in the blackout.

A WAAF driver takes aircrew to their
bomber disposal point.

The last goodbye? Waafs at the end of a Bomber Command runway wishing their sweethearts 'Good luck' and waving them off. Then began the ordeal of waiting for their return. Forty-nine thousand did not come back.

'Wish Me Luck, As You Wave Me Goodbye'

t: Mary Osborne, on left th WAAF friends, Pam, cy, Audrey and Norah, at recambe, 1942. Many of the AAF married aircrew but re widowed shortly erwards.

Jean Edge, WAAF.

Flying Officer Harold Lackland Bevan and his bride-to-be,
Marcelle Lestrange, looking at a ring.

Changing faces. Jean Black Kingdon, whose romance led to a
life behind the 'Iron Curtain'.

Ruth Newall Negus (on extreme left of picture) with ATS members of 576 anti-aircraft battery: Barrie Thomson, Joyce Morris, Mary Snowball, Joy Norval, Mary Shea and Margaret Shenton.

An American sergeant and his English girlfriend watch the bombers returning to the airbase.

Private Bill Hersey and Augusta, the girl from the Café L'Epi d'Or, he brought home via Dunkirk, dressed as a British soldier.

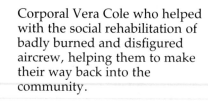

Corporal Vera Cole who helped with the social rehabilitation of badly burned and disfigured aircrew, helping them to make their way back into the community.

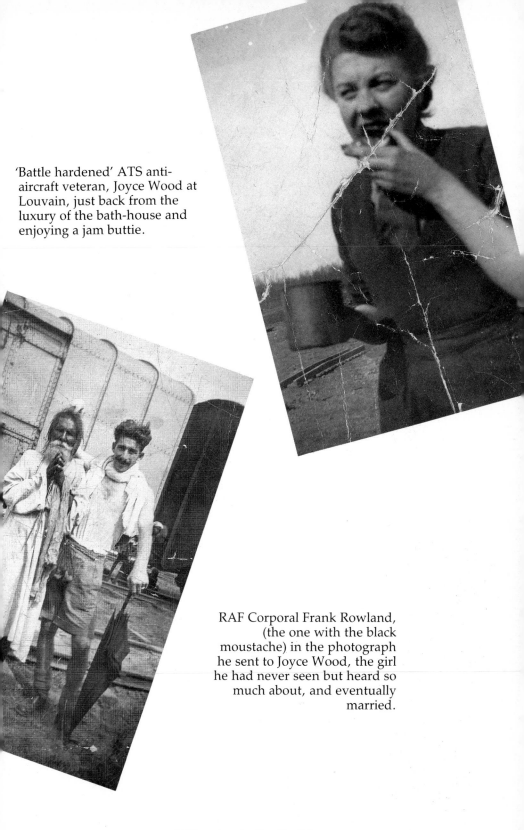

'Battle hardened' ATS anti-aircraft veteran, Joyce Wood at Louvain, just back from the luxury of the bath-house and enjoying a jam buttie.

RAF Corporal Frank Rowland, (the one with the black moustache) in the photograph he sent to Joyce Wood, the girl he had never seen but heard so much about, and eventually married.

Land Army girls and servicewomen invited US Army servicemen to their dances and, in return, received invitations to dances organized by the American Red Cross.

Soldiers of a US Infantry Regiment with ATS girls at a dance in the garrison gymnasium in 1943.

beneath. They learnt to recognize a look in the eyes, a tilt of the head which provided clues to a man's nature and mood.

Many of these mutilated men found that they were able to overcome anything through their faith and spirit, strengthened by the love and understanding of the women who took them back into their arms and their hearts. Together they were able to laugh away gloom and depression. Mary Osborne, who served in the WAAF, recalled how her friend's husband was shot down three weeks after they were married. He was badly wounded, lost his left arm at the shoulder and his left leg below the knee. Together though, they built a new life.

In October 1940 there were other men who were recovering after fighting hard for their country, the men of the free Polish Army.

After Hitler's triumphal entry into Warsaw on 5 October 1940, a new Polish government was set up (first in France and then in Britain) with Raczkiewicz as president and General Sikorski as prime minister. Soon Polish soldiers who had contrived to escape from Poland began to gather in Britain. And what better place was there than Blackpool for a well-earned period of relaxation and regrouping?

Ruth Nixon was there to enjoy it all:

I was evacuated from London to Blackpool with the government department I worked for. As an 18-year-old I could not have had a better time anywhere. Blackpool had the Tower Ballroom, the Winter Gardens, the Palace and Burton's Ballroom to dance in, the ice rink, theatres, cinemas and best of all hundreds of RAF boys – and the Polish Army!

Romances came thick and fast. Most of them were just for a short duration, as most of the RAF were in Blackpool for only a few weeks of their training, though some romances were much more long-lasting.

How romantic it was in those days to have a handsome Polish airman, who could hardly speak a word of English, bowing and clicking his heels before you to invite you to dance, rather than just being grabbed by the elbow and propelled onto the dance floor.

My particular beau was a pilot called Wladek. We couldn't converse much, and on parting he used to say, 'You bin Winter Gardens Friday?' by way of asking for another date.

Eventually he was posted and we wrote to each other for a long time, and then suddenly his letters unaccountably stopped. I never knew why until long after the war. I had settled down to family life, and we had moved to a house near Northolt, and one day I visited the Polish war memorial there and found his name upon it. That was a shock and I really was upset.

When letters unaccountably stopped for another young ATS girl, Brenda Beeston, she feared the worst, but there was a surprising twist to the events of her romance.

It had all started when she was just fifteen, happily walking home with her 21-year-old sister, Eileen, who was then a NAAFI manageress at HMS *Collingwood* Royal Naval barracks. They were chattering away, oblivious of what was going on around them, and stepped off the pavement right in front of a double-decker bus. A hand shot out and dragged Brenda to safety, and the stern, admonishing voice of a sailor said, 'Don't you ever look before crossing the road?'

For a moment Brenda was speechless, thankful for having been pulled back from the very jaws of death but somewhat ruffled nevertheless. 'I was on my dignity, all five foot one of me, black patent shoes and white socks too. So I thanked the sailor and we walked on.' They had not gone very far when they heard the sailor calling out to his friend across the road.

> Before we knew what was happening, two sailors were walking alongside us, saying they would make certain we arrived home safely. Once we reached our garden gate, my 'rescuer', Phil, said, 'We shall wait for you at the end of the lane the evening after next.' He kissed me quickly on the cheek and walked off.
>
> It was a great relief for us to know that my dad, a chief petty officer at HMS *Collingwood* barracks, was not at home to see his daughters being brought home by sailors. He was very strict about what we could and could not do. Mother only laughed when we told her what had happened but said that I could go to meet the sailors again only if Eileen came with me.

For several weeks the two girls met sailors Phil and Ted. They went to the pictures together, danced, walked and talked as only young lovers can. Then came the last evening. Phil was posted for duty with the Atlantic convoys.

Months went by. Letters arrived intermittently. Phil's twenty-first birthday came, and Brenda sent him a silver cigarette-case with cigarettes.

When Brenda was sixteen, she joined the ATS, and after initial training was posted to a heavy anti-aircraft gun site at Gosport. One day a breathless sailor, Phil, rushed into the camp. He wanted to see Brenda before going away on a mission that he knew would take him away for a long time. He left a forwarding address.

After that hectic hour together time went by without any letter, without any communication or word of any kind.

> I convinced myself that he had just taken this way of breaking off our relationship and that he did not really love me. (After all, I was still only sixteen, and at that age you can talk yourself into believing anything.) I took a twenty-four-hour pass one weekend and talked to my mother. She too thought it had just been one of those things – a short romance, and

that I would be best advised to forget all about Phil. So when I got back to camp I sat down and wrote a short letter to Phil at the forwarding address he had left, saying that I was sorry that it had worked out this way and that it would be better if we did not bother with each other any more.

Anyway, by this time I was revelling in Army life and had never enjoyed so much freedom before. Our battery was on the Isle of Wight, so there was plenty of social life. One night though, I was brought down to earth when I came off duty to find a strange-looking bundle on my bed, a soggy, wet bundle tied up with string. They were all letters from Phil, one for every day he had been away.

O ye of little faith! I thought, feeling very upset. I met my sister Eileen that night and told her what had happened. Her response was short and to the point: 'Write and tell him what's happened and why you wrote calling it off.' But I could not do it. I was too proud.

Young Brenda then got on with her work but felt as if something vital had gone out of her life, though she was making the best of what was left. She was taken by surprise one day when, coming off duty, she found a crisp new envelope on her bed. She recognized the writing immediately. It was from Phil. But how had he found her new address? The answer was simple. Eileen had written to him.

Phil's letter from the destroyer HMS *Wild Swan* was short and loving, as Brenda recalls:

All he said was 'Wait until I return and we will sort it out,' so I waited.

It was in June 1942, when I was sitting in the back parlour of Seaview sub-post office, run by the elderly and friendly Briant couple who made us welcome for 'a bite' every Sunday evening, that the shocking announcement came over the nine o'clock wireless news. The Admiralty was sorry to announce the loss of HMS *Wild Swan* ... Of survivors there was no news. No crumb of comfort or hope. After that I telephoned Phil's father every day. Nothing. Days became weeks.

Then, one afternoon when I was on duty in the command post, a telegram came. One of the guard-room orderlies brought it. The capital letters which stared at me from the buff-coloured form read: 'HOME. GET LEAVE. PHIL'.

No one ever moved faster than I did that evening. The major signed a furlough pass, phoned Cosham HQ and arranged for a jeep to take me to the Ryde ferry. I telephoned Phil, saying I would be arriving at High Wycombe. He was there waiting, in survivor's gear, as the train pulled into the platform. Three hours later we were engaged. He had bought the ring that morning. Inside, three words were inscribed: 'That's all settled.'

Brenda Beeston went back to her gun site the following day in a very happy state and blessing the night on which her sister had written to Phil explaining all that had happened with the delayed letters. For Brenda the future looked assured.

It was in June 1941 that another telegram arrived. In wartime no one liked seeing the telegram boy propping his red bike outside the house and walking up the path to the front door. More often than not, the news was tragic. That summer Brenda was away from the gun site, attending a radar course at Waltham Cross. She opened the telegram with fingers that fumbled nervously. The forthright message said, 'GET LEAVE. GETTING MARRIED. PHIL.'

Once again Brenda rushed home. She bought a 'war-gold' ring for 25 shillings, and two days later she and Phil were married at Fareham register office.

'I don't know how my poor mother managed it, but she gave us a roast beef dinner before we set off for London and the Union Jack Club. In the next four days we took in our stride the shows and the bombing – *Arsenic and Old Lace*, Richard Tauber, *Old Chelsea*, *Orchestra Wives*, and *Die Fledermaus*. It was only after our brief leave was over that I learnt how it was that Phil had got leave at short notice. He was bound for the Far East!'

Back in 1940, when Brenda was first grabbed by Phil from the pathway of the oncoming double-decker bus, the eyes of the world were focused on Britain. Hitler's promised invasion had been expected for some time. Indeed, in the United States people seemed more aware of Britain's plight than was the British public itself.

As early as 21 May 1940 Kathleen Kennedy, then safely back home in Bronxville, but with her fiancé in the Coldstream Guards, wrote to her father, America's ambassador in London, expressing the concern generally felt by Americans for Britain: 'At the moment it looks as if the Germans will be in England before you receive this letter. In fact, from reports here they are just about taking over Claridges now. I still keep telling everyone that the British lose battles but win wars.'[11]

The British war cabinet did expect a German invasion at any hour. It was believed that assault landings would be preceded and accompanied by heavy attacks from the air, and consequently anti-aircraft defences were considered to be of prime importance and were to be raised to the highest level of efficiency. Yet – paradoxically, it seemed – fit, trained men were being posted away from these anti-aircraft units to make up the depleted ranks of the front-line infantry regiments. The answer to the manpower shortage in Anti-Aircraft Command was seen to be in the recruitment of more women. A vigorous recruiting drive was set in motion.

Diane Lee, who had enlisted in the ATS in June 1939, was called upon to make her contribution to the campaign in York: 'At that time I was stationed at Northern Command Headquarters in York, and in typical Army fashion I was bamboozled/cajoled/ordered to go on stage of the Theatre Royal and make a recruiting speech.'

In fairness to her commanders, it must be said that Diane Lee was particularly well suited for that role, for she had been in the ATS since the first day of the war and knew very well from her own experience what sort of life the ATS could offer young women. Furthermore, she was well aware of the dire straits Britain was in following the retreat from Dunkirk. The situation had been made clear to her by the man she would one day marry, Captain Alan Hess, the former BBC motoring correspondent, who had been one of the last to leave France via Brest in June 1940.

'Having had no time to prepare the talk, I opted for playing safe and invoked the Official Secrets Act for reasons of not being too explicit about the work of the ATS. But I did stress the importance of work then being done and about to be done by women entering the service, and I emphasized the fact that more and more women were needed to spare men for front-line roles. It must have sounded reasonably convincing, because I got a blush-making cheer from the audience at the end of my talk.'

She must also have impressed her commanders, because she was commissioned shortly afterwards and spent the next five years as a junior commander in anti-aircraft signals – the only woman in the officers' mess. How did she cope with men's advances? 'I decided to adopt a sisterly role to one and all and develop only platonic friendships, and this worked very well.'

Her fiancé, Alan, perhaps thought that this was asking a lot, for he hitch-hiked back from Washington DC for her twenty-first birthday, which was to be one of the most memorable of her life: 'My presents included a second-hand Smith-Corona portable typewriter, one dozen grapefruit, one dozen pairs of silk stockings and a box of Hershey bars – popular American chocolate. Alan was a cigar addict, and at the end of the evening I had the best present of all. We got engaged. The ring? An Uppman cigar band!'

After all there was a war on, a job to be done, and women were going to play an ever-increasing role in the battles to come. More and more would be needed and all efforts were made to ensure there was never any scandal to reach the newspapers. Women's quarters were strictly out of bounds at all times, and infringements were punished rigorously. Occasionally there were amusing incidents though.

Robert Cowell, then a recruit in the RASC at Aldershot, was on a special parade one day when everyone was surprised to find that an ATS officer accompanied their own CO on his inspection.[12] Two other ATS officers were with her. Slowly the little party walked up and down the lines of men, peering into each face.

'There were only a few who managed to avoid looking guilty. At long last all three identified a tall young soldier as being undoubtedly responsible for the dastardly crime, whatever it was. He was marched off and put on a "252" charge sheet. He was confined to barracks under open arrest, but steadfastly refused to tell us what his "crime" was. Next morning he was up before the CO. The charge was this: Section 40 of the Army Act; conduct prejudicial to good order and military discipline, in that he did walk up and down outside the ATS quarters after lights out, ringing a handbell and shouting the word, "Crumpet".'

Naturally, stories of romantic experiences of servicemen and women gained much from being retold in the barrack-room – like, for example, the one about the night Jenny McKenzie slept with a sailor and an airman. Perfectly true, as Jenny recalls:

I was going on leave from London to Glasgow Central late at night. Trains were always packed and many had to stand in the corridor. At that time trains often had a three-tier luggage rack at the end of each coach. These were made from wooden slats a few inches apart. Being by this time a crafty member of the ATS, I put myself on the middle shelf and pulled my kitbag into place in front of me. The night passed and I slept fitfully but well enough, considering. Then, early next morning, a cigarette was handed up to me through the slats, followed by a lighter. Then a voice from above said: 'I bet you won't tell your mother you slept between a sailor and an airman last night!'

Plenty of stories there might have been, but in fact there were remarkably few instances of ATS personnel sleeping with soldiers, even though they were quartered together on the same camp. 'I never came across an instance all the time that I was working in the unit orderly room,' said Catherine Culbert, 'and I should have known, for I processed all the charge sheets.'

In her first few months in the ATS, Catherine Culbert matured and acquired a measure of polish and self-confidence she had never before possessed. In many subtle ways she was different from the woman who had left home in September 1939. She now saw all too clearly how depressingly restricted her life had been with Martin.

She had married very young, at only seventeen, full of love and hope for the future. They had bought a small terraced house with a patch of garden at the front, big enough to stand a pram in, and within twelve months she was pregnant. When Jennifer was born, they both doted on her: she was a gorgeous girl and never a moment of trouble. She was, though, a luxury they could hardly afford on one wage. Cash was always short; there was never enough left at the end of the week after paying all the bills, for Catherine and Martin to go out and enjoy themselves. It led to arguments.

At twenty-three, after six years of marriage, Catherine was bored with life – even Jennifer had lost much of her first charm. Catherine was sick of cooking, sick of cleaning, sick of the endless washing and ironing. All the love and excitement they had shared was gone. Sadly their happiest times were those they spent away from each other. Martin had his Territorial Army nights and camps; Catherine had her ATS training too, after 1938. The war had added new zest to her life. It had lifted her on to a high she had never experienced before. She relished her responsibilities as orderly room sergeant.

Then came the letter, totally unexpected, from her husband, Martin. The news left her stunned, so that she had to read the letter again, slowly. Martin had been invalided out of the Army.

He had always had trouble with his nose and also suffered with painful sinus problems. Recently he had gone to the medical officer and been sent to a specialist. His lungs were too stiff and inflexible to cope with the tough physical exercise a soldier might be expected to perform. Consequently the medical board had recommended a medical discharge, so that Martin could have treatment in a civilian hospital.

The point of his letter to Catherine was that she should now apply for her release from the ATS, so that she could look after him and also Jennifer, still with her grandparents.

Catherine's world crumbled. She felt as though she had been struck a hard blow across the face, and her legs trembled. Her eyes welled with tears. Holding the letter, she dropped heavily into one of the NAAFI chairs, appalled at the thought of leaving the life she was enjoying so much.

Gradually her composure returned, and it was then that she recognized the fact that she did have a life of her own to consider, as well as those of her husband and daughter. She was then acutely conscious of wanting to break away from the fetters of a past that had prevented her from making a success of her life.

And then she thought: 'Is it too much to ask?'

Her friend, Moira, a cheerful Huddersfield girl, sat down beside her and asked if she'd had bad news. Catherine explained and asked, 'What should I do?'

Moira sipped her tea for a moment or two and then delivered her considered judgement: 'I'd do nothing for the moment. I'm a great believer in the old adage, "When in doubt, do nowt".' She sat silently for a few moments and then said, 'You know, Catherine, relationships never stay exactly the same, and it's nobody's fault necessarily if they change because people change. Problems intrude, create tensions; opportunities come up, and it's not always easy to know when a wife should take an opportunity and when the husband should.' She squeezed Catherine's hand affectionately and said, 'What I should do now is write back to your husband, ask after his health – the usual stuff –

and say you're making enquiries. That'll give you time to come to a decision. Think things through to the end. What will happen if I do this, and what might happen if I do that, sort of thing. Now we'll have another cup of tea and I'll get you a special cake.'

The next day Catherine wrote to the problem page of one of the women's magazines, explained the situation and asked what she should do.

A reply came quickly and personally, instead of being printed in the next edition of the magazine. Catherine did not like it at all. But after she had read it carefully, she knew immediately what she would have to do.

Briefly, the letter said: 'There are difficulties all round aren't there? You were free when you went into the ATS with your husband away in the army and your child safely looked after by your mother. But now you are not so free. You can't deny that your husband has a claim on you and he is perhaps not the same fit man that he was. He needs you and has a right to express his opinion on how your child should be brought up. What does your child feel? Are you sure you wish to have no hand in her development at this time in her life? Would you consider doing some war work other than in the ATS?'

Catherine Culbert pulled out a writing-pad from her handbag and wrote a short letter to her husband. She hoped his painful sinus trouble had cleared up a little, advised him to go and see his own doctor about whether or not he should have an operation. She said it would be better, for the time being, to leave Jennifer with her mother, because she did not want to leave the ATS at this particular time of the war. And even if she did apply, she felt that there would be little chance of her being released because of the 'specialist nature' of her duties (she had taken a course in 'code and cypher' duties by this time). She looked forward to seeing him soon, when she had leave.

The way she saw it, the situation was clear. Naturally she loved Jennifer, was concerned for her well-being and sorely missed seeing her, but at the same time she felt that Jennifer was now far better off than the thousands of other children who had been evacuated from cities away from their parents and were being looked after by complete strangers in the country. At least Jennifer was with a grandmother who adored her and had time to spend with her. Martin could surely look after himself. If not, he would just have to learn. Frankly, she did not want to go back to the old way of life. Ever. She posted the letter with a certain amount of trepidation and went back to her unit lines.

As soon as she opened the door of the hut, she knew something had happened. The other women were in a state of excited chatter. They were gathered round the notice board, where the unit daily routine and general standing orders were posted.

'I'm going. Are you coming with me?' she heard one woman say in a voice that suggested she had just been offered a fortnight's free holiday in a five-star hotel. And that, as it turned out, was not far off the mark either, for at least there was a sunshine cruise involved.

Catherine walked straight to the board. Eyes were focused on a new order, lips moved as they read the small print.

The gist of the order was that an opportunity was offered to ATS personnel to volunteer for employment with the Middle East forces in the trades of cooks, clerks, orderlies and telephonists, and for one or two 'special duties' for which a good knowledge of German or Italian was required.

Suddenly everything seemed clear to Catherine, as she later recalled: 'It was as if the final piece of a jigsaw puzzle had just fallen into place and I could see the whole picture quite clearly. I'm not a fatalist but I've found in life that at critical times things happen, opportunities arise that just fit the situation and you know what to do then. The next day I volunteered for service in the Middle East. It was a chance to get on, and also, as I had already decided to stay in the ATS and not ask for my release, it was a way of making my position a little safer. I remember thinking too of my Dad's old saying: "In for a penny, in for a pound".'

4 'Dancing in the Dark'

> Back on day duty there were dances every night. Tired in the
> mornings, we would decide definitely to have an early night.
> But when the evening came, one of us would say, 'It does
> seem a shame to stop in.' And off we would go.
>
> Sister S.R. Brazell, QAIMNS

Twenty-six-year-old Second Lieutenant Ian Carmichael (looking all of sixteen) was about to join the 22nd Dragoons of the Royal Armoured Corps stationed in the breezy, North Yorkshire fishing port of Whitby.[1]

The newly commissioned Carmichael, who would one day star in a succession of brilliant comedy films such as *Private's Progress, Lucky Jim, Brothers in Law* and *I'm All Right, Jack*, was then a rather shy young man. He was not long out of RADA and had only a short, blissfully carefree life in the professional theatre behind him. It was not surprising that he approached the awesome headquarters of the Dragoon Guards with a good deal of trepidation. He felt even less secure when he reported to the adjutant, who eyed him up and down and said: 'What the hell are you wearing?'

Apparently Carmichael's tailor at Camberley had not got one item of his uniform correct. This young man's feelings can easily be imagined that evening when he assembled in the ante-room of the officers' mess with the regular officers of the two long-established cavalry regiments, the Royal Dragoon Guards and the Royal Inniskilling Dragoon Guards, brought together to form the 22nd Dragoons. Here was the new boy, from a comfortable middle-class home, 'improperly dressed' and having to cope with snobbery in its most nerve-shattering form.

He recalled that terrible first night: 'Most of the senior officers wore "blues", clanked about in spurs, referred to girls as "fillies", drank large "pinks" and kept saying, "Don'tcha know" with monotonous regularity.'

It was not the way to make anyone feel at home, but it was often the way in which senior officers treated young, newly commissioned subalterns coming into regular regiments. For example, sometime Foreign Secretary of HM Government Lord Carrington, who began his distinguished military career with the Grenadier Guards, later recalled with horror his first lonely months with his fellow officers:

'It was the custom of the Grenadiers to make newly joined second Lieutenants sharply aware of their insignificance, to induce humility and knock out any thoughts of grandeur upon joining such a distinguished regiment. The salient method was not to talk to him and so they behaved as though he wasn't there. This was the system and it generally went on for some months, three in my case. I went into the officers' mess and not a word was spoken, no glance of awareness that I even existed. For me to have said, "Good morning" would have been regarded as insufferable impertinence. It certainly induced a feeling of loneliness.'[2]

The customs of the service could be surprisingly hard on young officers with regular regiments. Even when Lord Carrington had reached the rank of captain, he could not get married without going through the regimental procedure. 'I marched into the Commanding Officer's Mess, known as the Orderly Room, and stood rigidly to attention. It was the hour when officers' applications were heard. I said, "I thank you sir for leave to get married." There followed routine questioning and I received congratulations.'

In view of such an atmosphere wherein young officers had to live by a code which kept them in their place, Ian Carmichael was delighted, three nights after joining his regiment, to be offered the opportunity of a night away from it all. A fellow second lieutenant, Haddock by name but known as 'Fish' by everyone, made a more than welcome suggestion. They would go down to the 'All Ranks' dance at Whitby's spacious Victorian Spa Hotel. Fish assured Carmichael that the twice-weekly dance there was generously supported by the local lovelies. 'Plenty of choice.'

Now Whitby in March can be as cold as Siberia, or so it seems to visitors and locals alike. That week was no exception. The black-out muffled the town like a dark cloak but did not snuff out its life. Groups stood shivering at bus-stops until the hooded, masked headlights of the bus appeared, the first trace of light in the blackness. The private motorist was non-existent; only a few essential categories of civilians, such as doctors, farmers and veterinary surgeons, could obtain a petrol ration, and they faced prosecution if caught using it for pleasure purposes. Taxis received only enough petrol for a few hours work each day, and the drivers eked it out by picking and choosing their fares, and doubling up where possible. Thus the streets in the town were almost bereft of wheeled traffic – but never in the whole history of Whitby had they been so busy, with three armoured regiments stationed there. In the early evening soldiers with greatcoats buttoned tightly to the neck clattered down the cobbles in their steel-shod boots. They marched noisily in step and laughed raucously and sang crude and dirty ditties. A particular favourite was one which recalled in a maudlin fashion sweethearts left behind by men who had not long to live anyway:

Along the street she wheels a perambulator
She wheels it in the springtime and in the month of May,
And if you ask her why the hell she wheels it,
She wheels it for a soldier who is far, far away.
Far away, far away, far away, far away.
She wheels it for a soldier who is far, far, away.

Above the shelf her father keeps a shotgun,
He keeps it in the springtime and in the month of May,
And if you ask him why the hell he keeps it,
He keeps it for a soldier who is far, far away.
Far away, far away, far away, far away.
He keeps it for a soldier – *who is six feet down.*

Along the main street of Whitby, soldiers and their sweethearts huddled in doorways out of the biting wind, and from these dark recesses came the glow of cigarettes, undertones of furtive murmurings and shufflings, so that the whole row of shopfronts seemed mysteriously alive.

On the pavements walked women with small flashlights sending a minute spot of light ahead, girls squealed with excitement as they hurried along in pairs and threes, all seemed to be making their way to that recess in the cliff between Monkshaven and the Royal in which the Spa is set.

Around the hall, women in bright dresses sat on chairs, side by side, or leant against the walls like sweet-peas decorating a garden wall. When the music slowed down to a slow foxtrot or waltz, the more amorous couples danced cheek-to-cheek, almost inevitably, and when the music slowed to a wistful tune and the crooner leant close to the microphone to sing 'We'll meet again', there came from the khaki or the blue uniforms and from the flowered dresses too, the well-known response, 'Don't know where, don't know when, but I know we'll meet again, some sunny day.'

Shortly before the end of the evening, when the band was playing a quickstep, 'Amapola', Carmichael and Fish spotted two likely 'fillies' at the other side of the floor. They made a beeline for them, hoping to be there before they were snapped up by someone nearer.

'I grabbed the taller of the two,' recalls Carmichael, 'she was wearing a salmon-pink dress ... her name was Pym, she was blond, just eighteen, five feet six, sensationally pretty and a beautiful dancer. Fish's half of the deal was apparently her cousin. They were of an age and having recently left school were occupying their time as telephonists at the local Civil Defence Report Centre. At the end of the evening we were driven back to the mess, all five hundred yards, by Pym in her mother's Morris Eight, and, after a brief and decorous "snog", went in.'

As young men will, the two of them wanted to know how each had got on. They sat down over a drink in the mess bar and quietly exchanged notes on their experiences.

'An interesting evening,' said Fish. 'What was yours like?'

Carmichael's reply astonished his new friend.

'I intend to marry mine.'

And he did.

In those grim years of the war which seemed to have no end in sight, dancing was not only the most popular social antidote to boredom, anxiety and depression, it also provided opportunities for amorous adventures.

Young married women with husbands away in the forces were tired of spending every night alone at home or with in-laws, and they soon began to join the ranks of the single women, the teenagers from school dolled up to look eighteen, and the unattached women who were having a marvellous time at dances and 'hops' many times a week.

At first some of these married women went to dances innocently enough with neighbouring wives in the same lonesome predicament. And they danced with each other. But not for long. It was almost impossible, for there were new conventions, such as 'Excuse-me quicksteps', 'chain dances', such as the 'Lambeth Walk' and 'Hokey Cokey', and the 'Black-out Stroll' which gave opportunities for a quick cuddle or snatched kiss when the lights went out for a moment, and sometimes for much longer. Then there were the 'change-partners' dances in which everyone changed partners when the music stopped, and the 'Paul Jones', which began by the men forming a ring on the outside of the floor and the women on the inside; as the music played 'Here we go gathering nuts in May, nuts in May ... ', the men and women walked in different directions, keeping a wary eye on the prospective partners coming ahead and then, when the music suddenly stopped, pouncing on the most attractive partner within reach.

It is easy to see that it would be almost impossible for even the most determined young wife going to a dance with the intention of dancing solely with her female escort, to avoid falling into the embrace of an equally determined young soldier.

'The top places for romances during the war just had to be dances and cinemas,' recalled Joan Dunhill. 'Being walked back to the "Wrennery" after a dance and in the "black-out" was in itself very romantic. There was a long driveway up from the road to the entrance of the camp, and each evening this would be lined with Wrens and their boyfriends saying a lingering "good night". About every ten minutes a naval sentry would shine his torch to make sure there was no "hanky-panky" going on! Generally speaking, though, there really was very little sexual activity. It was still an era when "nice" girls just didn't, and they weren't put under any pressure by the boys, and yet everyone had such a good time – and a romantic one too! Ah, happy days!'

Keeping the troops happy was a problem with which service authorities were very much concerned throughout the war. The value of entertainment in all its aspects was emphasized as an essential element in maintaining the morale and mental stability of forces personnel.

For example, in 1942, when Ian Carmichael's regiment was posted from Whitby to the much smaller North Yorkshire market town of Helmsley, the problem of entertainment was immediately obvious.

Helmsley was in many ways an ideal place for an armoured corps regiment, for there were open moorlands for tactical exercises and there was a plentiful supply of accommodation, but as far as entertainment went, it was, according to the troops, 'a dead loss'.

'There were four pubs in the main square but nothing else for us to do once training for the day was finished,' said one former soldier. 'It's all right now as a place for people to come for cream cakes and ice-cream on a Sunday afternoon, but frankly in our day there was just not enough crumpet to go round.'

Something had to be done. Ian Carmichael recalled how his commanding officer solved this problem: 'To relieve the boredom, a passion wagon was run one evening a week to York, our nearest oasis. The wagon used to pick us up for the return journey shortly after closing time of the pubs and dance halls.'

Most towns and cities then could boast of having three or four well-supported dance halls. Other garrison towns had even more. Blackpool, with thousands of RAF men and women, had its Tower Ballroom (with the legendary Reginald Dixon leading the dancers from his mighty Wurlitzer organ), the Palace and the Winter Gardens, as well as several smaller ones.

'It was a dreamland where young men could chase girls, and girls could go and hook a man,' recalled Peter Johnson who had many a dance there as a trainee RAF wireless-operator.

Naturally those activities in 'dreamland' could have far-reaching consequences, as Jean Kingdon found out to her misfortune: 'It all began when my friend and I went to a sergeants' mess dance. I went on the floor with several Czech soldiers attached to the 19th Armoured Fighting Vehicle Regiment. One of these troopers was an excellent dancer. It was quite a good evening, though nothing exceptional. For my friend, however, it was marvellous. Consequently she wanted to go again the following week. I wasn't too keen. However, I agreed to go just to keep her company and then, on the spur of the moment, I made a bet with my friend: *"If that good dancer is there again, I'll hook him!"* '

She was not to know until some time later that the young Czech in question had made exactly the same bet with his friend about her.

That night Jean Kingdon fell head over heels in love on the dance floor: 'I realized then that the sergeant-major "he-man" I had once been engaged to was offering not love but flattery. Alex, another flame, had been a "steady" affair that would probably have been the basis for a good marriage, but with my Czech, John, it was something different. We met, we danced, we went home to talk to my mother, we walked by the river, we married.'

On the balance sheet of that marriage there was the usual profit-and-loss account. The first thing Jean lost was her British nationality.

It didn't matter whilst I was still in the ATS, but that wasn't for much longer. When I became pregnant, I got a 'para II' discharge. Then my problems began.

I went to register at the hospital for the confinement and was stunned to be told: *'You can't come in here. You're not a British subject.'*

I could not believe what I was hearing. I had served all those years in the ATS; my husband, John, by this time had been gazetted for gallantry with the 51st Highland Division, and here was a nursing sister telling me that I could not have my baby in a British hospital! I was furious. But nothing would move the authorities. In the end I went to the Czech Army Headquarters and appealed for help. They paid for a private nursing home, gave me money for the layette and arranged for the proper allowances to be paid to me as a wife and mother.

But that rejection from the British hospital was only the beginning of my problems. Soon I was to become a 'DP', a displaced person. That was in the not-too-distant future. Meanwhile I got down to the business of looking after my baby and waiting for the war to end.

In the years that followed, the balance sheet of that marriage went steadily into a loss, and there were many times when Jean Kingdon must have regretted that rash bet to hook the good Czech dancer, as we shall see.

But then, back in 1942, young men and women in the services, not knowing what the future might hold for them, grabbed at every opportunity of being together. The phenomenon of war aphrodisia was really at work, and friendships begun on the dance floor soon developed into more serious liaisons.

War weddings were usually quiet, austere affairs, with the bride and groom in uniform. Clothing coupons were rarely available for the luxury of a white wedding dress, and the reception held in village halls depended much upon the generosity of friends and neighbours contributing carefully hoarded sugar and flour for the cake.

Occasionally though, there were exceptions, weddings which were remarkably opulent, like that of Catherine Roberts. But that perhaps was not surprising, for Catherine herself was a most unusual woman: the only American serving in the British Women's Auxiliary Air Force.

'My natural mother was an American Indian of the Penobscot tribe, my father was of Germanic-American descent,' wrote Catherine. 'When I was six, I was adopted by a Welsh couple, yet my father served in the US Navy and subsequently both he and my mother became American citizens and lived in America. Later they got *Hiraeth* – the Welsh for a longing for their homeland. So they returned to Wales. I was educated there and went on to take degrees at the London College of Music.'

Consequently she was still in Britain when the United States came into the war after Pearl Harbor, and she was given permission to join the WAAF.

'I went to Morecambe for six weeks of foot-slogging, then went to Cranwell, Lincolnshire, for two weeks of teleprinter school. I was so very proud of my Air Force uniform and especially of my USA insignia which I wore on my shoulders. After the course I was posted to Old Sarum, near Salisbury.'

Here it was that Catherine was literally swept off her feet in a romantic dance-floor encounter that speedily led to marriage and then to a dismaying phenomenon with which many war wives had to cope, as Catherine herself recalls:

It all began really at Tidworth, for near our camp was the magnificent ancestral home of the Duchess of Marlborough. She had lent this beautiful fifty-bedroom mansion to the director of the American Red Cross, Mrs Theodore Roosevelt, cousin of the US president.

She and the duchess became firm friends, and on five nights each week they invited different British and American service units to a dance in their ballroom and laid on plentiful supplies of free coffee and American doughnuts. One night it would be a dance for Americans and the WAAF, another night Americans and WRNS, another Americans or British and ATS, and so on.

It was on a memorable evening in August 1942 that I went to one of those dances, and there I met a tall, handsome and blond Nordic young man of the US Army, Private Eddie Swauger.

It must have been love at first sight on that dance floor. Six weeks later we decided to get married.

During the whirlwind courtship, Private Eddie Swauger became very friendly with Mrs Theodore Roosevelt, as he was able to help her with aspects of her Red Cross work. Consequently, when she heard of his engagement to Catherine, she insisted that an engagement party should be given and that the wedding reception should be held at Tidworth House. 'The Duchess and Mrs Roosevelt had been so kind that I just did not have the heart to tell them that I really would prefer to be married in my own village church in Wales.'

What a splendid wedding day it was! An unusually hot sun for February bathed the beautiful Gothic church of St Mary the Virgin in a bright golden light; 300 guests rolled up in a wide variety of cars, jeeps and trucks, to be welcomed by Mrs 'Teddy' Roosevelt and pack every pew in the church. Everyone had entered into the spirit of the occasion and given whatever help they could to get the couple away to a magnificent start. Even the groom's commanding officer, Colonel McNearney, had joined in by letting the whole of his unit have the afternoon off to attend the ceremony.

One can well imagine the awe-inspiring sight for the young bride as she paused in the porchway of the church on the arm of her father. Ahead of her were the rows of smart young men and women in the distinctive khaki of the US Army sitting together on one side of the church; on the other side of the nave was a mass of Air Force blue.

Catherine herself was a picture fit to bring tears to the eyes of the most hardened and distant relative. She wore a white satin gown with wreath and veil and carried a bouquet of red carnations. Her matron of honour, Flight Sergeant Richardson of the WAAF, added further colour to the scene in her borrowed pink gown, and the four bridesmaids were immaculately turned out in their 'best blue' uniforms with brightly polished buttons.

'Almost everyone was in uniform, a real wartime wedding. The only ones in civilian clothes were my parents, myself and the matron of honour,' recalls Catherine.

Following the American custom, Private Marty McKenna sang 'O promise me' and 'I love you truly' during the service.

As the bride and groom left the church, they passed through a guard of honour formed of members of the WAAF, American forces and American Red Cross. Catherine was mesmerized by it all:

For one brief shining moment it was Camelot. From the church, the Duchess and Mrs Roosevelt led the way across the old oak-lined driveway to Tidworth House, and there we had the most magnificent reception. I did not think there was so much food left in the world, but dear, kind Mrs Roosevelt had it all flown in from the USA via MATS and the compliments of FDR! The traditional American 'donut' was right there on the head table. My three-tiered chocolate wedding cake was also flown in, compliments of my husband's unit. The *Life* magazine photographers took many pictures, and after the reception Mrs Roosevelt allowed me to change from my wedding gown in her bedroom.

That was indeed an occasion never to be forgotten. So impressed was Mrs Roosevelt with it all that she wrote to President F.D. Roosevelt claiming that Catherine was the first American to marry a GI in Britain during the war, and this led to American magazines taking up the story too.

Unfortunately it was not to be a story with a happy ending. Less than a year after their baby daughter was born, Catherine's husband was posted to the US First Army, which became embroiled in one of the bloodiest battles of the war, 'the Green Hell of the Hurtgen Forest'. It was a battle that became known to the US infantry as 'the Death Factory'. Edward Swauger's regiment was caught in that hard slog to capture the first German city encountered by the US Army – Aachen.

There are very few accounts of that disastrous campaign, a six-month-long battle with ever-mounting casualties, but a recent book by military historian Charles Whiting gives the reader a vivid picture of what it was really like there and goes a long way towards explaining how it was that sweethearts and wives of survivors found their menfolk were never again quite the same men to whom they had waved goodbye on embarkation leave:

> From September 1944 to February 1945, every two weeks or so, a new American division of infantry was fed into those dark green sombre woods, heavy with lethal menace. Fourteen days later the shocked exhausted survivors would be pulled out, great gaps in their battered ranks, passing like sleep-walkers, the 'new boys' moving up for the slaughter. Seeing nothing, hearing nothing, muddy, filthy, unshaven, they had somehow escaped the Death Factory while all around them their comrades had died by scores, by hundreds, by thousands. In the six months of the Battle of the Hurtgen Forest, eight infantry and two armoured divisions, plus several smaller US outfits went into the Death Factory. In a matter of only fourteen days most of the rifle companies suffered up to fifty per cent casualties. In the case of two unfortunate regiments, the Ninth Infantry Divisions's 60th Regiment and the 4th Division's 22nd Regiment, the losses were a staggering one hundred per cent.
>
> By the end nearly thirty thousand young American soldiers died or were wounded there and many thousands cracked and went down with combat fatigue – unable to take any more.
>
> Few men who survived were ever the same again.[3]

Edward Swauger was amongst those evacuated back to hospital in the States, and in April 1946 Catherine was able to join him there with their daughter. Sadly though, neither Catherine nor Edward was able to recapture the bliss of their earlier relationship. Six months after their reunion in Beaver, Pennsylvania, they were divorced.

Perhaps it was that, though Edward's physical injuries healed, he was, like thousands of other veterans, scarred and maimed in other ways. In those days little was known of post-traumatic stress disorder, a condition now said to be prevalent amongst survivors of war and victims of terrorism, accidents and violent crime. All such shattering experiences are likely to impair physical and emotional health. It was certainly a condition which wreaked havoc amongst marriages and careers in the immediate post-war years.

That Catherine's wedding was front page news in 1943 is understandable, but by the end of the war GI marriages rarely rated a column headline, for by then there were more than a million women from war-torn countries about to sail to the United States to join their GI husbands. In Britain alone, out of two million GIs stationed there at some time, 70,000 took home a British bride. It was estimated that wherever there was an American airfield about twenty per cent of the men would marry a British woman. And naturally there were thousands more engagements that never came to anything, often through no fault of either of the two sweethearts. Military as well as parental approval was not always easily acquired.

In those days many parents believed that if their daughter married an American they would never see her again. As one war bride put it: 'Going to America was like going to the moon.' Parental approval was a vital part of the complex documentation process which the US War Department instigated in 1942. This deliberate bureaucratic red tape was part of the US policy of discouraging wartime marriages, based on the theory that the single soldier who was not distracted by family responsibilities was likely to be a more valuable soldier. It infuriated sweethearts but perhaps did ensure that the old adage of 'Marry in haste, repent at leisure' did not apply so often.

As events turned out, most of those wartime marriages, many of which had their beginnings on a dance-hall floor, were happy and successful. It is interesting in retrospect to contemplate how one dance could change the lifetime plans of parents and daughter. It happened with Margaret Carmarda, a Glasgow university student, as she now recalls:

Like most girls of my age then I was 'dance crazy', and I should have been attending a geology lecture instead of succumbing to the allure of an afternoon tea dance at the Locarno Ballroom in Sauchiehall Street. An American soldier there told me he was just getting his 'land legs' after a terrible voyage from Iceland during which he had been sick all the time.

I can still remember those soft lights, the revolving stage as bands changed without a break in the music. All the different uniforms from every nation, and of course Glasgow had sailors galore. They all won our hearts briefly, but for me the Americans were something special. They were exciting, full of clever talk, had a great sense of humour and were friendly in a way that I had never encountered before. And the idea of eating out after a dance was over, at 10.45 p.m. was unheard-of. I always had to scurry home in the black-out to catch the late tram. Fortunately my parents were understanding and trusted in my good judgement. They let me bring guests home and shared our rations with them.

Margaret's dancing partner, Luke, was a determined young man, and Fate, as well as Margaret's parents, was on his side. By sheer coincidence he had booked to spend his leave at the Red Cross Club in London and was about to travel down when Margaret received a letter calling her for an interview for a job in London with the Ministry of Supply for which she had applied weeks earlier. Luke immediately had Margaret's ticket altered to first class, instead of third as it was then, and they travelled to London together. He stayed in London until the time came for him to return to his unit in Iceland. Margaret thought she would never see him again.

But that tea dance at the Locarno had cast a spell on Luke, and Fate again intervened. Within the space of a few weeks his unit was posted from Iceland to Glasgow. Now it was Margaret's turn to act. She left her well-paid job at the ministry, having persuaded them that a career as a school teacher was more in her line than liaising with engineers and naval officers about submarine parts. However, her career was already being shaped by Fate in a much more drastic fashion.

She saw much more of Luke – they went dancing frequently at the Locarno, and it was no surprise to her parents when she told them that he had asked her to marry him and that they were now engaged.

Luke was posted to Germany after the invasion and never came back to Britain. His unit stayed with the Allied Armies in Germany until the war ended. He was then sent back to the United States in charge of a batch of German prisoners of war, and was himself discharged from the Army.

Although Margaret was engaged to be married to an American soldier, she could not obtain the official US travel documents or tickets to go to the USA. But on the spur of the moment one day she walked into a small shipping office in Glasgow, having seen a Pan American Airways sign in the window. Could she have a flight, she asked. The reply was that only people with special authorization as priority passengers were being allowed to travel, but if she would like to gamble on putting her name down and being ready to go at twenty-four hours' notice, they would see what they could do. A few weeks later she got a telephone call. Twenty-four hours later she was airborne, *en route* for Shannon, Gander, Chicago and Racine on Lake Michigan. There she was welcomed by her husband's warm-hearted family of Italian immigrants. She was married in May 1946 and started on a career completely different from the one she had planned those few months ago when she was skipping lectures to go dancing at the Glasgow Locarno.

Enveloped in the warmth of Luke's large Sicilian family, there was only one thing for her to do: to support her husband and be mother to his children. Luke went through university; she had his first child in 1947 and the fourth child when he graduated in business studies. With her MA degree from Glasgow, she was often able to help her husband through his work, sometimes doing his homework for him, all the time continuing her new vocation.

'I pursued the career of "Mother" – we had ten children, five boys and five girls. My dear husband died, of cancer, aged fifty in 1971. One of my daughters has married an Italian and lives in Florence, a son is marrying a girl from Manchester, England. I have so many happy memories. I still hum and sing the songs we danced to all those years ago. They had wonderful tunes with lyrics mostly about joyous reunions and sad partings.'

Dancing went on despite the air raids. Towards the end of the hot summer of 1940, when the battle for London had already been engaged, bombs fell by day and by night. Londoners had become accustomed to the sudden drone of a Luftwaffe bomber, the screech of a falling bomb, the dull crash of its explosion and the smell of cordite that filled the air afterwards. It was a time when, in the hour before dusk, crowds would file through the streets carrying suitcases and blankets on their way to tube stations and public air-raid shelters. Most restaurants would close, but some, such as the Hungaria and the Dorchester, stayed open, attracting far more diners than usual because of the reputedly stout structure of the buildings and also due to the fact that both places allowed their diners to doss down for the night on improvised beds. Wealthy senior officers on leave would sometimes take their sweethearts there for a final evening (and night) together before going overseas.

But the favourite of all these supposedly safe restaurants for the young officer on leave who did not care about the expense was the Café de Paris.

Originally the site of the Café de Paris was a bearpit sunk below ground level, and subsequently it had been remodelled as a replica in miniature of the ballroom of the greatest liner in the world then being built, the *Titanic*. Because of its construction below ground, it was advertised as London's safest restaurant. Unfortunately, as events were to prove on the night of 8 March 1941, this was quite untrue. A fifty-kilo Luftwaffe bomb landed right in front of the band, killing its leader, Ken 'Snakehips' Johnson, and thirty-two dancers.

Before that tragic air raid, however, the Café de Paris enjoyed tremendous popularity. Not only were the decor marvellous and the food excellent, despite rationing, but there was the special appeal of Ken Johnson's dance music, and consequently the dance floor was packed on most evenings with young men and women in uniform.

Dancing amongst them one evening in the late summer of 1940, was 22-year-old Primula Rollo.[4] The daughter of Lady Kathleen and Flight Lieutenant Rollo MC, she was tall and aristocratic-looking with blonde hair neatly trimmed and curled to clear the collar of her WAAF tunic, her figure set off attractively by her crisply tailored blue uniform. She had the refined air, as actor Peter Ustinov was later to say, of the best sort of English girl with the rose-and-lavender look.

When she got up to dance on one occasion, she caught the eye of a young commando officer at a nearby table. There was something familiar about his face, which was not surprising because his picture had been plastered on hoardings all over London as the star in two films currently breaking box-office records – *Dawn Patrol* and the Ginger Rogers film *Bachelor Mother*. The officer was David Niven. On the screen he played the part of the archetypal English gentleman: witty, debonair, immaculate in dress and behaviour. In real life he was an accomplished womanizer and connoisseur of female beauty if ever there was one.

Niven recalled that moment when their eyes first met: 'She looked at me for a long moment. Her eyes were the merriest and bluest I had ever seen and she had a divinely willowy figure.'

It was such a memorable evening of dancing that Niven went back to the Café de Paris frequently during the next two weeks, hoping to meet the beautiful WAAF, but she was never there. He could not get the girl out of his mind. Then, one lunchtime, Fate took pity on him and guided his footsteps into the National Gallery, where there was one of those free midday concerts provided by the government as a morale-booster, an opportunity for people to relax and forget the war for a while. On this particular day there was a cello recital. Niven was entranced. When it was all over and the audience had left the hall, he remained in his seat, totally engrossed in the experience. Someone else had remained, equally enraptured: the blonde WAAF. Two people alone in the gallery.

'Wasn't that beautiful,' she said.

Niven could but agree and asked her if she would like to take coffee and a sandwich with him.

'This was no time for the niceties of a prolonged courtship,' recalled Niven. Two days after that meeting in the concert-hall, he knocked upon the door of the house in which 'Primmie', as she liked to be called, was billeted. He was well received – so well, in fact, that by the end of the week he was invited to meet her father (her parents lived apart), with the express purpose of asking permission to marry his daughter. All three dined together. Halfway through the meal there was a terrific air raid. Primmie, her father and Niven huddled for safety under the heavy oak table. There it was that Bill Rollo gave his consent to the marriage. The wedding took place a mere ten days later.

Then began the happiest years of Niven's life. Everyone who knew the couple could see how utterly content they were. 'They were a champagne couple; just being with them and sensing their happiness in each other made you feel better,' said Mrs Eddie Hart, whose husband had starred in films with Niven.[5]

David Niven was happy with his military service too, for although he was a member of the SAS-type 'Phantom' commando unit, he was given frequent unusual detachments for 'special duties'.

In one spell of these temporary duties he was pressed into appearing in fog-filled cinemas all over Glasgow for the purpose of haranguing audiences about the need for more women to volunteer for the Auxiliary Territorial Service. But this was an appeal with a difference, for he directed his words more to *men* than to women. The gist of his short speech was to say to all men in the audience: '*Let your women go and do their bit for the country!*' Now this gave women just the support they needed to persuade husbands, fathers and brothers to agree to their joining the women's services. Only by recruiting more women could men be redeployed for front-line service.

This campaign for more women volunteers was intensified nationwide, in the press and on the radio. Posters and magazine advertisements appealed to men to be more trusting and not to stand in the way of their wives, sweethearts and grown-up daughters who wanted to volunteer. A woman in *Good Housekeeping* magazine wrote with feeling about the work that women could be doing for the war effort if only they were given the chance by the men in their lives. She backed up her arguments with the words: 'Separation is difficult to bear but it is nothing compared to what happened to the people in occupied Europe, and what could happen in Britain if Hitler took over'.[6]

This was just the sort of encouragement that a young woman like Joyce Rowland needed. She had been trying to join the ATS for a year. Today she recalls: 'As an only child with loving parents it took me a full year to persuade my parents to agree to my joining the ATS. Even at eighteen, in those days a parent's signature was needed on the application form.'

Once she had this consent, Joyce Rowland immediately joined up and began a period of service that was both exciting and romantic. It ended in a way which she never for a moment could have believed possible:

After the initial weeks of foot drills and technical training I was posted to a mixed anti-aircraft battery of the Royal Artillery. The men manned the guns, and we sat a little way from them, operating the predictors. It was our job to lay on to enemy aircraft, its height, speed, direction and then shout 'Fire!', allowing ten seconds for them firing. It was marvellous how the system worked. We were a happy crowd calling out, 'Elevate',

'Depress', 'Traverse right', 'Traverse left', and so on, with all the confidence of veterans.

We operated from sites all over Britain and were fortunate enough to have officers looking after us who kept us all well disciplined but at the same time were considerate enough to make sure that we had enough healthy social contact and entertainment to keep morale high. The Army seemed to recognize the fact that men and women needed to meet each other, to talk, laugh and share experiences together, and so they organized entertainment on the unit and provided transport to nearby towns for dances. Naturally, many romantic and exciting relationships were formed.

Joyce was posted to a training unit at Cromer on the Norfolk coast, for firing practice, and was billeted in one of the old high Victorian hotels on the sea front. During a fire drill at the hotel, Joyce was badly injured, and the prospects for her recovery seemed grim. Few gave much for her chances of returning to her unit fully fit. And as for her chance in the matrimonial stakes ... well, it didn't really bear thinking about. However, the young woman herself was determined to prove all doubters wrong. It was a long haul. Not until the autumn of 1944 was she discharged fit for duty.

By that time the Allied armies had raced across France and were over the Rhine. The Germans, though holding out in The Hague, were striking back with V1 and V2 rockets launched from within their own frontier. The main target was the newly captured port of Antwerp – the greatest port in Europe and of particular importance to the Allied advance, for its use would shorten the supply lines to the forward troops. Consequently the Germans aimed to obliterate it completely. Horrific rocket attacks were launched, far worse than any experienced in London. Over 5,960 rockets fell within eight miles of the city centre, killing more than 4,000 people.

Antwerp then had no anti-aircraft batteries with previous experience of shooting down flying bombs, and, moreover, those units already there were desperately needed to cover the crossing of the Rhine. Consequently calls were made for ATS volunteers to serve in mixed batteries being sent to relieve the Antwerp ack-ack batteries.

Now, after her previous experience of volunteering, Joyce Rowland might have been expected to settle for the soft option and stay in the United Kingdom. Not so. Once again this irrepressible young woman stepped forward. Before long she was in one of the five mixed batteries in Antwerp engaged in the most hectic anti-aircraft activity of the whole war. One of them, 139(M) HAA regiment shot down nineteen flying bombs in one month!

Life for those gunners was not only hectic, it was hard. A War Office report stated: 'Throughout this time the hardships endured were great. For six weeks the batteries operated in frozen snow and one of the chief off-duty occupations was sawing wood. Electricity was cut during the day, there was no coal and at one time nothing but "iron rations" and dehydrated vegetables to be eaten out of mess tins!' ('The Auxiliary Territorial Service', War Office, 1949.)

Naturally, both men and women serving under such conditions needed some relief and relaxation of a social nature. And they got it.

Every fourteen days, gunners were sent on leave for forty-eight hours to a luxuriously appointed rest centre housed in a five-star hotel. And every six months both servicemen and women could get together for seven days to enjoy the luxury – at no expense to themselves – of clean sheets, hot baths, meals with an orchestra playing, and hairdressing salons. But way above all these attractions was the dancing. Every night there was a dance in the huge hotel ballroom, with plenty of eager partners. Inevitably in that cold winter of 1944–5, many a servicewoman met, on that ballroom floor, the man whom she was to marry.

Joyce Rowland's enjoyment of those facilities was cut short – 'tragically', in that she was hastily repatriated due to the unexpected death of her mother during a minor operation, but 'fortuitously' also, because, through this repatriation, a most unusual chain of events began which was to lead within a few months to a strange and romantic courtship and marriage.

Quickly she established herself in her new unit, and she was able to work from home and so help her father to run the house when she was not on duty. But after Belgium, with its alluring dances so full of promise, life was dull and depressing until one memorable day. A letter arrived for her, addressed in an unfamiliar hand. The writer was an RAF corporal recently repatriated from Belgium. He said he had been talking to Joyce's ATS sergeant, who had spoken so much about her courage and cheerfulness that he felt compelled to write. Joyce lost no time. She recalls:

I was prompted to reply without delay. From then on letters passed between us at regular weekly intervals. Curiosity finally got the better of me, and I asked if we could exchange photographs. The upshot was that I received a snapshot of a young man in shorts and vest and sporting a handlebar moustache.

He must have found my photograph to his liking, because his next letter arrived asking me if we could meet in the not-too-distant future.

'You must go and meet him,' said my friend. But I needed no encouragement. Life at that time in Manchester was so boring, and I felt the need for a little excitement. A date was picked – depending of course on whether or not he got leave. However, in the run-up to this meeting, my corporal wrote to say that he had had an accident. Then all letters stopped. No explanation. I came to the conclusion that it had all been too good to be true.

Then one day I got a letter with a Durham postmark. It was from my Air Force corporal. He told me that he had been granted some sick-leave and would be passing through Manchester on the way to see his mother and that he would like to meet me there if I still wished. We agreed to meet under the clock of the Mancheter City Bus Department's office. He'd be wearing a red carnation in his jacket, carrying the *Daily Telegraph* and whistling 'Chewing a piece of string', which was a popular song at that time.

The day came. I got there early enough to position myself so that I had a good view all round, for I had already decided that if I didn't like what I saw, I would just leave and consider the matter closed. It would avoid awkward explanations and the possibility of hurting his feelings. At exactly the appointed time there came into sight an airman with his right foot and leg encased in plaster. He hobbled his way towards me with his arm outstretched. 'Are you Miss Wood?' he asked. And then after I'd nodded he added, 'Shall we go to the pictures?'

To many young people today, 'going to the pictures' might seem a rather unimaginative way for two people who had just met to spend their first afternoon together. But going to the pictures then was somehow different. The cinema had much to offer other than entertainment. It was not just a place where you could forget the grimness of war: it was a dark and intimate place where men and women could find the romance and glamour that were missing from their own lives. A lot of the films were about love – romantic, splendid love, usually at first sight, consummated eventually with a kiss, on which 'THE END' was superimposed. Of all these films, pride of place went to *Gone with the Wind*, starring Vivien Leigh and Clark Gable, which opened in London in 1940 and was still showing four years later, by which time Lieutenant Clark Gable of the US Air Force had already completed thirty operational missions with US 7th Bomber Group Flying Fortresses.

The cinema then was a great attraction and sold no fewer than 30 million tickets a week! Many people went twice, some three times. It was an occasion, a treat for which one got spruced up, a night out; you never knew who might be sitting next to you, and you could always live in hopes that the right partner might come along.

Going to the pictures also provided one of those rare opportunities for people to get to know each other better. On the back row of the stalls there were two-seater 'banquettes' in which sweethearts could sit close together without being separated by the bar of the chair arm. It was a dark, romantic world in which hands could touch for the first time and fingers intertwine, and where the daring Don Juan could casually drop his arm over the chair back and gradually lift it until it was round his girlfriend's shoulders. If she snuggled closer, hearts would beat just that little bit faster.

In the interval between the main feature films, from somewhere under the stage the mighty Compton organ would rise and warble out familiar tunes for the audience to sing together in between chattering and eating ice-cream. In front of the spotlight the organist swayed rhythmically, keeping a thousand or more young men and women in time to his music. He set dreams free. As the harmony subsided into a lake-like calm whilst the organ disappeared into the bowels of the earth again, it left a warm, enchanting groundswell of good fellowship in which romance could flourish.

So, after all, it was not such an unimaginative way for Joyce and Frank to spend their first afternoon together. And events proved this to be so, as Joyce today recalls: 'That was the first of many meetings. We went out dancing whenever we could, as well as going to the pictures. I took him home to meet my dad, and it was he who suggested some time later that Frank could use the spare bedroom instead of staying in the servicemen's hostel in town.

'Five months after that first afternoon in the pictures we were married, and I often thought how strange life is, that two people could have the whole of their lives changed just because one of them had an impulse to write a letter to someone right out of the blue.'

But that was the way life was in wartime. A look, a letter, the briefest of meetings could take on an intensity that led men and women to commit themselves unreservedly to each other. Was it surprising that in the darkened cinemas and the softly lit dance halls of Britain romance blossomed in lives blighted by war?

5 'Yours'

Love letters straight from the heart
Keep us so near when apart.

Popular wartime song

Saturday was always a very busy day in the Shropshire market town of
Whitchurch, named after its famous Norman white church. Farmers
from the surrounding countryside came in on roads which converged
like spokes of a wheel onto the hub by the old Bull Ring. With the
farmers came their wives, holding long lists of shopping to tide them
over the next week.

In the spring of 1941, this old town, which had once housed the
Roman legions, was host to an even greater army of foreigners. They
were the Czechoslovakian Airborne Divisions training in parachuting,
and for hush-hush activities, at RAF Ringway. Their camps were in the
lush parkland belonging to Lord Cholmondeley (pronounced
'Chumly'), seven miles to the north. Consequently at weekends the
ancient streets – with such quaint names as Bargates, Bluegates,
Watergate and Highgate – were absolutely packed with people:
shoppers, soldiers and those just out for a change of scenery.

Amongst them one Saturday in April 1941 were two sisters, Edna and
Lorna Ellison, who had come to town as usual by bus from their village
of Ightfield. It was getting towards the end of the afternoon, and they
were on their way back to the bus-stop, filling in time walking slowly
down a street which was full of interesting small shops and several pubs
with splendid swinging signs. They browsed in a book shop, looked at
the bric-à-brac in the adjacent junk shop and paused at the
greengrocer's, whose wares spilled out onto the pavement on a stall
covered by a mat of lurid artificial grass piled high with country
vegetables.

It was then that they became aware that they were being followed.
Both of them had been conscious of the fact that whenever they slowed
down the footsteps behind also slackened pace. The two girls looked at
each other and then at the reflections in the shop window. They gave a
knowing look. It was the handsome soldier who had passed them in the

opposite direction a few minutes earlier. The one with the floppy hat and bronze cap badge, the one who had smiled. A Czech.

Now Lorna, aged sixteen, and Edna, fifteen, were torn between their curiosity to look back at the soldier and their anxiety not to become involved just when they were at the bus-stop where neighbours from the village were standing, seeing everything, noting who was doing what, and storing the information ready for reporting later at the village gossip shop. So the two girls climbed quickly on to the bus as it arrived. Then, from the safety of their seats, they turned to look through the window. The soldier was still there, this time smiling happily, mouthing words and making signs. Then he stopped, patted his pockets, took out a pencil and a scrap of paper and laboriously wrote a few words. He folded the paper and slipped it through the narrow gap at the top of the window.

Lorna and Edna opened the note. It read: 'Please meet here tomorrow.' The girls smiled, lifted their eyebrows and shrugged in a way that could have been interpreted as meaning: 'We'd like to but don't know.'

When they reached home, they were buzzing with excitement and could hardly wait to get into the farmhouse to tell their mother what had happened. She soon dashed any hopes they had of meeting the Czech soldier again. 'That you will not!' she said. She had heard all about those Free French, Free Poles, Free Norwegians, and she had heard tales too about the Free Czechs, the squat men with droopy berets and broad epaulettes, who tended to kiss ladies' hands at the slightest opportunity. The girls were slightly taken aback at their mother's categorical 'No!'

The following week, in town with their mother shopping, they suddenly met the same Czech soldier, almost colliding on the busy pavement. He stopped politely, saluted, inclined his head towards Mrs Ellison and, in his carefully enunciated broken English, tried to make conversation. There was something about this young man that immediately appealed to the motherly instincts of Mrs Ellison. She no longer saw him as a possible threat to her daughters but as a lonely soldier in a foreign land, like her son in the RAF far away from his home and country. She thought it would be nice if some mother was kind to him. Introductions were made. His name was Jan Kubis.

On the spur of the moment Mrs Ellison asked him if he would like to come with them to the pictures. They went to the first house, and it was fairly early in the evening when they stood to attention for the national anthem at the end of the show. Then Mrs Ellison asked Jan if he would like to come home with them for a cup of tea and a bit of supper. Before he answered, she warned him that it would be a long walk back from their village, as the last bus would already have gone.

The young man did not hesitate and accepted the invitation in his polite, stilted English. On the walk from the village bus-stop to their little farmhouse, Edna and Lorna noticed how his eyes seemed to linger over the farmyard and cowsheds they passed. Mrs Ellison noticed too. She said in the most simple way she could manage: 'You a farmer?' The young man smiled broadly and nodded vigorously.

In every way he seemed a likeable, pleasant young man, well enough educated, and he often surprised people in Whitchurch with his knowledge of music. He had even heard of Whitchurch's own son, Edward German, composer of *Merrie England*.

Jan was so profuse with his thanks as the evening came to an end that Mrs Ellison surprised her daughters yet again by saying: 'Why don't you come and see us on your days off? Come and stay here if you get any leave. If you'd like to, that is.' He gave her a look of sheer pleasure.

For the next eighteen months the Ellisons' red-brick house became home for Jan Kubis. He was very fond of the girls and also of their mother, and always acted with utmost propriety. He never took anything for granted. He had his own bedroom to the right of the front door, tastefully furnished in blue – the wallpaper, curtains, counterpane, all of matching shades of blue.

Days of delight passed, and their affection for each other grew. They joked and they laughed and they enjoyed playing simple games together. But there were times when Mrs Ellison found Jan sitting in the front parlour looking immeasurably sad, as if grieving for what he had left behind in Czechoslovakia – or for what lay ahead.

It was after one of these occasions that Mrs Ellison suddenly had an idea. She had guessed partly what was troubling Jan, and she made a second significant suggestion: 'Would you like to bring a friend to stay with you here?'

Jan jumped at the idea and on the next weekend he arrived with his friend Josef. He was a dark-haired, brown-faced and volatile young man who was forever flashing his teeth and slapping his thigh as he roared with laughter – a complete contrast to the shy and more serious Jan. Josef spoke nearly perfect English too.

Occasionally on such weekends Mrs Ellison would take her two boys a tray of tea in bed before they got up in the morning. Spoiling them. One such morning they were both asleep, and she had time to stand looking at them for a moment. The covers were off Jan's bare back and buttocks, and what the good lady saw nearly made her drop the tea tray. She counted the scars of seven swastikas which had been branded on his buttocks. She put the tray down on the bedside table and was about to leave the room when her eye was caught by two dark objects lying on the wickerwork basket at the end of the bed: two automatic pistols complete with magazines. What task was it, wondered Mrs Ellison, that caused them to have such deadly weapons to hand?

Then came the last hectic weekend, when the two young men rushed up to the cottage to say goodbye. They emptied their pockets of gifts, cap badges and all they held precious. 'Keep these and we will come back for them later,' said Jan.

They had no time to spare. At the doorway Josef turned and stood for a moment as if wanting to say more. He was outwardly composed but his mild, sad eyes spoke of the futility of all that lay ahead. He was taking a last look, as if to fix in his memory all that stood for the real love and affection that had grown between them all. Finally Josef found the words he wanted: 'Please remember us. We shall never forget all your kindness and loving care you have given us.'

Mrs Ellison reached out, her fingertips resting lightly upon his arm. 'Do take care of yourselves. We shall all look forward to the next time we meet. The war can't go on for ever.'

And, in a way, Mrs Ellison was right. For Jan Kubis and Josef Gabchik the war was indeed almost over.

It was several days before Mrs Ellison found the single sheet of blue notepaper propped behind one of the ornaments on the mantelpiece, for it was folded many times into a small, square shape. She saw it early one evening, opened it and read the carefully written lines:

Remember please your Czech friend
who will never forget the nice time
he spend with you.
         your sincerely,
         Jan

And as she stood there, note in hand, in the dim, empty room, vivid and contrasting pictures came into her mind: Jan lying peacefully asleep, seven swastikas branded on his buttocks, and the loaded automatic pistols by the bed-end; Jan laughing cheerfully as he skipped down the path to the house, carrying a big bunch of daffodils. She felt that saying goodbye to Jan and his friend Josef was like saying goodbye to spring, and in the stillness of that small room, tears stung her eyes.

The Ellisons were not to know what happened to their Czech friends for several years.

A short time after leaving Whitchurch, Jan and Josef were looking down at their homeland through the coffin-shaped exit hatch of an RAF Lancaster bomber. The red light had come on, static lines and parachute harness had been checked. The sergeant dispatcher stood looking intently at the other unlit bulb. Then it happened. 'Green on. Go!' he shouted, slapping Jan's shoulder.

Jan Kubis and Josef Gabchik dropped into the snows of Czechoslovakia to carry out the mission for which they had been trained: the assassination of the ruthless SS General Reinhard 'Butcher' Heydrich, one of the most powerful men in the Nazi hierarchy, a man who controlled the secret police of the Gestapo and all the apparatus of terror. He was now 'Reich Protector' of Czechoslovakia. They planned to kill Heydrich at a hairpin bend in the road down which he drove every day to his office in Prague.

On the morning of 27 May 1942 all was ready. At half-past ten, Heydrich's green open Mercedes appeared. Josef Gabchik sprang into the roadway. He raised his gun and aimed. He could see Heydrich's pale face through the windscreen. He pressed the trigger. Nothing happened. He cocked the gun and squeezed the trigger again. Again nothing happened. Behind him Jan Kubis shouted; he lobbed a grenade at the car as it slithered to a stop. The explosion blasted the horsehair stuffing from the seat into Heydrich's spine. He died eight days later.

Jan Kubis, the shy boy the Ellison family had loved, had got his revenge for his branded buttocks. The British government had got what it wanted too: a wave of terror that would raise hatred for the Germans as they took their revenge for the death of Heydrich. Ten thousand Czechs were arrested, 1,300 were shot and the village of Lidice, which was supposed to have harboured Heydrich's assassins, was razed to the ground.

And Jan and Josef? Inevitably, as they had known from the start, they were caught. They came to a bloody end in a Prague church. The details of their final capture and death were given to Edna Ellison many years later by the man who researched the assassination, Alan Burgess.[1] But part of the gory story is still missing. And no one will tell. Who in Britain gave the order for the operation which deliberately had as its main aim not the death of Heydrich but the murder of all those innocent Czechs in reprisals, so that hatred of the occupation forces would be intensified and all co-operation in the Czech arms factories – producing weapons for the Germans – would be affected?

The files are still closed. No one will tell.

In a quiet village near Ightfield today, Edna Ellison is not concerned with all that but she remembers as clearly as if it were yesterday that sunny spring when a young soldier smiled shyly and tried to date her as he pushed a note through the open window of a bus.

On 23 April 1941 Mabel Baguley was asleep in her bed in the cosy little house she shared with her widowed mother in North Horton, Bradford. By day, Mabel worked very hard at the English Electric works, winding wire coils for RAF engines, and she was so tired each evening that she went to bed and slept soundly. Never was she troubled with nightmares or disturbed sleep of any kind.

On one particular night, the house was perfectly quiet, no sound came from her mother's bedroom, the air outside was still. Suddenly Mabel sat up in bed. There it was again. Her name being called, softly. Part of her still denied what she had heard. She pushed herself bolt upright, waiting. Was she mistaken after all? A pale moon stared blankly at her through a gap in the white lace curtains. Softly the call came again: 'Mabel, Mabel.' No doubt in her mind this time, she felt a rush of happiness surging through her. It was Bill, her sweetheart. He was back on leave!

In one sweep she flung off the bed covers, stepped onto the cold bedroom floor and in the half-light walked towards the stairs. Now fully awake, she did not put on the lights, because the black-out curtains were down ready for the morning, and not wishing to waken her mother she crept silently downstairs into the living-room, where she thought Bill was waiting. No one was there. She stood bewildered, looking about her in the pale moonlight. Lost in thought, she gripped the table and screwed up her eyes momentarily, concentrating on her thoughts. Had she been dreaming? The voice had unmistakeably been Bill's.

Shivering now from cold or fear, she staggered up the stairs, this time only vaguely aware of what she was doing. She *had* heard Bill's voice. White and shaking all over, she dropped on to her bed, pulling the eiderdown round her trembling body, and eventually fell into a stupefied sleep.

When she awoke next morning, she did not know what to make of the experience. It had all been so real. Her mother sensed there was something wrong but made no comment, thinking her daughter was depressed because the post had been and still there was no letter from Bill, who had embarked weeks ago for the Middle East. As she got ready for work, Mabel tried to push all thoughts of the night's experience firmly out of her mind. But they kept coming back.

Consequently, when she got home that evening after work, she took out the diary which she had kept assiduously every day since the war started, and wrote an account of the strange incident she had experienced the previous night. Could Bill really have been calling her? Had something terrible happened to him? Who could she tell who would not inwardly scoff at her as being a silly, overwrought woman imagining things?

Mabel was not alone, however, in receiving such 'messages'. Many wives, sweethearts, mothers and other close relatives had similar experiences.

She had met Bill Smyth, a veteran of Dunkirk, at a dance in Gledhills, Bradford. He had come up to her saying, 'I can't dance but would you dance with me, please?' They had struggled round the floor a few times, sat out and chatted for more tunes and at the end of the evening he had taken her home. For the next few weeks they had spent all their spare time together, dancing and riding on the rattling, blacked-out trams to different cinemas.

By Christmas time they knew each other so well that Mabel invited him home to stay for his short leave. They walked on the smoke-blackened moors above the city, and he had talked about his job at Abingdon. For the first time they kissed passionately, and Bill then told Mabel that he loved her and asked if she would wait for him. All of which Mabel committed to her diary.

A few days later, early in January 1944, Bill was warned for an overseas draft. He managed to slip out of barracks for an hour, a wonderful hour with Mabel. 'The last memory I had of Bill was of him walking away whistling "I'll be with you in apple blossom time", and I wondered if he would.'

From the boat, just before departure, Bill wrote a short letter to Mabel. It was really only an official form giving the address to which letters could be written for forwarding onward later. After that there were no more letters from Bill. Days passed into weeks, weeks into months, and still no mail. Mabel noted the fact in her diary.

When April came with still no news from Bill, Mabel's mother said philosophically, 'Oh, Mabel, Bill's forgotten you by now. He's just another soldier. Forget him.' But Mabel had no intention of forgetting Bill. She would wait. But it was not going to be easy.

So many wives and sweethearts had to face the problems of separation, and it was not made any easier when advice and temptations came from all sides. It was particularly difficult for women in the services not to be influenced by their friends. The very nature of service life, with its long periods of separation, not only gave women a newly found freedom, new opportunities for meeting other young men and financial independence for the first time: it also put them in a totally new environment of women living together after work was finished. In a barrack-room, with no men present, they could talk freely. They could talk, and did talk, of sex as they had never been able to talk before. And from all accounts, many young women took advantage of wartime life to express their rebelliousness against the traditional, male-set archetype of a loving wife and mother sitting dutifully at home whilst the husband had a night out with the lads in the local.

It must be recognized also that the strain of separation could make even the most devoted sweetheart and wife susceptible to chance encounters with lonely men who offered temporary emotional solace. The susceptibility increased with the length of time apart, especially if the partners were not regular and fluent letter-writers providing frequent messages of reassurance about the constancy of their love. Front-line soldiers suffered pangs of gnawing anxiety; they worried terribly as they waited for letters from wives and sweethearts.

And even when servicemen and women were assured of the true love they had found, they still had to overcome difficulties caused by censorship – it was not easy to write passionate personal love-letters knowing that they would be read for censorship before despatch by section or platoon officers. The situation was made worse by the irregularity of military mail which was often delivered in batches, in no chronological order and weeks late. But better late than never, as long as the link with a loved-one was established.

There was one letter though that no man wanted to receive: the 'Dear John' letter. Next to a direct hit by a mortar bomb on his trench, nothing devastated a front-line soldier as much as the letter from his wife confessing infidelity or from a sweetheart saying she had met someone new. Jilted soldiers reacted in frightening ways.

Sister Winifred Beaumont recalls vividly the day a wounded soldier in her ward severed his jugular vein with a razor blade after receiving a letter from a neighbour informing him of 'goings-on that he should know about'.

Questions of whether or not a wife should write and tell her husband of her infidelity often appeared on the problem pages of women's magazines. The advice usually given was quite definitely against 'kiss and tell'. It was usually more on the lines of 'wait and don't tell yet'.

On 10 December 1943 for example, the letter of one poor woman who had been agonizing over the question appeared in *Woman's Own*.[2] She explained that her husband was a prisoner of war and that in her loneliness she had become terribly depressed. Then she had met two Allied officers who took her out and roused her from her depression. The friendships developed into something far more serious. 'Now I realize I am going to have a baby and I don't know which of the two is the father,' wrote the worried wife. Her sick and wounded soldier husband was about to be repatriated, and she did not know how to tell him. What should she do?

The Agony Aunt, 'Leonora', in her reply said that she appreciated the woman's problems of being depressed and lonely but said that how a woman could do such things with two men passed her comprehension. Her advice ran as follows: 'The main thing to do is to avoid hurting him, isn't it? I advise you, as soon as you know he has reached this country, to write to the matron of the hospital or the commander of the next camp to which he is sent, tell them the whole truth, and ask them how you can arrange some way of not seeing him until your condition is not apparent. Wait until his health is better before you tell him the truth. It might be the finish of everything for him if he knew it now.'

When some readers questioned the justification for withholding the truth from servicemen abroad, 'Leonora' replied that it would be unfair for a man fighting for his life, thousands of miles away and thinking of home and his wife, to have such a ghastly shock, and that she could not see how the situation could be improved by his suffering. She went on: 'Let her wait until he comes home and can face the position with his time and mind at his own disposal, not taken up by the business of fighting for his life.'

The harm done by women who felt impelled to write letters telling their husbands of their infidelity was roundly condemned by journalist Stephen Francis in *Women and Beauty*: 'What untold harm a foolish, unthinking woman can do with a scrap of paper, a pen, and ink, just because they want to ease their conscience.'[3] He went on to quote a journalist who asked: 'Are half the wives in Britain demented? Won't they realise the men out here have a job on that's more important than the heart-burning and soul-searching of all the silly females who have nothing better to do than pour out on paper their silly "confessions"? Don't they know what they are doing to the morale of the men?' Francis's advice to such women who were about to begin a letter with such stock phrases as, 'I don't know how to write this to you ...' was 'Why write the cursed thing? Tear it up. Wait till the war's over – you may have learned more sense by then. Or if not perhaps he'll have died happy.'

There was never any possibility of Mabel's deserting her Bill, and though during those long months when no letters came from him she could not communicate directly, she still felt she could 'talk' to him as she wrote up her daily diary.

On 7 April 1941 she wrote: 'British troops landed in Greece.' About to join those troops was Bill Smyth.

The Italians had attacked Greece in November 1940 but had met vigorous Greek counter-attacks supported by RAF aircraft which drove the 'macaroni' army back into the desolate mountains of Albania. After this brief campaign, Greece enjoyed a peaceful lull, but everyone knew that some day soon the Greek Army would have to deal with a more formidable enemy – Italy's ally, Germany. Reinforcements of Allied troops began to arrive in Athens to be ready for the inevitable attack.

In that brief respite between the Italian defeat and the German assault, a magic spell was cast over the whole of Greece, a feeling of euphoria in which people turned to love and romance. Betty Wason, an American journalist with the Columbia Broadcasting Corporation, reported: 'Love not war was the order of the day then in Greece. Never had the sunlight seemed so golden, the skies so blue. The sight of British officers in trim RAF uniforms strolling arm in arm with Greek girls over the white pavements added to the illusory gaiety, until it seemed less like war than a scene from some old-fashioned play.'[4]

Soon Athens was seething with men in uniform. There were tough Australians with wide-brimmed hats pulled rakishly down over their ears, and New Zealanders who charmed Greek girls with their simple, easy-going manners as they sprawled in cafés with tankards of beer before them. After weeks of fear and austerity the women seemed to become more animated and excited as social functions got going again. The war for the moment was over. It was spring, a glorious time to be alive.

It was boom time for the night clubs. British troops had never seen any floor shows like those in their lives. They clapped rapturously whenever the strippers came on and when the half-gypsy dancer in Maxim's finished each swirling dance with a leap into the nearest British officer's lap. In the dim light men from Britain and Commonwealth countries learned how to say '*Se agapo*', 'I love you', and '*Kukla mu*', 'My sweetheart doll', and brief encounters developed into engagements and long-term relationships.

'Suzy, the Romanian cabaret artiste, got engaged to a New Zealand pilot,' recalled Betty Wason, 'and even Niki, the tall, cross-eyed girl who danced a sailor's hornpipe in a satin sailor-suit uniform, had her own British boy friend.'

Here, too, was war aphrodisia at work. Colin McGregor writes:

Let no one think that these night-club girls were just tough, ill-educated tarts, though. Many were well educated, speaking several languages intelligently; they were talented and cheerful young women who had found that night-club work was far more interesting and much better paid than dreary office work. They were not girls of easy virtue.

I used to park my fifteen hundredweight Bedford truck just outside Maxim's, and on one very hot night, Bebe, a hostess there, said she would love to go for a swim. So we drove down the coast road, away from the filthy harbour area and onto a lovely field and grassy beach, sloping down to the sea. We dashed into the warm, shimmering water absolutely starkers. It was wonderful. Every time you moved your arms in the water, you left a trail of luminous sparkles behind.

We swam vigorously, splashed, larked about, revelling in it all, coughing up swallowed water; we hung gasping onto each other and marvelled at the thrill of one warm naked body against another in the water. Then we staggered up the beach and dried ourselves on our vests, underclothes or whatever, because we had no towels. I have never forgotten that lovely night!

However, the point I want to make is that, though we all had little flings of one kind or another, we weren't always thinking about sex. There was nothing wrong with us, but we didn't think we had to have sex to have fun and enjoy ourselves with women. Somehow it was different. The pressure was not there. Nor the expectation.

When Bill Smyth disembarked, he had no time to ogle Greek girls and drink ouzo. Once ashore, he was detailed to drive troops up to the forward defensive positions. Speed was now of the utmost importance. Troops and artillery had to be in their positions before the German Army attacked. There was hardly time to eat. Gone were the days when a soldier could sit down and write a leisurely letter home. Womenfolk once more would have to wait. Fears grew for their men when they heard on the news that Hitler had loosed his formidable army of fifteen divisions. Nazi tanks smashed their way across the Macedonian frontier. Two days later, Salonika, the second largest city, fell and then, to everyone's utter amazement, only eleven days after the start of this new war, the German Army passed right through the Olympus defence line. The entire front was in confusion. And once again Bill Smyth's troop-transporters were busy evacuating bemused British soldiers back through Athens and on to the beaches and into ports they had left not many days earlier.

As the troops left the doomed city, the sweethearts being left behind demonstrated their affection for the soldiers and airmen in a magnificent fashion. Betty Wason wrote: 'On that last Saturday, when a final lorry full of British soldiers drove through the outskirts of Athens in the late afternoon, girls all along the street threw flowers after them. One young woman went into a flower shop and spent all the money she had on flowers.'

Once again the British were left trying desperately to evacuate their troops by sea. Historian William Shirer was later to write, 'It was a minor Dunkirk and almost as successful.'[5]

But not for Bill Smyth. Not for 9,000 other troops left that night on various Greek beaches. As the German Army's advance patrols drew near, the Royal Navy pulled out. Men ran to the water's edge shouting desperately for one more small boat. Bill remembers that he too was shouting – but not for a boat. He shouted for what he was losing – life with his loved-one. He shouted her name over and over again: 'Oh Mabel! Mabel! Mabel!'

That was the cry Mabel Baguley heard in Bradford. It provoked her to write a spate of letters, for she was sure something had happened to Bill. She wrote to the Army Postal Service, the War Office, his former unit and in the end to the firm Bill had worked for in Abingdon. From them she got the address of Bill's mother. Being the next of kin, perhaps *she* had heard something.

Eventually Mabel heard from Bill's mother that Bill had been taken prisoner and was in Germany.

For the next 4½ years their courtship was continued by letter-writing. Mabel also kept in touch with Bill's mother, who wrote some weeks later to tell Mabel that there was something she ought to know if she had any ideas of marriage. Mabel was by this time really anxious and began to wonder what was coming. The news was simply that Bill was a Roman

Catholic. What a relief, Mabel felt. Though she was a devout Church of England communicant, she felt perfectly capable of dealing with the problem of religion. The next day she went to see the local priest and sought instruction for conversion to the Catholic faith. She told Bill in her next letter that she had chosen the saint's name Bernadette. In Bill's next letter he told Mabel that his real name was not Bill – that was just what his mates called him: it was Bernard!

All Mabel's letters to Bill had to pass through a British censor to make sure she was not inadvertently giving any useful information to the Germans. Similarly all Bill's letters to Mabel had to pass through the German censor. Occasionally they were allowed to send photographs, but these had to be sewn onto the letter. 'It was those letters that kept us all going,' said Bill. 'Even though we were allowed to send only one letter a month, it gave us something to look forward to, a positive link with our loved-ones.'

Mabel agreed: 'We knew we had something good that was going to be ours one day. And when I got the letter I prized most of all, I hugged myself for sheer joy. In the letter, Bill wrote: "I'm wondering when I'll be with you to change your name to mine. Some day in May, I hope." I remembered then how he walked away that night before the draft left Bradford and he was whistling that same tune – "In apple blossom time". And I sang to myself the lines of the refrain again: "Some day in May, I'll come and say, happy the bride the sun shines on today".'

Bill Smyth did return home in May 1945, the apple blossom was out, and as they sat talking together into the small hours that first night, he told Mabel how bereft he had felt as the last naval boat pulled away from the beach, leaving all the soldiers behind. 'I suddenly realized that I wouldn't be seeing you, and I shouted your name,' said Bill.

Mabel's reply surprised him: 'I know,' she said, 'I heard you. Look here in my diary.' She turned back to the date of 23 April 1941, and there it was written: 'Bill called to me last night.'

'Our story had a fairy-tale ending,' said Mabel, 'but it might have ended quite differently if we had not kept writing and telling each other how much we were still in love. And, you see, we have lived happily ever after.'

Letter-writing paid handsome dividends for Violet O'Brien, too. She must surely hold the record for her output of letters to her soldier sweetheart, William.

Violet, a Land Army girl in October 1943, recalls how it all started, at Rudham:

Our only social life there was in going to the Crown Inn and sitting with a shandy which had to last all evening. It was on such a night that I looked up from my drink and saw a soldier standing in the doorway. He was deeply sun-tanned, as if he had just come back from abroad. He came across and sat down beside me, and we talked all that evening. He told me his name was William. At closing time he asked if he could walk me back to the hostel. I said, 'No, thank you,' and then sat there as if turned to stone, until the pub was empty. Then suddenly I found myself making a mad dash to tell him he could walk me home after all.

From that night on, we sat by the fireside in the hostel each evening, content with each other's company. Sometimes, if the other girls in the hostel had stayed in, we would go to the summerhouse in the garden, with the door shut. It was very cosy. There it was that William one night asked if I would wait the next four years he had to do in the regular army and then marry him. I said I would.

At Christmas time we had to part. I had promised to go home. I cried when I left him but still managed to leave him with a smile to remember.

That Christmas Eve, my mother and I were alone when there was a knock at the door. Mother went to answer it. I heard William's voice, and my heart leapt. It was a marvellous two days we had together then.

In January William was posted away. Letters came from Scarborough every day, and soon everybody in the village knew about my William, and they were always asking how he was getting on. I carried each letter in my pocket throughout each working day, treasuring it. Sometimes they were very long days, getting up at five and at haymaking and harvest time not finishing until ten. (We had double summer-time then.)

Once William was posted back to a camp just eight miles from the hostel, and I used to cycle through hail, rain and sleet, slithering all over the place. The girls used to say I was mad. But I wasn't. Just madly in love.

Then he was posted away. He did not say where. All letters stopped coming but I still wrote to him. Weeks went by and still no letters came from William. I didn't know what to think. Surely he hadn't found someone else. We had meant so much to each other. My good friend Stella gave me a shoulder to cry on. One afternoon she came bursting into my room and pushed a letter into my hand. The familiar hand writing was William's. She left me alone to read it. All it said was that he had been posted somewhere but was not able to tell me when or where.

Then, a few weeks later, he came back suddenly on leave, and we got married by special licence. I did not have to wait four years, after all, until he came out of the army in 1948. But during all those years when he was still away from me, we still wrote to each other every day. I've never bothered to work out just how many letters we did write to each other. And during that time we both travelled hundreds of miles to spend precious moments together, sometimes just in cafés and on railway platforms. It was all worth it, and in 1948, when he finally came out of the Army, we got married again, but in church this time, and this, we felt, made our happiness complete.

Now we have been married forty-five years, and after three sons and nine grandchildren we are still very much in love.

The words of the popular song were proved to be so true: 'Love letters straight from the heart keep us so near when apart.'

Men and women separated by wartime service needed reassurance that all was well and that their love for each other had not waned with the years apart. This was the idea behind a series of programmes broadcast then by Vera Lynn – now Dame Very Lynn DBE. Her unmistakable voice, pitched somewhere on a fine edge between the beguilingly sentimental and the soothing and reassuring, did much to link servicemen and women with their equally lonely loved-ones, wherever they were.

Her romantic delivery did not, however, please everyone. Stuffy generals at the War Office wanted more rousing marches or even waltzes, and the hierarchy of the BBC thought light, cheerful music was what the troops really needed. In fact, both the generals and the BBC pundits believed Vera Lynn's singing could even be bad for morale and 'sap a soldier's spirit'! The forces knew better. Men and women wrote by the thousand to Vera to say that her songs helped to bolster their courage to carry on as they thought of their own loved-ones far away.

No matter how trite the words might seem, the sincerity of delivery got the message across. And so the BBC planned a new programme, now so well remembered. It would be in the form of a letter to send to the forces overseas each week. It would be called *Sincerely Yours, Vera Lynn*.

The 'Yours' touch was an inspiration, because at the time the first programme went on the air in November 1941 that was the title of the most popular song, one that reassured parted loves:

Yours till the stars lose their glory,
Yours till the birds fail to sing,
Yours till the end of life's story,
This pledge to you, dear, I bring.

The programme soon developed into the realm of personal contact and individual messages, as Vera Lynn recalled:

I had the idea of visiting hospitals where Servicemen's wives had just had babies, and conveying the news to Gunner Smith, or whoever, within hours of the event. To be able to say to some poor boy serving out in Burma or North Africa, or somewhere at sea, that I'd actually been to see his wife and that I'd taken some flowers and talked to her, was like getting hold of their hands and putting them together ... It had the effect of reducing the distance between them, or bringing them all a little closer ... I was simply acting as a message carrier between separated people, and through the words of a song I told one what the other wanted to say.[6]

A similar programme to keep American servicemen in touch with their loved-ones back home was presented by Bebe Daniels and called *Here's Wishing You Well Again*.[7] Apart from messages and entertainment by guest artistes, there was always a feature of requests called 'Sounds from Home', and this included anything from fish and chips frying in a fish shop or a Hyde Park orator or the roar from their favourite football stadium.

Immediately after D-Day and the invasion of 6 June 1944, Bebe Daniels made history by flying into Normandy – the first woman civilian to join the assault troops. There she recorded reassuring messages from home and cheerful interviews with wounded soldiers close to the front line.

There can be no doubt that the efforts of Bebe Daniels and Vera Lynn, who also visited forward positions in Europe and the Far East, helped sweethearts to feel more in touch with each other. By requesting a particular song, they could express – convincingly and without embarrassment – deep feelings of love and longing to be together.

For men and women serving in remote areas overseas this contact through radio and letters was vitally important for morale. A letter or a message meant they had something definite to which they could look forward – a wife or sweetheart waiting for them at home. And for a few precious moments they could forget the sand or the flies or the mud, and the attack that was going in tomorrow.

6   'Love Is All'

What with the war, and the heat and I think with being so far
away from home as well, it played havoc with our feelings. I
know it was quite easy to fall in love.

Margaret Dippnall, ATS

Randolph Churchill was stony broke![1]

The commando lieutenant, son of Prime Minister Winston Churchill,
was beset with money problems: debts galore and angry creditors
threatening to sue him. And now he had little time to solve his problems.
He was to embark with No. 8 Commando to the Middle East.

His young wife, Pamela, daughter of Lord and Lady Digby, was to be
left, literally, holding the baby, Winston, (now Winston Churchill MP).
This was a situation many wives were to find themselves in as husbands
were posted abroad and they were left with a pittance of a service
allowance from which to provide food and shelter for the family.

'It's going to be terrible, parted like this,' said Randolph to his wife,
'but if you live economically off my army pay, we will pay off some of the
bills and that will be glorious!'

Twenty-year-old Pamela, whom he had married after a whirlwind
courtship of three weeks in 1939 and now left in a small house rented
for a pound a week, was not so sure. She could see nothing in the future
that seemed at all glorious. The future looked decidedly grim.

Three weeks after Randolph left, a telegram arrived for Pamela. She
naturally feared the worst. Telegrams to servicemen's wives in those
days usually began with the ominous words: 'The War Department
regrets to inform you that ... ' The telegram that day was different. It
was not bearing news of a death or of someone being missing; it was,
nevertheless, a harbinger of disaster. The short message came from her
husband. He confessed to having lost a fortune gambling with his rich
friends on the troopship, but begged Pamela not to tell his father.

No wonder! Winston and Clementine Churchill were no different
from other parents who were having to worry over the marriage
problems of their children. The Churchills had had more than their
ration of that. Their daughter Diana had married a wealthy South
African, John Bailey, but their marital happiness was very short-lived. In

91

less than a year they separated, and they were divorced shortly afterwards. Diana, now serving in the WRNS, had married again, to Duncan Sandys. Another daughter, the actress Sarah, had become a chorus girl, and this had certainly worried her parents. 'Even though,' as younger sister, Mary, wrote later, 'several ladies of the chorus had become duchesses.'[2]

Winston's apprehension was soon more than justified when Sarah fell in love with a comedian, Vic Oliver, who was seventeen years older than her and twice married already.[3] Nothing the Churchills could do – and they tried many devices – could prevent the marriage. Sarah did not have the nickname 'Mule' for nothing. She bolted off to the United States, where Oliver was then acting, and married him. This caused her parents much pain and public embarrassment.

In 1941, when Randolph was having his financial problems, Sarah and Vic Oliver had just separated. The marriage had collapsed, but to avoid adverse publicity Sarah hurriedly (with father's help) joined the WAAF as an aircraftswoman second class and to all appearances remained with Vic Oliver throughout the war years, after which they quietly divorced.

The concern for his daughter and the publicity added to the stress Winston Churchill was already carrying as prime minister.

It was at this time also that his youngest daughter, Mary, caused yet another diversion on the domestic front. When only eighteen and much to the consternation of her parents, she became engaged to a man she knew only slightly – a situation typical of those wartime years when sweethearts rushed into long-term relationships.

Her mother, Clementine, thought this was just a bit too rash and felt that her daughter had been swept off her feet with excitement. 'They do not know each other at all,' she confided to her friend Max Beaverbrook. (How many other mothers were saying exactly the same words then?) As events were to prove, she was right. Mary saw the light too, and the announcement of the engagement was postponed – amidst sighs of relief all round. But Mary still gave some cause for parental anxiety, for she joined the ATS to serve in one of the new 'mixed' anti-aircraft batteries.

With worries enough over three daughters, what father would relish yet another family domestic problem from his son? Hence Randolph's plea to his wife, Pamela: 'Don't tell my father!'

Such was the bombshell in the telegram that shattered the marriage of 20-year-old Pamela Churchill, who had never before been a penny in debt.

Every week welfare societies and agony aunts were dealing with similar problems which came to them in letters from servicemen's wives who also had been left 'holding the baby'. They were desperate for advice on how to cope with financial problems caused by husbands' being called up from well-paid civilian jobs to serve on the low pay of the armed forces.

Pamela Churchill's way of dealing with the problem was also typical of solutions found by other poverty-stricken young mothers. She parked her baby, 7-month-old Winston, on a friend and got a job. She worked at the Ministry of Supply for £12 a week, sold her wedding presents and jewellery to pay off the debts, and cut her losses in more ways than one, as husband Randolph began his tour in the Middle East.

In the summer of 1940, following the British Army's withdrawal from France, Churchill's prime concern was for the defence of Britain against a German invasion. But whilst planning for this he suddenly had to consider a threat from a new quarter.

The Italian dictator, Mussolini, obsessed with dreams of his country's destiny, decided to declare war on Britain to realize his crowning ambition – the conquest of Egypt, with his legions lording it over the riches of the Nile Delta, with garrisons in Alexandria and Cairo. And at the head of that empire, controlling the Suez Canal, *Il Duce*.

But it was madness. His army was not ready for war.

'We haven't even enough shirts for our army,' said his military adviser, General Badoglio. 'How is it possible to declare war? It's suicide.'[4]

But Mussolini would not listen. His mistress, Claretta Petacci, who would one day die violently by his side, pleaded with him not to risk a war in which the country had no heart. Employing all her charm and guile, she implored him to be patient and wait until the country was better prepared for war. On many occasions before, she had succeeded in influencing Mussolini, as mistresses throughout history have influenced commanders, but this time she failed.

At six o'clock on the evening of 10 June 1940, Mussolini went out onto the balcony of the Palazzo Venezia and said to the well-drilled crowd below that the hour of Italy's destiny had come. 'A declaration of war has been handed to the ambassadors of Britain and France. Italian people, rush to arms and show your tenacity, your courage, your valour!'

Glumly the crowd dispersed. It would not be very long before many of them would be giving succour to British prisoners of war, tending their wounds and falling in love with them. Meanwhile they were committed to fighting the British Army in the Western Deserts of Libya.

Consequently, in the autumn of 1940, when the Battle of Britain was over, Churchill took a calculated risk. He depleted the forces for the defence of the United Kingdom against invasion and sent drafts of fresh troops, mixed with veterans of the old British Expeditionary Force, to reinforce the Middle East garrisons before the Italian Army took the initiative. By February 1941 they had covered 700 miles to reach the vital Italian base at Benghazi. An Italian army of ten divisions was destroyed.

It was during this victorious campaign that the Commander-in-Chief Middle East Forces sent an urgent request to the War Office for more ATS units. Early in November 1940 an ATS unit was hurriedly dispatched to Egypt for administrative duties at headquarters MEF and for special duties of a secret nature at a camp ten miles from Cairo.

So it was that Margaret Dippnall, Catherine Culbert and close on fifty other ATS women found themselves being hustled aboard the troopship SS *Georgic* one foggy autumn morning.

The first few days at sea were pretty horrific for everyone. Margaret Dippnall was seasick for the whole week. 'But it was not too bad for us,' she recalled. 'I was a sergeant then and shared a cabin with another sergeant. I slept in the top bunk, and there was not room for two of us to be out of bed at the same time. With both of us being seasick, life was not easy. But we were far better off than the troops.' Later the voyage took on the faint air of a pleasure cruise. Margaret Dippnall recalled thoroughly enjoying herself:

We steamed leisurely and peacefully along, and what a lovely time I had strolling round the deck. There were New Zealanders, RAF aircrew and ground crew, Royal Signals and Royal Artillery and umpteen British Army regiments. In fact we were surrounded by men in all kinds of uniforms. It was lovely.

We had been issued with khaki dresses at Aldermaston, where we were kitted out for overseas, so we walked round in those. I soon made friends with a New Zealander; we strolled round together and sat together in the evenings. The night sky was so clear and the stars shone out so brightly from the black velvet sky. It was really so 'story-book' romantic.

Most of the ATS girls soon found a partner, and we gathered together some evenings on one side of the deck where a soldier played his accordion for us and we sang with him those sentimental songs, many of them with a faint nostalgic flavour of Edwardian music halls, such as 'Daisy, Daisy, give me your answer, do' which was a favourite. Every time I hear those tunes now, I'm taken back to the boat and I'm wistfully singing with them all again in my mind and in my heart, 'Over the rainbow' and 'All the things you are'.

There was one man, called Fred, who wanted me as a 'stand-in' for his wife – not in the intimate sense but just as a *listener*. You see he wrote love poems to her and wanted to read them aloud with feeling to me, to see if they were all right.

Everyone at some time or other began to exchange confidences. They sat around talking of home, of their wives and sweethearts and of all the things which fill the minds of men and women who have recently left

home and fireside. Creased photographs would be pulled out of battered
wallets and handed round.

Margaret Dippnall had butterflies in her stomach as she disembarked:

'I felt then for the first time what a long way I was from England and my
legs wobbled in a strange way too, though I think that was just because we
were on firm ground again.

We travelled by train across the desert. We could see nothing but sand,
and I did begin to feel excited about what lay ahead of us. At last the train
pulled up. Not at a station but at a siding. There, soldiers were waiting to
escort us to our camp. It was early morning – as usual – and we were so
glad to lay our blankets down on the hut floor and try to get some sleep.
When I woke up, I strolled to the door of the hut and opened it on to
blinding white light. What a beautiful sight, a marvellous sunrise. And it
was November! On the ground the ants were already busy running
around.

The camp of the Combined Services Detailed Interrogation Centre
(CSDIC) at Maadi was situated on the edge of the desert among
casuarina trees. There were a few huts surrounded by a wall of dried rush
to make it more secluded from the road, but it was not quite finished.
There were no proper toilets, showers or baths. There was one gate into
the camp on which was an armed guard from the Hampshire Regiment.
The work of the unit was highly secret, and visitors were rigorously kept
out.

These Hampshire soldiers just loved the job of being guards to the
ATS quarters. They were regular soldiers who had just come from many
years of service in India, and so they were delighted to meet real English
girls again. Soon I got friendly with a corporal, and we used to go down
into Cairo for our off-duty hours. Sometimes we'd be roller-skating and
at others we would go to the pictures. I also had an Egyptian who fancied
me as well, and one day when my corporal and I arrived at the Picture
House we found that it was full and we were just wondering what we
could do instead when this Egyptian friend came up to me and said that
he had three seats if we would like to join him. What an uncomfortable
evening that was! I sat in the middle with one of them holding my right
hand and the other my left.

However, it did not seem to put my Hampshire boyfriend off, and by
Christmas I was engaged to him.

Shortly after our engagement he was posted to Malta. A few days went
by without a letter, but I had expected to have to wait for new mail to
come through. The days turned into weeks, and then I knew that was the
end of the affair. However, there were so many men worrying us for dates
that I soon got over my disappointment. Soldiers coming down from the
desert – 'out of the blue', as we used to say – were ravenous for female
company, and it was hard to resist their approaches without seeming to be
churlish or mean.

It was a few months after my arrival that the main body of troops for the
interrogation centre arrived and we settled down to a steady routine. For

the officers, Maadi was a 'cushy' number and one in which women's presence was very much appreciated.

Actor Michael Denison was surprised: 'To a newcomer to Middle East Forces, the war being waged by CSDIC seemed extraordinarily unreal. It followed strict office hours and stopped completely for a prolonged siesta every afternoon,' he later recalled.[5] Though married to Dulcie Gray, he too felt this need for female company and soon found it: 'Among the girls I was fortunate to have as my assistant, Elizabeth Angas (now Bancroft) of the ATS, as attractive as she was efficient. We became and remain firm friends and I am grateful across the years for the gaiety of her companionship, both on and off duty which helped to fill the aching void of Dulcie's absence, and, even more important, sought to do no more.'

The other ranks had to work somewhat harder but still had time to relax and enjoy themselves. Margaret Dipnall's day started at five in the morning:

I had to wake up cooks and all men on early call. I did this the same way each day by singing Deanna Durbin's song at the top of my voice, 'Love is All'. My singing was not universally appreciated, but the song became identified with me.

It was a fairly long day for me but we still had time for socializing. A truck took us once a week to the Slade Club in Cairo, where we danced the evening away. There were bazaars, visiting concert parties, cycles to hire for rides along the Nile, and swimming in the freshwater pool. I suddenly became aware that by 1942 something had happened to me; the shy girl who had joined the ATS to broaden her horizons had gone for good. Now I could handle all the back-chat the troops had to offer.

It was just about this time that I was sent on a desert cooking course for a month. It was really a testing time, for the sun blazed down and the heat was barely sufferable. By the time I came back, my skin was almost black. Things had changed in the camp too since I had been away. I noticed a lot of fresh faces around. One in particular was a soldier who had been sent to us for a break as he had been 'up in the blue' for a long time with a tank regiment. It was not long before he too was asking for a date. At first, all this amounted to was a walk around camp to the Maadi tent. Then we progressed to the Slade Club for dancing. Later we managed to get a day off together to take a trip to the Pyramids. Soon Henry and I settled down to a steady relationship, as did many others there.

We came to the conclusion that, as we got on so well together under difficult wartime conditions, we could certainly cope in peacetime and we decided to get married there and then.

We knew though that marriage would immediately bring one big problem. The Army would let us get married but would not let us serve together. We would be separated by postings to different units.

Noon

Marriage by deception! Helen Martin was about to be married
when all leave was cancelled. Her fiancé had other ideas; his
friend, another Able Seaman put on his best 'officer type'
voice, impersonating a Naval lieutenant and telephoned
Helen's Commanding Officer to say that special arrangements
has been made for AB Jones to marry and requested similar
leave for Helen. This was granted. Jones was then smuggled
out of his barracks and the wedding took place as arranged,
with Jones 'Absent without Leave'. No wonder the newly
weds look so happy and relieved.

Jan Kubis and Josef Gabchik who
found love and family affection
before parachuting into Czechoslovakia to
kill SS General Reinhard Heydrich.

Right: The farewell letter from Jan to the
two sisters and Mrs Ellison.

Above: The wedding of Bill and Mabel Smyth,
after his return from prisoner-of-war camp,
1945.

The photograph which Mab
had to stitch to her letter to I
in the prisoner-of-war camp

Bill and Mabel today with th
diary in which she wrote: 'B
called to me last night' on th
same day as he did in fact ca
her name as the rescue boat
turned back from the Greek
beaches leaving him to be
captured by the Germans.

The 'sun-tanned soldier', William O'Brien, and his Land Army sweetheart Violet who wrote letters to each other every day.

Major Ian Carmichael and Pym Maclean on their wedding day and with their daughter Lee.

Margaret Blenkinson Dippnall *(top right)* at Maadi Camp, Middle East.

6 'Love is All'

Henry 'Jim' Dippnall back from the desert where he had been in action with a tank regiment, just before meeting Margaret.

Margaret and Jim today, still enjoying dancing at Heywood, Manchester.

A last quick cuddle for Minnie
Chappell from Peter Jeffrey at
Ismailia, November 1945, prior
to her departure for the UK.

The wedding of Sister Marjorie
Doyle Bennett, Syracuse, Sicily,
June 1945.

D-33

Marlene Dietrich – 'the fabulous queen of glamour' delighted troops
in the Algiers Opera House in 1943 with jokes about the romantic
philanderings of their officers.

7 'Let's Do It, Let's Fall in Love'

Studying Form? Which do you fancy? Eighth Army officers of Number Four Pack Transport Group, down from the front line for the day at the races seek help from Italian signorinas before placing their bets.

Nurses in the forefront at the parade ring during the horse racing organized by Number Four Pack Transport Group, Northern Italy, 1945.

Calls Ken Barker has ignored, too happy with his contessa to trust the amnesty for deserters granted by the Ministry of Defence.

8 'Che Sará, Sará!'

Former POW Ronald Hankinson and his Italian wife Rosina (in 1971).

The village of Vestea in which Ronald Hankinson found refuge and romance.

Brigata Garibaldini of Bologna. Girls served with their sweethearts in these partisan groups. Paratrooper Medic, Ronald Hankinson served with one such group.

Nevertheless, on 21 July 1943 we were married in the church hut of Digla Garrison, Maadi. We had a little 'do' in the camp afterwards. One of the ATS officers made a cake and sandwiches for the buffet, and then off we went for a honeymoon at Port Said.

Talk about a cheap wedding! It did not cost us a penny. We were given railway warrants, the officers let us have one of their drivers to take us to the station, and then we got settled into a hotel in Port Said for a magnificent week. We went to the beach, lazed in luxury under sun umbrellas, swam in the clear blue sea whenever we felt too hot, and had a honeymoon never to be forgotten.

But then came the heartache.

We had steeled ourselves for the blow, for we had seen it all before. The posting orders came. Jim was sent to Alexandria, I was left where I was. Married couples were considered bad for good order, efficiency and military discipline.

A few months later I found myself in another situation, not entirely unexpected, which meant that I too would be on the move. I was pregnant.

The Army was no place for a pregnant woman. That was the attitude taken on both medical and welfare sides of the War Office. The difficulty of finding light duties for her, the question of night duty, the problem of booking in for her confinement and, if she was unmarried, of finding accommodation – all made early discharge desirable. In addition there was always the possibility of a miscarriage, and although doctors agreed that Army service did not predispose miscarriage, rather the reverse, the authorities feared that it would be difficult to convince an unhappy husband that the baby had not been lost through his wife's lifting a heavy object or rushing about during an air raid. All these arguments strengthened the case for an early discharge. On the other hand, the medical officers had to be reasonably certain that a woman *was* pregnant, for a claim to pregnancy by a serving woman was seen as an easy way out of the service. When pregnancy was positively diagnosed, the discharge of the serving woman was carried out usually at three months.

A pregnant auxiliary serving in the Middle East had to return to the United Kingdom by troopship, as air travel was rejected on the grounds of discomfort and because of the possibility of having to land at airfields far from medical aid. In 1942 an instruction was issued to Middle East Command that an auxiliary was not to embark if her pregnancy was more than twenty-four weeks advanced. Thus, if the pregnancy was late in being diagnosed and if there were few troopships sailing to Britain, there was always the possibility of missing the boat altogether.

Margaret Dippnall was caught in this trap. At first she was told that she qualified for a home posting and that she would also be told when there was a ship sailing to the UK. But, as with many arrangements in wartime, there was a SNAFU – Situation Normal All Fouled Up (as the polite version put it). She was not told, and she missed the boat. 'But don't worry,' said her commander. 'You can carry on cooking for the ATS and then, nearer your time, you can go and stay at special accommodation which we have for pregnant ATS personnel.' Margaret went to this special flat in Cairo.

It was a magnificent four-bedroomed place. There were Wrens, NAAFI girls as well as ATS, and we had a lovely time waiting until we moved into hospital. On 14 April my baby boy was born. We called him Fred.

I had then to wait from April until August before I could get a passage on a ship home, and we sailed on a boat coming with troops from India. This time though we sailed on the short route through the Mediterranean, a lovely calm voyage in pleasant sunshine for most of the way.

On the next to the last day of that trip I had a very moving surprise. 'Jock', one of the girls who had come out with me and served at Maadi in the same unit, made a special request to the officer commanding troops. So it was that as we sailed towards the entrance to Liverpool port there came over the ship's loudspeaker system the unmistakeable voice of Deanna Durbin singing my reveille song, 'Love is all'. What a fitting end to such a memorable period of my life!

We edged slowly into the port of Liverpool through a typical Lancashire drizzle. That too was lovely. I lifted up my face and let the cool raindrops pour down my cheeks and those of the baby too. I had not felt or seen any rain since leaving England so many years ago.

I had a big smile on my face as I walked down the gangway in my smartest ATS uniform, and it grew into a broad grin when I heard a passing soldier say to his mate with typical Liverpool scouse wit, '*Hey look! Do you see what the ATS are getting issued with now?*'

It is evident, in retrospect, that the war intensified emotions. Casual relationships between servicemen and women developed so easily and naturally into friendships, then through a more affectionate stage into a serious romance and marriage. And what is interesting too is that the marriage was for the commitment it brought and not for any excitement of the big white wedding day. These were, in any case, rare.

The marriage of Minnie Chappell of No. 3 Air Formations Signals serves to illustrate this point. Minnie's meeting with Leading Aircraftsman Peter Jeffrey was far from a case of love at first sight, for though they began the relationship with the usual sort of chitchat, they never actually saw each other for weeks: Peter fell in love with a voice! He recalls:

I was a wireless mechanic specializing in teleprinters. These machines were like typewriters connected to each other through a pair of lines inside a land cable, and whatever operator A typed on his machine would appear on B's machine at the other end. Sometimes these machines went out of order due to a fault in the machine or a landline failure. I would then report the fault to our local Faults Control Centre.

Each time I telephoned, I was answered by a very pleasant and friendly-voiced ATS operator. It turned out that she had only recently left Britain, whereas I seemed to have been away for ages, and so naturally I was curious about what life was like there now. I asked her about food rationing, the bombing, leave travel on trains and buses and that sort of thing. She was willing to chat and told me more each time. She also told me her name was Minnie but she preferred to be called Mickie. I said I would call her Min.

I often wonder now, was it the hand of Fate or just a strange coincidence that my early calls were always answered by her? Before long, though, Minnie took over from Fate. When my shift of duty changed and someone else took my calls, Min would always ring me back as soon as she came on duty. That gave me a real thrill. The pace of my pulse and our relationship then began to race ahead.

The breakthrough came one day when she telephoned to say that her ATS unit was holding a social evening in the lounge of the block of flats in which they were billeted, and she asked if I would like to go as her guest. I was keen to meet her, and she must have known how pleased I was by the sound of my voice. Afterwards I sat wondering what I had let myself in for and tried to put a face to the voice. But I gave up. I knew it could be setting expectations which might not be realized. However, I had agreed and was looking forward to the night.

There was no problem in getting a lift to the ATS quarters, and I was at the appointed place dead on time. There stood a young ATS girl, and she looked really stunning. Could this be Min? It was. And she was absolutely charming to me all night: she looked after me, guiding me to the refreshments and to comfortable chairs afterwards where we could relax and talk. The evening passed so very quickly as we sat just absorbing the genuine pleasure we were giving each other.

When I next spoke to her on the phone, I took a deep breath, crossed my fingers and asked if she would like to go to the cinema with me and perhaps have a meal afterwards. She said she'd love to, so we agreed a time and place. Oh how exciting it was waiting for the next meeting! You sometimes forget how it was when you were young and in love.

We met outside her billet at Heliopolis, took the 'Brown' tram to Cairo, went to an air-conditioned cinema and then to a restaurant to complete the evening. After that our meetings became more frequent. Sometimes we'd go to Geziero Island, which was just over the bridge across the Nile from Cairo. This was the pre-war social centre for those with money and position. The grass there was green, for every so often the island was closed so that it could be flooded by opening the Nile sluice gates until the lawns and sports fields had had a good soaking. At other times we would go to Groppi's, the ice-cream parlour, where we tried all the marvellously different concoctions in turn.

The next stage in our relationship was memorable. We took our leave together, went to Alexandria and stayed in the Southgate Hotel, which was run by an elderly Englishwoman. Min had a room looking out over the sea, and I had one at the back overlooking a side-street. We had a wonderful week. We rode on the tram to the 'servicewomen's beach' at Sidi Bishri, swam in the clear blue Med and sunbathed. We took in a couple of tours to Pompey's Column and the catacombs and of course went to the cinema in the evenings. The cinema was an essential part of courting in those days.

I suppose then we were in the 'affectionate stage' – nothing too serious or advanced. It wasn't the 'done thing' to go any further then than the kiss and cuddle. Also, because of the local customs and religion and especially their attitude to women, one did not walk arm-in-arm or outwardly show any signs of affection, as we might have done back home in the UK. In the hotel we did not want to do anything that would make the elderly English proprietor raise her eyebrows, for we were sure that there was nothing that went on in the hotel that she did not know about.

Time rolled on, and our repatriation date came nearer. Neither of us said anything about getting married, but I think we both knew that eventually everything would work out in the way we both wanted. So we stayed how we were. Min left for home on 18 December '45, and I went back to UK in February '46. We promised to keep in touch.

Minnie Chappell and Margaret Dippnall were still in the Middle East when Catherine Culbert moved on. Her situation had changed: she was no longer a private but an officer. The opportunity for promotion came when the role of the ATS in the Middle East changed, with many new trades being opened for servicewomen. With the expansion of the ATS by enrolling local recruits as well by drafts sent from Britain, more officers were needed.

Catherine's merit was recognized just as it had been at her school. Her annual reports marked her out for promotion, and her name was eventually submitted for officer selection. She was interviewed by the assistant director of the ATS, and by the spring of 1943 had completed her officer training. She was then transferred for staff duties at Allied Forces Headquarters, Algiers.

There she had two surprises. The first was the remarkable atmosphere in the headquarters itself. Women there were agog with talk of romantic liaisons between men and women of all ranks and between the mixture of nationalities there, American, British and French. The second surprise came in the form of a rather disturbing letter from her mother: she said that everyone was fit and well, Martin earning big money on overtime, Jennifer happy at school, but wouldn't it be better if Catherine could now come back into the home again? Otherwise, well, a man needed a wife to come home to at night, and it really was time Catherine was home ...

Catherine reasoned with herself that her problem would have to be solved after she had settled into her new job. Meanwhile there was a war to be won, wasn't there? And she couldn't start asking for a posting back to the United Kingdom just after being newly commissioned, could she? In any case, had she not just heard how troopships were now in great demand, reinforcing the armies in the Far East? For the time being then, she did nothing about her mother's letter.

On one of those Far East convoys sailing into Bombay at that time was actor John Le Mesurier, who later would make films with Ian Carmichael, Peter Sellers and Kenneth More and be remembered affectionately as Sergeant Wilson in the television series *Dad's Army*. He recalled vividly that morning the ship docked, and in his book *A Jobbing Actor* he relates how as a young Army officer he leant over the ship's rail and was immediately struck by the stench.[6] Nevertheless, despite the smell, he later returned to Bombay to spend a few days' leave. He stayed at the Taj Mahal Hotel and, like so many young servicemen who had gone before and who would follow after him, he asked the waiter where the 'action' was in Bombay. The speedy reply surprised him: 'Number 4 Grant Road.'

This was the famous address visited by so many wartime soldiers in search of further education, sexually. And John Le Mesurier's experience was probably far from unique when he discovered that buying sex was like lighting a damp firework: it didn't go off. But it made an amusing tale to relate over a drink with friends and even partly on television. Years later, when he appeared on a TV quiz show in Bristol, he was handed a piece of paper on which was written, 'Good girls go to heaven. Where do bad girls go to?' To this question he replied, 'Number 4 Grant Road, Bombay'. Some men in the audience laughed rather too loudly.

On the particular evening on which young Lieutenant Le Mesurier entered Number 4, he followed what appeared to be the accepted procedure: he ordered a drink and eyed the coffee-coloured girls swinging their tightly covered buttocks round the room. At last, with resolution bolstered by drink, he made up his mind.

'I chose a very beautiful Eurasian girl and finally took off with her to her room,' Le Mesurier recalled. But once inside, his interest in the whole sordid affair began to wane: 'I looked round at some dreadful pictures on the wall, and examined with great care her dressing table, as any sexual urge I might have had on arrival, drained away despite her physical appeal.' The fact that she became impatient, telling him to hurry up, at the same time as an Indian outside was beating on the door shouting that his time was up, was enough to put an end to the whole pathetic proceedings.

John Le Mesurier must have left with rather confused feelings, but he might have felt better had he known then how many other young men had experienced a similar reaction to Indian brothels once the moment of truth arrived.

Another media celebrity, BBC disc jockey Jimmy Young, had a similar experience.[7] He recalls, in his amusing biography, *J.Y.*, how he was once an RAF physical training instructor waiting for posting orders in a Bombay transit camp. Whilst knees got browner, everyone got increasingly bored. There were a number of distractions to keep them amused, such as 'Housey Housey' (the original Bingo) and the camp cinema, and there were also the Indian prostitutes in the 'out of bounds' district.

It was on one of those evenings of boredom that Jimmy's friends decided that his education should be extended, sexually. He well remembered that night: 'I was still a virgin airman, a situation that some of my colleagues were impatient to bring to an end.'

In all his innocence, Jimmy allowed himself to be taken along the dingy back streets beyond the black-and-white military police signs suspended from wires across the road. Eventually he found himself standing in a queue of self-conscious soldiers, smoking, sweating, waiting and trying to put on a bold face. It was then that he realized he had no inclination whatever for what the others were waiting for, and that he didn't like the situation at all. It could land him in trouble with the military police. There was only one thing for him to do: turn and run. He did. He dashed downstairs, side-stepped a red-capped policeman and lost himself in the crowded street.

Jimmy Young's sexual further education would have to wait a little while. He preferred to take his instruction in more civilized surroundings. He would not have very long to wait.

There followed one or two other postings before he was moved to Chakrata, where his services would be needed in more ways than one. He was going to join the 'Entertainments Section', for by this time he was spending more of his time singing and playing the piano than taking PT classes. He was not to know then just what the extent of those 'entertainment services' was going to be. Nor how pleasurable, how romantic.

At Chakrata, 8,000 feet up amongst the snow-capped Himalayas, two military rest camps were situated, and the air was pure and clear. Chakrata was full of men, the other camp, Kailana, full of the wives and children of servicemen. The whole set-up was a relic of the pre-war British Raj, when wives and daughters of soldiers and airmen were considered too fragile to withstand the dust and heat of the plains during the summer months. So, whilst the men sweated it out below on the plains, their womenfolk relaxed in the cool comfort of married quarters in the hill station of Kailana. Husbands came only for brief periods when they had leave. Men without families spent leave in the neighbouring camp of Chakrata.

When World War II broke out, however, women were packed off immediately to the safer confines of the hill stations, where they took up permanent residence. One can well imagine the boredom of such an artificial life of leisure they would have had to endure, were it not for the fact that across an easily negotiable ridge were hundreds of virile young servicemen who were equally in need of entertainment. Here it was then that so many of these young innocents, like Jimmy Young, were introduced to what were then still delicately called 'the Facts of Life'.

In Kailana, infidelity and adultery were an inevitable and acceptable part of expatriate life. It had always been so. In pre-war days the annual migration of wives and children to the cooler climes had set the pattern for women to experience exciting periods of liberty in those mountain resorts. Maud Diver, in her detailed study of *The Englishwoman in India*, written back in 1902, declared that the women thought nothing of extra-marital affairs. 'Their time,' she wrote, 'was filled with flirtations with and without issue ...'[8]

The situation had changed little in the intervening years, as Corporal Jimmy Young discovered on his arrival. He found that in Kailana there were wives who could cope without the companionship of their menfolk, and those who could not. Jimmy soon realized how things were done. Contact was established, a relationship developed and then you simply moved in. 'It was,' he wrote, 'to all intents and purposes like being married, and, accompanied by one's lady friend, one moved around, mixed with and went to parties with other couples just like husband and wife.'

After work each day he would 'go home to the little woman', to his slippers and supper. After supper there were lessons to be learnt, as he was to write later in his biography *J.Y.*: 'I could not have been taught what little I know about the art of making a woman happy in bed by a nicer person.'

Jimmy had a long course of 'instruction'. Others, like Harry Carling of the Royal Engineers, had to be content with a three-week crammer.

Harry had been laid low by a serious illness and was sent to Chakrata to recover on convalescent leave. He said:

> Those women knew what kind of entertainment they wanted, and no two ways about it. Frankly I was astonished and shocked by the forwardness of some of the wives at that place. Their manner and talk carried an unmistakable message – they were available. I don't know if it was the heat or the remoteness of the place or the exotic background of Victorian India which affected them, but affected they certainly were. To put it

bluntly, my first thought then was that I'd never seen such a randy lot of women.

But I was wrong, in a way. It's true that half of them seemed to be after a man, but not necessarily for sex. They missed having a man about the house. Some of them wanted both sex and companionship, but you never know really. People don't always tell the truth. And when it comes to the subject of sex, probably very few men or women tell the truth. One thing I must say too is that many of those women were models of propriety and decorum. They really were faithful to their husbands.

Anyway, to get on with my story, one night shortly after I'd arrived at Chakrata, a fellow sapper asked me if I'd like to walk over the ridge with him to have dinner with a lady he knew well. He had mentioned my debilitating illness to her, and she had immediately suggested that I should be brought over to dinner one evening.

So, off we went. I had a very good time, with six or seven others gathered for drinks first and then round a table for dinner afterwards. Usually I'm not very good at circulating and making small talk at such parties, and so when one lady, who introduced herself as Celia, started talking to me and showing an interest in what I said, I was relieved to stay with her. She was a close friend of the hostess and said I could call to see her whenever I had a spare evening or was at a loose end any time.

Two or three nights later I wandered over. She lived in a nice four-square bungalow with steps leading up to the veranda. She must have been watching for me coming, for as soon as I put my foot on the first step, she bounced down the others to meet me – and I mean bounced, because she was a well-made woman and I don't think she was wearing a bra, which in those days must have been the height of wanton behaviour.

She smiled and reminded me that her name was Celia and took me by the arm. The movement released a little wave of scent. As I've said, she was inclined to be chubby and well-shaped round the hips. Did she walk well! I judged her to be in her mid thirties, and her whole manner put her in the class of the Raj – born to breathe that rarified oxygen-starved air of the upper slopes and peaks. She was supremely self-confident, with the air of women who have been to Cheltenham Ladies' College or Roedean and know everybody's place and are determined to have people recognize their own. It was this attitude that had, at first, made me reluctant to accept the invitation, but when the alternative was a game of bridge, with all its inevitable post-mortems on why had I not led with my king or that I should have known all the spades had gone, pontoon or Housey-Housey, I thought I would give it a go.

We sat down in reclining chairs on the veranda. Exactly on cue the curtains behind us parted and a bearer floated in with a large tray of drinks which he put down on a table before us.

'Help yourself to a drink,' said Celia.

There was a generous selection: whisky, gin, soda, angostura bitters, bottles of Murree beer and a wide variety of squashes and cordials. I chose a whisky – an Indian version of Scotch which I diluted well with lemonade and added cubes of ice from a zinc-lined container. For her I made a large gin and tonic.

We sank into our chairs. I sipped my drink and waited. She was obviously in command, and I was overwhelmed by it all. I remember thinking it was all so much like a play, and we were actors on stage. We chatted, or at least she did most of the talking, speaking in a slightly nervous fashion. She was one of those women who giggle a lot, bare their teeth and look knowingly into your eyes as if sharing an intimate secret with you.

Eventually, after we had helped ourselves to more whisky and gin, we went inside to eat. Over the table a fan revolved slowly, squeaking and clicking. There were just the two of us. She said we were going to have something which sounded like 'Pudding wally cleaner', but when I tried to repeat it, she burst out laughing and insisted on writing it in capital letters in my diary. I still have it. 'PUDINE WALA KHEEMA'. It was marvellous. Succulent minced lamb mixed with mint, pulses, ginger, garlic, cayenne pepper and spiced with cardamom pods and coriander. On top of it all we squeezed fresh lemon juice. The odour of it was just too tantalizing for words. It would make anyone smack his lips.

A bearer, turbaned, sashed and barefooted, hovered in the background, bringing one dish after another onto the table. After the first course I never asked what I was eating. I just enjoyed everything that was set before me. My wine glass was continuously topped up by the well-briefed, attentive bearer.

Vaguely I recall the meal ending and gramophone music starting up. Celia took my hand and led me to a patch of floor behind the table. There she swayed with me to the slow rhythm of the music.

Now you've got to remember that I was then a young lad of twenty-two, and I was excited by the closeness of her body so that I could not help feeling my sexual response stiffening against her thin dress. It was then that she began to dance me towards the open door of her bedroom, and we gravitated on to the bed without releasing our hold of each other. I soon found out I was with no novice to the game. When we kissed, her tongue parted my lips firmly and her fingers ran over the back of my head, slid over my shoulders to the small of my back, pressing her body tightly into mine all the time. Makes me quiver to remember it. I had never known anything like that before. Nor have I since.'

Early next morning I walked back along the ridge to Chakrata camp through a fine mist which smelt of wood smoke and dung fires. It was an eerie sensation, like being in a dream, as the sun gradually burned away the vapours of the night. I was to become familiar with that dream during the next three weeks. It was only when I was back in the men's camp and sitting at a deal table with a pint mug of tea in front of me that I again felt down to earth and no longer in Kipling's India with the lonely ladies of the British Raj.

The next time I went to Celia's house I took my small overnight pack. I stayed there every night for the rest of my convalescence.

Nobody thought anything of my activities. I gathered from others at the camp that it was quite the normal thing. Kailana was always like that. Always had been.

I decided though that when I got home to England and at some future date when my children asked me the question, 'What did you do in the war, Daddy?', I would never tell them the story of Celia and Kailana. But sometimes now, as I lie awake in the small hours of the night, I tell it again to myself. And I marvel that it ever happened.

In those brief weeks of convalescence Harry had learnt a lot about life. Then he went back to his unit and the horrors of Imphal and Kohima, where he learnt more about death.

7 'Let's Do It, Let's Fall In Love'

We are concerned about the love-life of various members of
staff. The steamy heat, like a Russian bath, is particularly bad
for women.

Harold Macmillan MP
Resident Minister in North Africa, Algiers, 1943

Catherine Culbert, who had abandoned husband and child to stay in the
ATS, had been at Allied Forces Headquarters, Algiers, only a short time
when she realized what a 'military love-nest' it was. 'All the girls, British
and American, seemed to be having affaires,' she recalled. 'There were
whisperings by the filing cabinets, guarded conversations behind the
typewriters as officers supposedly amended drafts of letters, and so
many telephone calls of a personal nature rather than operational. It was
an eye-opener for me to work in that strange set-up. Raw sex was in the
air!'

It was indeed an unusual headquarters, established after the biggest
invasion fleet the world had ever seen had landed American and British
troops at several points along the French North African coast between
Casablanca and Algiers. They had brought with them their brass bands
and 'number one' uniforms, expecting to be welcomed by cheering
crowds greeting them as liberators from the jackbooted Germans. The
French were not so welcoming. In three days of bitter fighting they
resisted the landings. A thousand Allied soldiers were killed by French
troops before they grudgingly laid down their arms and allowed
themselves to be 'liberated'.

Now Allied troops could press ahead with their strategic objective of
'closing the ring' around Germany, which meant clearing all German
troops from North Africa. The headquarters for this campaign, taking
place some 300 miles east in another country, was established at the
elegant St George Hotel, Algiers. And, somewhat appropriately as many
were later to comment, the commander-in-chief of those Allied troops,
General Dwight Eisenhower, occupied the 'Bridal Suite' on the third
floor, with windows looking down over a magnificent sweep of the
harbour and the Mediterranean beyond.

In the high-ceilinged rooms of the St George and neighbouring

107

hotels, middle-aged staff officers, who would, but for the war, have been preparing for their pensions and poultry farm in the south of England, were enjoying a new lease of life. And of their sex life in particular.

A few hundred miles to the east of these exotic hotels, the starved mongrel of an army which the staff officers serviced – the British First Army and the Americans – was battling against the odds, short of equipment and learning very quickly that Tunisia was not a land of sun and sand as they had expected of Africa. It was bitterly cold, with icy rain and mud which turned into such thick brown glue that it would almost wrench off your boots. It was also a land of craggy hills and dense scrub. Supplies came in by jeep and mule train up treacherous mountain tracks and along machine-gunned roads without air cover. For weeks infantrymen engaged in a gruelling fight had lived in open slit trenches with only their ill-fitting waterproofs to cover them. Their nights were spent shivering under wet blankets slung over their battledress.

Exhausted though they were through lack of sleep, they fought on through formidable hills against German infantrymen counter-attacking from defensive positions with tanks, venomous and accurate mortar fire and complete air superiority.

Meanwhile, back at Allied Forces Headquarters, the tedium of service life was being lightened by the arrival of ENSA artists. They quickly sized up the steamy love-life of the city and parodied it on stage. In March 1943, for example, the Queen of Glamour, Marlene Dietrich, the star with the fabulous legs, delighted Allied troops packed into the Algiers Opera House with her skits. Soldiers had joked often enough about the philandering of their officers – now it was even better to see it exposed by outsiders.[1]

They roared with laughter at the opening gambit of Marlene's show. It began with a comedian coming on stage with a doleful face and announcing that Miss Dietrich would be unable to appear, as she had gone out to dinner with an American colonel. Groans of disappointment and anger erupted from the audience, but quickly they were quenched by a shout from the back of the auditorium – an unmistakeable deep voice calling: 'No! I am here.' And there indeed she was, 'the Flame of Orleans', the star of *Destry Rides Again*. Whilst all heads swivelled towards her, the immaculate khaki-clad figure ran down the centre aisle. In her hand was a small attaché case.

Once on stage she immediately apologized for her lateness and captured one hundred per cent attention as she slowly opened the case and took out first a pair of evening shoes, which she put on, and then a silky evening gown. She took off her tunic and was apparently about to change on stage when she was discreetly led away to the wings, much to the loudly vocalized disappointment of the troops.

But she was back in a flash and had her audience with her all the way as she crooned the song which might well have been written for so many of those men and women of the Algiers garrison:

Falling in love again,
Never wanted to …
What am I to do?
I can't help it.

After the show, jeeps, staff cars and light trucks tore through the blacked-out streets back to their messes and officers' clubs, with captains, majors and colonels yelling good fellowship at one another like kids on an outing. At the Centre District Club, Italian prisoners of war in white linen coats served schooners of cool beer and tall, emerald Tom Collinses. On stage there a Negro band played smoochy tunes for the officers dancing with civilian women and servicewomen, in the scented gloom on the dance floor. Eventually the late-night revelry broke up, and once again, jeeps, staff cars and trucks raced down the Rue Michelet in drunken convoys.

The next day the officers, some looking decidedly the worse for wear, would be at their desks again, lighting cigarettes with shaking fingers and trying to deal with the daily deluge of mail which flooded the in-trays and pending baskets. Press releases informed the world that a German attack on the Medjez El Bab front had been repulsed, with some casualties.

In the intelligence section Catherine Culbert read a summary of activity on other fronts. 'Patrol activity. Nothing further to report.' Words could not convey how it really was.

They were living in worlds apart.

Catherine had been sent to Headquarters Algiers from the quiet backwater of the Maadi camp in the spring of 1943 after being commissioned and posted for duty with the intelligence and field security section. Although ATS Controller Maud Baillie was then exploring possibilities for posting more ATS officers and other ranks to Algiers, they did not arrive in any numbers until 1944, and Catherine found herself amongst a mere handful of ATS officers.[2]

I was lucky enough to fly into Algiers airport at Maison Blanche because I was acting as courier for classified documents. It was a tremendous experience for me as I had never flown before. My first sight of Algiers was breathtaking, it was all so glaringly white, cradled in steep hills and nestling round the harbour which seemed to be packed with ships of all shapes and sizes: warships, tankers, merchantmen and smaller craft. When we taxied into the reception area and got out, the contrast could not have been greater. Clouds of dust blew over the airfield on which dozens of military aircraft were dotted. It was all noise and bustle. No one was there to meet me. No transport. No directions. I was sitting on my kitbag wondering what to do next when a portly, dapper British Army major in 'brothel creepers' (those suede soft-soled boots worn by those who had been in the desert for years) came up to me, flicking a tropical flywhisk of horsehair, and asked me where I was going and would I like a lift. When I told him, he seemed to know exactly where I should report, and so I was happy to jump in the front seat of his Humber staff car alongside him.

Instead of taking me directly to Allied Headquarters, the major said we'd better go and have something to eat first, as all the meals in the military messes would be over by the time we arrived. So we drove to the Hotel Aletti, one of the few hotels not requisitioned by the military and where we could get good 'local fare'. I must say that I was glad to go with him because I had set off very early that morning, and not only was I very hungry but thirsty too. We went straight to the bar, where he ordered mutton couscous for two. 'You'll love it. Might find it a bit hot at first, but if you can take curry, you'll soon be hooked on couscous,' he said.

For about half an hour we sat drinking thin, cold beer at the bar whilst the meal was being prepared, and I felt quite light-headed by the time the waiter called us to a table in a cool, shaded corner of the dining-room partly hidden by broad-leafed potted plants.

On the table was a carafe of Algerian red wine. I took one sip and did not care for it at all, and anyway I knew the beer on my empty stomach had already made me a little woozy, so I decided not to drink any more. But despite this resolution I just had to take occasional sips to put out the fire in my throat. The tasty mutton which floated in a gravy generously seasoned with a murderous mixture of chopped chilli peppers, cayenne, paprika and ginger just set my whole mouth afire. I needed a little wine to cool it.

By the time we'd finished eating, I was hot, sweaty and drowsy. It had already been a long day. Then it was that the major moved on to stage two of the operation. He told me that there was no point in reporting to Allied Forces Headquarters at that hour of the afternoon because most of the offices would be on siesta. The sensible thing to do, he said, would be to take a room upstairs, have a shower and relax for an hour or so. And just in case I was left in any doubt as to the form that relaxation would take, he dropped his hand quite naturally on to my thigh.

I thanked him, retreated to the ladies' room and then, with a wave, made a run for the safety of the bright afternoon sunshine.

There was not much 'safety' in that bright sunshine though. Algiers had not earned its place in history as the wickedest city in the world for nothing. A Special Investigation Branch (SIB) policeman, C.V. Hearn, was stationed there in 1943 and shuddered as he recalled how it was:

The city reeked of sex, vice and violence. The young unshaven men seemed to have no work to do. They stood on street corners, uncaring which way the war went. Their only interest seemed to be in caressing with smoky eyes the figure of any passing female. It was a pitiless place.

People who stole often had their fingers or hands cut off. Men who got young girls into trouble often had their sexual organs cut off.

Frenchmen shot their enemies in the back, Arabs slit the throats of infidels. Into this cauldron of humanity the reserved, stuffy, obstinate, pious, antiseptic British were flung ...[3]

It fell to the SIB to protect innocents abroad, like Catherine Culbert and simple Allied soldiers, from their own folly. No one was safe from the vice kings. Troops marching around the city would be accosted by young pimps who offered 'gals and exhibishon', and a big job for the SIB was to clamp down on the widespread vice before too many young soldiers came to grief.

Typical was the night when Hearn and another policeman, posing as privates in the RASC, allowed themselves to be led to one of the houses where 'exhibishons' were offered. The young pimp led them to a dimly lit establishment under the sign of the 'Black Cat'. When they got inside, a shock awaited them. The place was seething with troops out for vicarious sexual enjoyment. Here was the mysterious East they had all heard so much about in barrack-room tales told by old soldiers who had served pre-war in Cairo. Here was the opportunity to further their sexual education and see something they would never have the chance to see in their own country. And these young lads were determined to cram in as much as they could, in the spirit of adventure. ('All,' as one squaddie put it, 'at His Majesty's expense.') During the show there was a good deal of chaffing, joking and good-natured badinage, and afterwards most of them left without further involvement, but there were the few, the drunken few, who stayed behind for something more and who, but for the intervention of the SIB, would have got more than they bargained for.

Algiers was indeed a wicked city, certainly not one which a young woman should venture through alone, even in the bright afternoon.

Catherine Culbert found it was a long walk up the hill to the Allied Headquarters housed in the Hotel St George. In pre-war days the terrace would have been set out with chairs and tables at which men and women in white tropical kit would sit sipping from long glasses in which ice tinkled. When Catherine finally mounted the steps, there were dark patches of perspiration staining her desert-bleached tunic. The terrace was crowded with red-tabbed senior officers waiting for their staff cars to arrive. She walked into the main foyer, reported to the desk and filled in the inevitable form, stating her business.

'Very soon I was absorbed – that's the best way I can put it – into the Allied Command. There was obviously a definite policy of integration, a friendly atmosphere between American and British troops of all ranks. Right from the start of the campaign, so I was told, this had been the deliberate policy of AFHQ. The genial General Eisenhower was determined to have no squabbling between the Allies.' Consequently, as part of a 'togetherness' policy, British and American officers messed together; they shared bedrooms which were also their offices; they shared billets and grew to respect and like one another.

In such an atmosphere it was not surprising that romance flourished. And especially when the lead came right from the top. Many was the time when GIs whistled and hooted as they saw their four-star general driving up to the front on the 'Red Ball Express' route alongside his attractive British driver, Kay Summersby. And no wonder! Kay's looks were enough to turn any soldier's head. Especially in North Africa. On those cold, hazardous trips, dodging through miles of thundering trucks hogging the centre part of the road because the shoulders were soft, 'Ike' was not so much worried by the traffic as by the stick he was getting from the drivers, as Kay later recalled in her book *Past Forgetting*: 'The General's sole concern was the continual collection of grins, whistles, wolf calls and coarse remarks I harvested in this exclusively male territory. He cursed and tried to look as stern as possible, muttering about the lack of discipline.[4]

Eisenhower was not so good on discipline, especially in an embarrassing situation, as one of his generals, Patton, was to note in a letter to his wife. Eisenhower had ruefully confided to him that when he was out horse-riding with Kay one day, a soldier had 'yahooed' at him. 'He told me that he glared at the man disdainfully,' wrote Patton.[5]

Kay, an Anglo-Irish divorcée with red hair and green eyes, had been a fashion model for Worth before becoming a driver with the FANY Motor Transport Corps. Her close and romantic relationship with the man who was to be Supreme Allied Commander in Europe (and future President of the United States) had begun in May 1942. She was then a newly enrolled FANY driver, detailed to pick up a VIP passenger at London's Paddington Station, a certain major-general with a German-sounding name.

On that foggy May morning of 1942, Kay drove General Eisenhower to Claridges Hotel and was thereafter his personal driver. She had been allocated to him, she tells us, because she knew the intricate London streets better than any of the American drivers.

During that time Kay had another officer to think about too. He was a man who was very much a 'VIP' in her own life, though not so senior in rank: Lieutenant-Colonel Dick Arnold of the Royal Engineers, whom she hoped to marry as soon as her divorce was finalized. It was a very busy time for Kay. General Eisenhower had so many calls and commitments at his office, and back at his hotel suite too.

In order to get some peace and quiet he took refuge in a quaint country retreat, mysteriously named 'Telegraph Cottage', off the beaten track near Richmond Park. There he could relax. It was on one of the first evenings on which Kay drove him out there, she recalls, that he turned to her and said, 'Kay, I never seem to have much fun and I get so bored. Must be boring for you people around me too. What can we do? What do you like?'

That was the beginning of many evenings, and later many nights, spent together. Thus, in the secret cottage and at his office in Grosvenor Square, months went by until, on 14 October 1942, Kay received news that her fiancé, Dick Arnold, was leaving for Scotland to join a draft getting ready for overseas. The tempo of Eisenhower's work increased at that time too, until the first week of November 1942, when he confided to Kay that he would be flying to Gibraltar for the North African landings, 'And,' he added, 'you'll be off to join me before long.'

It was, in fact, many weeks before Kay finally arrived in Algiers. There she was shown to her new quarters in the Clinique Glycine on top of the hill above the city. With a rare sense of humour, the army had billeted the new draft of women in the French maternity hospital.

Work for Kay started the next day, and she had little time to think of her fiancé on his way up to the front in Tunisia. By day she was driving the general and in the evenings she was helping him with the mass of paperwork which landed on his desk. Frequently she dined with him and ministered in many ways to his health, impaired by a lingering touch of flu.

During this busy period, however, there were two romantic interludes. On one occasion she drove the general to one of the forward positions on the Tunisian front at Tebessa, where the battle situation was serious. From headquarters he went forward on foot to look at the defensive positions. This gave Kay time to enquire at the corps headquarters, to see if Colonel Dick Arnold was available. But her fiancé was so busy chasing from one meeting to another that he and Kay were able to snatch only a few minutes for conversation. The fear was that the whole American front was crumbling under a furious German attack, as if they were staking everything on one big gamble – win all, lose all. Kay waited in the contagious atmosphere of apprehension. Later that evening, however, she and Dick did manage to have some memorable minutes together in which they were able to talk about their forthcoming wedding. By that time it was obvious that General Eisenhower would not be driving back that evening.

Kay tells in her book of an amusing incident that happened later that night. She had been given the VIP tent in which to sleep – it had a dry pebble floor instead of wall-to-wall mud. She had fallen into a deep sleep but woke in the early hours to hear the angry raised voice of General Eisenhower expressing dissatisfaction with the defensive arrangements. Muttering angrily, he finally squelched through the mud to the VIP tent. Kay heard a voice say, 'We put your driver in there. We'll wake her.'

'Jesus Christ!' growled the general, 'Don't do that. Let her sleep.' He pulled the flap aside, crawled into his sleeping-bag fully clothed, pulled a woolly hat well down over his bald head and ears and within minutes was snoring away.

A week or two after that night, Kay was taken aside by Colonel Ernest, who was on Ike's staff. Obviously embarrassed and stumbling over his words, he conveyed to her the gossip that was going round headquarters. 'People are saying ... that you ... that you ... ' he was too embarrassed to continue.

'That we what?' Kay prompted him.

'That you ... uh ... well, that you sleep together when you go on trips.'

Kay apparently enjoyed the colonel's embarrassment, for she added to it by bursting out laughing and replying, 'We did, Tex! We did!'

Kay's next romantic interlude with her fiancé was under much pleasanter circumstances than that at Tebessa. Dick was on leave in Algiers, and thanks to General Eisenhower they had a wonderful day together. He gave Kay time off work and a most considerate present. Kay recalled the general's words: 'You and Dick can take over my villa and be alone for once. I'll make a point of going out for the evening. With this wedding of yours coming up you must have a lot to talk about. Have a good time!' They did exactly that. Swimming in the afternoon, dinner for two prepared by the mess sergeant, and they spent an exciting evening talking about plans for their marriage.

In May 1943 the war in North Africa suddenly came to an end. The wedding day drew near, and Kay drove about in an orange-blossom world. She was in such an ecstatic mood, chattering airily away one evening as she drove General Eisenhower up to the villa, that she did not realize for some time that much of what she was saying was going unanswered. Ike was unusually quiet.

Kay pulled into the narrow driveway in silence that was oppressive. The general climbed out slowly. He called over his shoulder, 'Won't you please come in, Kay? I'd like to talk to you.'

She followed him into the villa, on into the library, and he motioned her to a chair. He lit a cigarette and stared at the floor. 'Kay,' he said finally, 'I don't know how to tell you this. Guess I'd better give it to you straight.' He looked up and said, 'Dick has been killed.'

The second disaster for Kay.

In one of war's tragic ironies, Dick had been killed after the fighting had finished in North Africa. He and a friend in the Royal Engineers Regiment were inspecting one of the well-taped German minefields when suddenly his friend stumbled on a trip-wire. He was seriously wounded. Dick was killed instantly.

Like so many thousands of other women bereaved by war, Kay bore her grief by immersing herself in work. And in doing so her relationship with General Eisenhower became closer.

Fruity speculations began all over again – Kay was later to confess that she felt at times like the girl in the hair-colouring advertisement of whom people were asking: 'Does she ... or doesn't she?' General Everatt Hughes expressed surprise in his diary one day at the way in which Kay seemed to dominate General Eisenhower and noted how she had once summoned him from the table. Indeed, it seemed odd to many of the Allied leaders that she had such a special place with Eisenhower. On one occasion later in the war, the Chief of the Imperial General Staff, General Sir Alan Brooke, arrived to take lunch with the Supreme Allied Commander and found Kay Summersby presiding over the table, with Prime Minister Winston Churchill on her right!

Eisenhower, it seemed, was trapped in the conflict that so many soldiers, sailors and airmen had to face in wartime: conflicting emotions for two women. He wrote passionate letters to his wife, Mamie, who was something special to him, but she was 3,000 miles away, whilst his British driver and aide, Kay, was with him constantly.

Was there, however, another reason for this close relationship? Another kind of speculation has at times emerged about Kay Summersby's privileged position with Ike – speculation as to 'was she ... or wasn't she' a special kind of driver/secretary, an agent of MI5? After all, she was a member of the elite FANY, which provided almost all the UK's 'female operatives', special agents and spies.

Officially, she was assigned to Eisenhower as a driver because of her knowledge of London's intricate network of streets, but there could have been another reason. The security services knew full well that the presence of an attractive, sympathetic woman in the front seat of a car could encourage VIPs to loosen their tight lips and become quite human as conversation flowed. Neither driver nor passenger faced the other directly, and there could develop a 'confessional box' type of situation, with thoughts and anxieties being put into words that should never have been uttered. General Patton, for instance, was always suspicious and would not have a woman driver, although he was an inveterate womanizer.

In the murky world of espionage and counter-espionage revelations are not encouraged, and if there were any substance in the speculation of Kay Summersby's other role, we are now never likely to know. But it *is* rather strange that a lowly driver should have her service recognized by the award of the British Empire Medal. Surely a curious honour for driving a Packard staff car?

Those senior American officers who refused to be driven by women were, however, not averse to sleeping with women drivers. General

Hughes noted in his diary that Brigadier General Henry B. Sayler, the chief ordnance officer ' ... was looking very tired. He has his chauffeuress back and is red eyed.'[6]

So many of these mature men, away from their wives were 'making hay whilst the sun shone', and it shone generously in Algiers in 1943.

Adultery brought inevitable feelings of guilt. Deputy Theatre Commander General Everett Hughes, wrote of his own affair with 'J.P.' and guiltily recorded in his diary that one night he had a terrible nightmare in which his wife had unexpectedly come to visit him, and J.P. had had to 'run like Hell down the back stairs!'[7]

The flamboyant General George Patton, one of the legendary commanders of World War II, had for his mistress Mary June Cooper, and also his niece, Jean Gordon. This young girl, the same age as George's daughter, had lost her father when very young and spent her vacations with her uncle George and family. At exactly what particular time in her life Jean and George's relationship became intimately close is not known, but once, after a drinking session, Patton confided to General Hughes in an oddly old-fashioned manner: 'She has been mine for twelve years.'[8]

Another very senior officer who quickly got organized with female company was the ambitious Air Chief Marshal, Sir Arthur Tedder. As a boy he was so shy that when he first went to school he hid under the table and would not say a word, but he quickly came out of his shell in Algiers. Soon after the death of his first wife, Rosalinde, he became very fond of Mrs Marie de Seton Black, who just happened to be unhappy with her own marriage at that time. Work helped her to surmount these personal troubles, and she set herself the task of organizing the first RAF Malcolm Club. (Named after Wing Commander Malcolm who was awarded the Victoria Cross for his low-level raid on an enemy airfield holding up the First Army advance in Tunisia.) It was not easy, and to get supplies Mrs Black had to work very closely with those who knew the Algiers black market.[9]

Everett Hughes was surprised at the speed at which the relationship between Tedder and 'Topper' Black moved. In no time at all they published the banns to be married. Hughes commented upon the speed of Tedder's remarriage in his diary, saying: 'Eyebrows were raised', but concluded: 'What the Hell!'[10]

No wonder. At that time there was no way of telling who was going to take up with someone else. Forty-nine-year-old Walter Bedell Smith, Eisenhower's chief of staff, who made enemies faster than friends, certainly did not seem to be a romantic character, yet he too jumped at the opportunities offered. When, in the early days of the campaign, a ship with five WAAC and 200 British nurses was torpedoed, Smith flew to Oran and took over the WAACs – and the five were promoted to captains. 'The English nurses got nothing except an English battledress,' wrote Hughes.[11] Later, in 1943, Hughes again twittered in his diary about Bedell Smith's saying he had ' ... gotten into some personal entanglement with a Nurse Wilbur who had returned a "Chief Nurse".' He certainly had a way with women.

And so the pattern went right down the line, affecting all ranks. It was perhaps somewhat strange that Eisenhower got on his high horse about these extra-marital love affairs and general promiscuity, in view of his own involvement, but he made no bones about admonishing his own Women's Army Corps personnel. In August 1943 he castigated them publicly, accused them of 'unsoldierly comportment' and told them straight to mend their ways or quit; forty-one obliged and went home. Eisenhower's distaste for these WACs perhaps caused him to utter the scurrilous definition of a WAC that found its way into Hughes's diary: 'a double-breasted GI with a built-in fox-hole'.[12]

It was not just the military men and women who were afflicted with high-octane passions: civilians were just as vulnerable to this war aphrodisia.

A few miles down the road from Allied Forces Headquarters the British minister resident in North Africa, Harold Macmillan, MP, was also having 'love problems' in addition to his official ones. His task in Algiers was to be the link between Eisenhower and the British government, and in many ways he was an ideal man for the job, for he had strong ties with the United States. (His mother was born in the small town of Spencer, Indiana, a state close to Eisenhower's birthplace of Abilene, Kansas.) On the other hand, though, Macmillan, with his baggy trousers, his gold-rimmed glasses that gave him the air of a Bolshevik teacher, and his toothily diffident half-smile, looked totally out of place in the military setting of Algiers.

He set up his headquarters in a sumptuous villa, the envy of his colleagues. 'Everything is of marble or gold,' he wrote to his wife, Dorothy. 'The pictures are by Botticelli or Murillo.'[13] All in extravagant contrast to the austerity and deprivation of wartime Britain. In such splendour it was not long before romance began to flourish. A worried Macmillan wrote to his wife saying: 'We are concerned about the love-life of various members of our staff. The steamy heat, like a Russian bath, is particularly bad for women. Miss Williams (my secretary) falls passionately in and out of love. The Sergeant archivist is now in love with her and since this passion seized him he has neglected his work. Fortunately this is now being done by a large, plain, red-faced and red-armed girl who has arrived recently and is very good. I suppose she will soon be a spoilt beauty in Algiers, where there is a definite shortage and therefore a correspondingly enhanced value is put on feminine society.'

Macmillan was often called upon to sort out other people's love-affairs, even that of his own political agent. In another letter to his wife he said: 'I expect you will remember Mrs G. coming to see me at Stockton [his constituency]. She telephoned me and wrote to me again before I left London. Apparently that silly fat husband of hers has fallen in love with a French nurse. He is thoroughly entangled, and I have to disentangle him. It's a great bore because he was a very bad agent and I should prefer to see him settle down in Algiers than return to Stockton, if I only thought of my own interests. But I suppose I must try to do something for her and her children.' Not very imaginatively, he resorted to the time-honoured military solution for solving love-affairs: 'I saw his chief tonight, a very nice officer called A.T. and we are trying to take some action to get him posted elsewhere.'

Passion might well have been a problem for Harold Macmillan in the Algiers of 1943, but in London he had his own pressing and personal problem to contend with. His wife was having a love-affair with his close friend and fellow MP, the raffish Robert Boothby, a former Chancellor of the Exchequer. This man was the exact opposite of Macmillan, described as an excitingly handsome bounder who dashed about in an open two-seater Bentley and was socially at ease wherever he went.[14] Macmillan, in his Edwardian manner, would undoubtedly have called him 'a cad', but Macmillan's wife doted upon him.

Yet it was a strange love-affair for Boothby, who, it was said, had enjoyed being chased all over the place by homosexuals in pre-war Nazi Germany. Nevertheless Lady Dorothy Macmillan, from the wealthy Cavendish family of Chatsworth, clung tenaciously to him and one of her children is said to have been his. Macmillan's biographer wrote of the Boothby affair: 'Cavendish women had a reputation for being highly sexed and it seems that Macmillan, like Churchill, attached little importance to the physical aspects of love. Indeed, President Kennedy, who was well acquainted with the Cavendish family through his sister Kathleen's marriage to Billy Cavendish, might well have been aware of Macmillan's lack of sexual appetite and given more offence than he realized when he casually remarked, many years later to the British Prime Minister: "I wonder how it is with you Harold? If I don't have a woman in three days I get a terrible headache".'[15]

There is no doubt that in 1943 Macmillan was deeply in love with his wife, Lady Dorothy, and he did work hard to save the marriage. As he confided to his biographer, Alistair Horne, 'I never loved anyone but her, never had a woman friend, or even knew anyone.' Of course, divorce would have ruined his political career. In any case, he was very proud of his marriage to a Cavendish and once said, 'I have it either way, my grandfather was a crofter, my wife's father was a Duke.'[16]

Consequently the man whom Churchill had made virtual pro-consul in North Africa and Italy wore a mask of unflappability whilst grimly enduring the pain and humiliation of his wife's adultery.

The scandal was widely known. Lady Dorothy made no attempt to hide the relationship, but Harold Macmillan played the traditional British stoic role of the husband who pretends there is nothing wrong. To those in Allied Forces Headquarters it might even have seemed that the resident British minister was having a rather enjoyable tour of duty.

There were frequent social occasions at which the blood of staid middle-aged generals and politicians was stirred in romantic ways. One of the ladies most adept at this was Lady Maud Baillie, ATS controller since 1942. Her husband had been killed on active service in June 1941, and in the following year Lady Maud spent a good deal of her time in the Central Mediterranean and Middle East Commands. An elder sister of Macmillan's wife, Lady Maud frequently dined with him and went out on picnics when time permitted. She was certainly a hit with the visiting generals, as he reported to his wife: 'Maud was at dinner, looking very smart. I gather she is having a great success here, and I think she is enjoying it. All the generals and colonels are inviting her to parties.'[17]

But the noses of these senior officers were rather pushed out of joint by the British commander-in-chief, General Alexander. He too was attracted by Lady Maud's charm.

Alexander was a dashingly handsome, sun-tanned man who wore his hat at a jaunty angle and sported a Clark Gable-type moustache. He had a certain way with women. And he had the ultimate aphrodisiac – *power*! The recently widowed Maud appeared to respond to whatever romantic signals Alexander was sending, for he decided to see much more of her, as Harold Macmillan was to report in a letter to his wife: 'A very amusing evening, everyone in good characteristic form. Alex, with his rather delicate mischievous twinkle, took a great fancy to Maud and has asked her to stay with him ...'

'Alex' – as he was generally known, though his name was Harold – was a charming, aristocratic Anglo-Irishman with all the easy assurance of his upper-class background (Harrow, Cambridge, the Guards), but with it the talent to reach the top of his profession without appearing to work too hard. He was a classic example of a man born with a field marshal's silver baton in his knapsack. He had commanded the last British corps to get off the beaches at Dunkirk, proved himself in Burma and the Western Desert and was deputy to Eisenhower in North Africa. Through all these trials he had emerged with an enviable reputation of imperturbability when things were going badly, and for apparent fearlessness under fire.

He was going to need those qualities. When Eisenhower returned to Britain to prepare for 'Operation Overlord' – the invasion of north-west

Europe, Alexander became supreme commander in the Mediterranean. Romantic interests would have to subside for the man who was to oversee the bloody and protracted Italian campaign.

8 'Che Sará, Sará!'

> I remember a British prisoner of war in the Val d'Orcia helping
> the peasant's wife to draw water from the well, with a ragged,
> beaming small child at his heels. I remember the peasant's wife
> mending his socks, knitting him a sweater, and baking her best
> cake for him, in tears, on the day of his departure.
>
> Iris Origo's Diary, *War in Val d'Orcia*

At precisely three o'clock on the morning of 3 September 1943, a
mighty barrage of 600 guns descended with demonic fury upon the
beaches of Italy's toe.

Later that same morning, people all over Britain and the USA heard
with mounting excitement how, after the biggest bombardment since
Alamein, Allied troops had crossed the narrow three-mile strip of water
dividing Sicily from Italy and landed at Reggio di Calabria, *unopposed*! It
was exactly four years to the day from Britain's entry into the war.

Now there was new hope for all those wives and sweethearts of the
70,000 British, Commonwealth and American servicemen held as
prisoners of war in Italian concentration camps. Soon perhaps they
would be liberated by the invading divisions. Had not Prime Minister
Winston Churchill said that Italy was 'the soft underbelly' of Hitler's
'*Festung Europa*' – his 'European Fortress'? Had he not assured the
nation that the Italians, with no real heart in the war, would soon give in?

Nancy Walley, then serving in the ATS at RASC OCTU, Southend,
certainly gained new hope for the release of her fiancé, Lieutenant
Leslie Adams, who had been taken prisoner at Tobruk along with
35,000 others in Rommel's big offensive of 21 June 1942, which drove
the Eighth Army out of Cyrenaica. He was then in Camp PG 21 at
Chieti, a few miles inland from the shores of the Adriatic at Pescara.
Soon, surely, he would be on his way home.

Hopes soared again five days later when the BBC radio broadcast
tremendous news. Italy had surrendered! There followed an extract
from a speech made by General Eisenhower: 'The Italian government
has surrendered its armed forces unconditionally … Hostilities will
cease at once and the Italians can have the assistance and support of the
United Nations to expel German oppressors from Italian soil.'

The news was heard by prisoners of war in Italy an hour and a quarter

121

later that evening. Music on the Rome radio was interrupted for a special announcement. Eric Newby was then lying in a hospital near Parma on the Via Emilia. He recalled: 'Someone began reading a message in a gloomy subdued voice. It was to the effect that the Italian government, recognizing the impossibility of continuing the unequal struggle against overwhelming superior enemy forces, and in order to avoid further grave calamities to the nation had requested an armistice of General Eisenhower and that the request had been granted.'[1]

Newby had been captured whilst on a Special Boat Service operation against German Luftwaffe bombers on a Sicilian airfield south of Catania in August 1942. Whilst in captivity he had fallen down a flight of stairs and broken his ankle. He was taken to the nearby hospital and there, in the maternity ward, had his foot plastered and treated by friendly nuns and medical staff.

A frequent visitor to the hospital was an attractive Slovene, Wanda, the daughter of the local schoolmaster, a notable anti-Fascist. Wanda paid particular attention to Newby and gave him lessons in Italian whilst he improved her English. Quickly things began to happen.

> Our relationship changed a great deal since we first met. It progressed far beyond the stage of giving one another language lessons. I had begun by thinking her a very good looking girl and being flattered that she should take any notice of me. Then I began to admire her courage and determination; now I was in love with her.
>
> These feelings were not entirely one sided. Now, when we were alone together, we sat as close as we dared to one another on the seat in the garden knowing that we were under observation by one or other of the *suore* [sisters] but on several occasions I managed to kiss Wanda in one of the dark corridors on the way back to my room.

That evening Newby had a visit from the *superiora*, who told him that a special *carabiniere* guard had been put outside his room, for the Germans wanted him personally supervised. It was at lunch the next day that he received the note that was to change his whole life. It was in Wanda's handwriting and hidden under a very hot dish (to discourage the *carabiniere* from lifting it), and it read: 'Get out. Tonight 2200, if not Germany tomorrow, 0600. Go east 500 metri across fields until you reach a very little street, then turn right and go on 500 metri until you reach a bigger street. Wait there. Don't worry about clothes and shoes.'

That evening, feigning stomach-ache, Newby rushed to the lavatory, made various groaning and grunting noises and then quickly wriggled through the tiny window and slithered down the drain pipe. Bootless and in pyjamas, he hopped and clattered away down the path as best he could with his plastered foot. Across the fields and on to the track he hobbled, to find a small Fiat car waiting there, with the doctor and Wanda's father. That was the beginning of a long and bizarre series of adventures and incidents, many shared with Wanda, the young woman who had helped him to escape and who would one day become his wife and share many more long and interesting journeys.

Captain Ken Barker heard the news of Italy's capitulation in the dining-hall of Italian prisoner-of-war camp on the Via Emilia:

Really it left us too stunned to raise even more than a cynical cheer. In fact, the Italian guards outside made more noises than we did. They scampered about embracing each other as if they had just won the war and a prize of a million lire into the bargain. Our senior officers got together and 'took charge'. This in practice meant turning the prison camp into something resembling a barracks in England, with regimental police-type sentries at the gates. 'We shall wait until we hear further from headquarters as to the disposition of Allied troops and instructions as to what we should do,' was the announcement at a special parade.

Frankly, after watching the hash senior officers had made of the war in my three years of service, and then in prisoner-of-war camps, using their rank to gain privileges, I was not inclined to be part of any further bungling. I decided to look after my own future for a change.

Quietly I made my way to the Italian cookhouse and bartered some of my precious possessions, and by writing a few glowing testimonials, which I said would get them jobs with the British when they arrived, I got sufficient food to last me a few days and co-operation in the next stage of my plan. Fortunately my year in the modern languages department at Sheffield University and the impulsive purchase of Charles Clark's *Italian Lessons and Reading*, which I had seen in a Cairo secondhand bookshop, were now to stand me in good stead.

The book had been a good companion, reliable and amusing throughout my imprisonment. At the end of each lesson there was a short list of Italian proverbs. One in particular determined my actions that day: '*Quando viene la fortuna, apri le porte*' – 'When fortune comes, open the doors.' From now on, *I* was going to be the one opening doors.

The other proverb certainly bolstered me up when I was feeling exhausted during the next few weeks and has guided me many a time since: '*Chi la dura, la vince*' – 'Whoever sticks it out, wins.'

Later that evening the senior officer called a meeting which everyone had to attend in the dining-room. Whilst men were moving down the corridors and pathways to the meeting-place, I was strolling, hatless and with an Italian jacket flung cape-like over my shoulders, through the camp gates, with my Italian accomplices on each side engaged in excited conversation with all the typical gesticulations.

Once through the village my two companions bade me farewell. '*Anche noi andiamo a casa. Guerra finito*' – 'We're going home too. The war is over,' they said as they pointed me in the direction of the hills. But for me the war was not yet over.

There were indeed many exciting and romantic times to come for Captain Ken Barker.

Lieutenant Adams was not fortunate enough to be amongst the thousands of escaped Allied prisoners of war. The Germans were quick to take over his camp at Chieti. They transported him with other prisoners of war to Sulmona, the birthplace of Ovid, and on to camps at Moosburg in Bavaria, Mahrisch Trubau in Czechoslovakia and finally Brunswick, to Oflag 79, from which he was released in April 1945 – a six-footer weighing only 6½ stones.

Nancy, true to her promise, was waiting for him on his return. Their romance had continued and thrived through letters, and it culminated in a wedding at St Michael's Church, Blundelsands, Liverpool, in May 1945. A fellow prisoner from Chieti, Lieutenant T. Lynch, was best man.

Corporal Ronald Hankinson of the Royal Army Medical Corps had parachuted into the heart of southern Italy in February 1941 with a team of demolition experts to blow up a vital aqueduct which fed the Italian naval ports of Bari, Brindisi and Taranto, which were being used to supply Italian troops in Greece and the Western Desert of Cyrenaica. The operation had been given the code name 'Colossus'.

All went well up to a point. The aqueduct was successfully blown, and the plan then was for the team to split into small parties which would make their way south-west down the Sele valley to the Mediterranean coast, where they would rendezvous in five days' time, ready to be picked up by a submarine which would be waiting for light signals. The only rendezvous members of that team made was in an Italian prisoner-of-war camp.

Except for Ronald Hankinson. He had broken his ankle on landing from the parachute drop, and once the noise of the explosion had roused the *carabinieri*, he was soon captured and taken to a military hospital, where he received good medical care. Once his ankle had healed well enough to take his weight, Hankinson escaped and headed for the hills – 'I was able to cover a good distance from the hospital, marching by night and lying up in culverts and under bushes by day.' The higher he climbed, the steeper the going became. Every so often he had to pause, bending forward with his hands on his knees, panting like a loose-tongued dog until he was ready to drive his stiffened legs forward again. After three days and nights he was at the end of his tether.

I was ravenously hungry and parched with thirst. I was also in great pain from my ankle, which had swollen enormously. I knew that if I took off my boot I would never get it on again. An idea came into my mind that if I came to a village with a church I would knock on the door of the nearest house and ask for a priest. Added to all my discomfort was the thought that I was completely lost and had no idea where I was. Just when I was feeling desperate, I saw ahead of me a few buildings clustered together around a church. Cautiously I walked up to the door of the cottage nearest to the church, took a deep breath and rapped loudly on the door.

It opened, a curtain was pulled aside and a man stood there holding a lamp. He was a typical Italian mountain farmer with a lined weatherbeaten face, black jacket, black trousers and a kind of cape. 'What do you want?' he asked.

I had rehearsed my answer to such a question all the way up the last rise. '*Bisogno parlare con un prete*,' I said haltingly – 'I need to speak to a priest.'

'*Non ce sta*,' said the man, shaking his head to emphasize the point. The priest had gone.

The farmer then asked me who I was and where I was going. I decided to take a chance and trust him. '*Sono inglese. Soldato!*' I said.

'*Ah! Inglese. Avanti*! You come inside.'

There were three women in the room hovering behind the old man. I say 'old', but I found out later he was just turned forty. He explained that he spoke a little English, for he had worked in America before the war. He introduced me to his wife and two daughters, Giovina, the elder, and Rosina, the younger one, who was wearing a bright, flowered frock which did not seem in keeping with the drab outfits of the rest of the family.

With typical peasant hospitality they made me feel welcome and soon had a meal of *mortadella* and bread on the table for me. The wife bustled round and filled a large glass with red wine which she set down at my elbow. When I had finished eating, I was shown to the back room, where a few chickens sat silently on their perches at the far side of the room in which a couch had been made up into a bed. There they left me to undress, and when I pulled the covers back, I had the surprising luxury of sliding between clean white sheets. After the rocky mountain naps, I felt I was revelling in voluptuousness. I fell into a wonderfully deep, refreshing sleep.

The sun had risen high in the sky when I awoke the next morning. Its powerful rays penetrated through the old wooden shutters, and when my eyes focused, I found myself looking upon the figure of Rosina. What a fine picture she made: a perfectly oval face in which were set dark, sparkling eyes, her long black hair tied back with a ribbon, leaving a bunch of curls to fall luxuriantly over her shoulder. She bent down to offer me a big cup of coffee, and I gazed upwards into the cleft of her breasts buttressed in her brightly coloured frock. The coffee was awful but the awakening magnificent.

I thought she was lovely. I still do.

She told me in words and signs as I sipped the hot coffee that the priest would be coming to the village that morning to say mass. Her mother was the church caretaker, and so the priest always called at the house for something to eat and drink after the service. Meanwhile I was to stay out of sight in that back room.

Later that morning the priest did come to see Ronald Hankinson. He was a big man with a red, unshaven face. He spoke a little English but, whilst being sympathetic, was not too encouraging about the prospects of being able to help. 'We are in God's hands!' he said. 'I will come back when it is dark and talk again.'

When he came back, he brought with him an old English–Italian grammar book. 'It is one I used when I learnt English,' he said, 'At the moment it is too dangerous for you to move from here. You must stay hidden.'

In the weeks which followed, I spent most of my waking hours studying Italian, and it was during one of those long evening sessions that Rosina surprised me by coming into my room and quite out of the blue said: 'Would you like to go for a walk with me?'

I jumped at the opportunity. It was already dark when we left the house, but the moon was rising as we made our way across a field to join a goat path which meandered over the hill. I gave only a passing glance to the landmarks we passed, because I was filled with a new and exhilarating sensation, a strange feeling of belonging, strengthened when Rosina linked her arm in mine. We said little, and the silence was broken only by the crickets and occasional barking of a dog. I took in huge lungfuls of clean, cool air which I had so missed being cooped up in the cottage. It was a marvellous feeling out there beneath the moon and the stars all out in array. Overhead was Orion in all its magnificence. It was hard to believe there was a war on at all.

When we reached the crest of the hill, we sat down for a rest and gazed upon the little white dots of the houses in the village of Penne. Illuminated by the bright moonlight, they looked like something from the backcloth of a stage setting. Towering darkly on our left were the peaks of the Gran Sasso mountains, which we both knew were soon likely to become my home. I did not relish the prospect.

Rosina must have known what my thoughts were, for she disturbed my reverie by reaching for my hands, which she pulled deliberately to her waist and placed them just where she wanted.

'I know,' I said, 'I'm afraid.'

'It happens to everyone at times,' she murmured, snuggling closer.

'I would much rather stay here with you,' I said as she lay down and put my head in her lap. Then for a while all talk ended. I dreamt my dreams and she dreamt hers. Neither of us dared to think how they might one day be realized.

Two hours later, when we got back to the cottage, our serene mood was abruptly shattered. In the middle of the kitchen stood the red-faced priest, hands on hips and feet apart like an irate housewife to give a severe tongue-lashing to a late-home husband. His face was screwed into a censorious frown, and in his formal grammar-book English he launched right into the attack with that oft-used question: 'Where on earth have you been? It's an affront to decency to be out so late with this young girl.'

With difficulty I kept my temper.

'Padre, for reasons of my own I went for a walk. The girl came with me to make sure I did not get lost.'

The priest unbuttoned his cassock at the neck and sat down heavily with a snort of disgust.

Rosina's mother took her by the arm and bustled her into a side room. She was obviously alarmed and angry. Rosina's father stood glaring at me like a bull about to charge and then followed his wife into the room, slamming the door behind him. The priest reached for the wine bottle, poured himself a generous glassful, then stood up, adjusted his cassock and stalked out of the house without another glance in my direction.

I felt absolutely rejected, like something filthy that had been left on the floor. What had I done to deserve this? I walked into the back room and tried to take my mind off the situation by studying Italian, but it was no good. Anger nibbled away at my concentration all the time.

'Tomorrow I will leave,' I said aloud.

That night I hardly slept at all, but I must have dozed off in the early hours, for I remember being wakened by a voice I now knew so well.

'*Buon giorno, Rinaldo. Ecco, una tazza caffè. E una bella giornata*' – 'Good morning, Ronald. Here's a cup of coffee. It's a lovely day.' And then she asked if anything was wrong.

I tried to apologize for the trouble I had caused, and began to wash my face in the bowl of cold water she had put on the chair. Whilst I was stumbling through my words, she came over and kissed me on the cheek, and she was just wiping the soapy lather from her nose when her sister, Giovina, walked in and, seeing what had happened, passed some scathing remark which neither of us answered. However, I realized that I had to restore the family's respect for me by not compromising them any longer. I had to leave.

My good intentions evaporated quickly though when Rosina said, 'Drink your coffee and stop worrying about what the family thinks.'

Later that day Rosina's father tapped me on the shoulder and motioned me outside with a nod of his head. He sat down on a low wall and patted a place for me to sit down beside him. He took out his pipe, filled it and, when he was satisfied that it was drawing well, turned to face me.

'You know,' he said, in his halting American-English, 'I am sorry about the row last night.'

Reconciliation had begun. It was the first of many such talks, sitting on the wall, at the end of the day. The more we talked, the better his English became as he dredged back words from his memory. We became good friends.

In the following weeks there were many frightening incidents when German patrols came searching the villages for Yugoslavs who had deserted from labour camps. At such times I was pushed into all sorts of hiding-places – once with an old sow in the pig-sty! And there was such relief after each incident that tears fell and I was hugged and kissed by everyone, including Giovina.

By this time I was allowed to walk out at night with Rosina, and our relationship developed so that we became closer and closer, with a deep understanding and love that was mutual. And then the inevitable happened. We made love.

With such a close-knit family, it was also inevitable that they sensed intuitively what had happened as soon as we got back. There were embarrassing silences, whispers in corners. I was made to feel unwanted. But I now knew how to put everything right. Later that night I came out of the back room with my grammar book in my hand and my finger pointing to one word on the open page. I spoke clearly so that everyone could hear. '*Moglie*,' I said, 'Wife', pointing to Rosina and her wedding-ring finger.

Even then the situation was not redeemed. There was a further complication. Rosina was promised to an Italian soldier who had been taken prisoner in Africa. However, everyone went to bed that night in a happier state of mind.

Two weeks later, 'Rinaldo' had just gone to bed when he was roughly wakened by Rosina, who was pushing his clothes into his hand saying, '*Tedeschi, tedeschi, vengono subito*! Germans are coming! Get up quickly. You are to go up to the mountains tonight. A big search is on.'

Swiftly he dressed. A neighbour, Tomasso, was waiting to lead him up the mountain track. Hasty goodbyes were said. Rinaldo hugged Rosina and said, 'I will come back, one day,' and then he thrust into her hand a piece of paper. 'On this paper are my name, my Army number and my home address in England too.' With that he was hustled away out of the house and onto the track, with Tomasso tugging urgently at his arm.

They had gone only a hundred yards when they heard footsteps running after them. They turned. It was Rosina. 'I want to come with you,' she panted.

Rinaldo wrenched himself free, took hold of her and told her firmly that it would be better for both of them if she went back home. 'Wait for me there,' he said, 'I shall come back.'

'I will wait for you,' she said, and stood watching as the two men climbed upwards towards the high peaks of Gran Sasso.

After a hard two-day march, Tomasso delivered Rinaldo to a partisan group. He was welcomed with open arms when they learnt that he was in the British Army Medical Corps. They immediately appointed him medical stores officer – they called him '*il medico*' and '*il dottor Rinaldo*'. But the appointment was short-lived. Three weeks after leaving Rosina, he was captured and sent to Prison Camp 112, near the ancient university city of Bologna. And Rosina then seemed part of another existence.

In prison the routine was always so tediously the same that men found that even thoughts of women faded into the boring background of sleep, breakfast, roll-call, an hour or so of reading or study, the midday meal and a repetition of the same in the afternoon – boredom mixed with an eternal longing for freedom. Some accepted the situation philosophically, consoling themselves that at least they were alive and not horribly maimed or buried, as were so many of their former comrades. Others planned escapes which invariably failed and brought loss of privileges upon themselves and their fellow prisoners.

'Why do you do it?' asked Anthony Deane Drummond's commandant. And then he proceeded to give the answer to his own question. 'Of course we know why you want to escape, and we sympathize deeply. It's because of women, beautiful women. We don't understand why you don't all go crazy. We would give you some women from the bordello, but we don't think your authorities would do the same for our prisoners in England. Still, we know where to look if you do get out.'[2]

Italian High Command obviously thought along the same lines, for all prisoner-of-war standing orders laid down a procedure in the event of an escape, included in which were instructions to contact all brothels within ten miles.

The reality of the situation appeared to be the exact opposite – captivity depressing the desire for women rather than stimulating it. Anthony Deane Drummond recalls: 'I was not seriously worried by lack of female company after the first month or two. Civilisation seemed so far away, and our life and thoughts so introspective and self-contained that sex became a very unimportant subject. It was no good longing for the company of women, there just were not any. We were not in a position to covet our neighbour's wife, he had not got one with him.'

Other former prisoners have voiced the same opinion. Eric Newby agreed that, 'We were not unduly troubled by the lusts of the flesh – perhaps it was something to do with the diet.' Perhaps, even in Italy, there lurked the myth then common in the services that 'bromide' was put in their tea.

But there is perhaps a more interesting explanation for that depression of the sexual appetite in prisoners of war. They were suddenly freed from the brutal conditioning process which most armies used to transform the peace-loving civilian into an aggressive fighting soldier. Deliberately, wartime military training was in many ways designed to suppress the natural individual instinct of self-preservation and also to make a soldier capable of killing a fellow human being and be willing to sacrifice his own life for the sake of a cause. At the end of such a conditioning process a man was a soldier, a statistic, no more than a Government Issue (a 'GI'), expendable.

Part of this conditioning process was the notion that a sexually aggressive man made the best fighter. 'If a man won't fuck he won't fight,' said the legendary wartime commander General George S. Patton. This pistol-packing general pulled no punches when he talked to troops going into combat for the first time. To one such division he said: 'All this bull about thinking of your mother and your sweetheart and your wife is emphasized by writers who have never heard a hostile shot or missed a meal.'[3]

A US Navy medical officer wrote: 'Men in a successfully trained army and navy are stamped into a mould. Their barrack talk becomes typical, for soldiers are taught in a harsh and brutal school. They cannot, they must not be mollycoddled, and this very education befits nature, induces sexual aggression, and makes them the stern dynamic type we associate with men of the armed forces. This sexual aggression cannot be stifled.'[4]

In such a world of ritualized aggression, weapons came to be regarded as extensions of a soldier's masculinity. But in the subdued reality of the aftermath of battle, found in prisoner-of-war camps, crude expressions of swaggering masculinity disappeared. The need had gone, and perhaps the brutalizing conditioning process went into reverse.

Whatever the reason, it is interesting to find that the lust for a woman was not the motivating factor for escapers that Anthony Deane Drummond's camp commandant believed. But certainly a determination to get back to a loved-one – a wife or sweetheart – was a most potent stimulus. John Verney, once a prisoner of war in Italy, would agree. Of his own escape he wrote: 'It is a POW's duty, we had so often been told, to escape in order that he might continue to fight for his country. My own reasons for escaping were entirely different. I escaped to rejoin my wife, Lucinda, and son, Comus, and for nothing else. So far as I was concerned, the country could look after itself.'[5]

Ronald Hankinson was determined to get back to his beloved Rosina too when he escaped from Camp 112 near Bologna. He took to the hills again, heading south-west to the mountains, where Garibaldi partisan brigades were forming. He joined one of the Reggio Emilia groups, and by this time, as a result of his studies and practice, his Italian was fluent.

Good news came towards the end of September 1943. The American Fifth Army had broken through the German lines on the Salerno mountains and entered the plain of Naples. But from then on, progress was slow, almost imperceptible,

January brought the first severe snowfall. The Allies were held up at Cassino and Anzio. On 15 February the abbey of Monte Cassino, fourteen centuries old, was destroyed by Allied bombers, but still there was no progress, and all the time the risks of hiding former prisoners of war grew greater.

In May Cassino fell to the Allies and the Gustav Line was broken. In June Rome fell. Then it was that Ronald Hankinson decided to go it alone and get back to the Allied lines so that he could start to make arrangements to marry Rosina. Before that aim could be achieved though, he had a more formidable enemy than the Germans to fight – British bureaucracy!

At first all went well. He slipped through the German defensive positions unscathed in the autumn of '44, joined a base hospital staff and began making the first of many applications for his marriage to Rosina. He seemed to be thwarted by everyone concerned.

The war in Italy finished before I had got very far with the paperwork. I was posted up to Austria before I could see Rosina again. We were both going through an agony of suspense and frustration. I was also having difficulty with opposition to my marriage from my parents back home. The Italian civil authorities were not at all helpful, and neither were my own military superiors. It became clear to Rosina and to me that we must take the matter into our own hands. And for a very good reason. Rosina had now given birth to our child. Twice she travelled up to the Austrian border, and twice she was turned back because her papers were not in order. Once she and the baby were arrested and spent four days in a civilian gaol.

That did it! Enough was enough. For the Army I had jumped out of aeroplanes, risked my neck on airborne operations, actively evaded capture for three years and deliberately made my own way back through German lines to rejoin British forces. And what was I getting for all that? Red tape and procrastination.

Well, I could escape from all that too. I was half-way down Italy before they discovered I had gone 'absent without leave' and left no forwarding address! In Rosina's parish church we were married by an Italian priest with the help of the local bishop. All this despite my being a Protestant!

But there was to be no fairy-tale ending to Ronald Hankinson's love-story. At least not for some years to come. He was arrested, court-martialled and sent back to Britain, and his marriage was not recognized by the British authorities.

Added to all Ronald Hankinson's troubles was the fact that his own family 'disowned' him. He was left to fight bureaucracy on his own. It was a long battle of attrition, but Hankinson was not one to give in easily. In the end victory was his. On 7 March 1952, almost eleven years to the day since he had dropped by parachute into Italy, Signora Rosina Constantini Hankinson, living at Contrada Madonna delle Grazie, Vestea, Pescara, received a short letter of six lines beneath the stamp of the lion and unicorn. It was from the British ambassador in Rome. It authorized Rosina and her daughter to join Ronald Hankinson in Britain. As Hankinson was to say to this writer close on forty years later, 'Compassion over bureaucracy can prevail.'

He might well have echoed also the words of the Italian proverb that had kept Captain Ken Barker going after escaping from his prison camp – 'Chi la dura, la vince' – 'He who sticks it out wins.'

After Ken Barker had said goodbye to the two Italian soldiers who had helped him out of the camp and on the way out from Forlí, he made for

the foothills around Meldola. There he planned to bide his time
somehow or other until the Allies made a landing further north to cut off
the German troops, which was the plan which everybody generally
expected. For the next few days and nights he walked mainly at dusk and
in the half-light of dawn, not trusting himself to navigate by the stars.

I plodded on, more on will-power than physical energy, and by dawn
every bone in my body ached. My scraps of food were finished and I was
about at the end of my tether when I came off the hillside and onto a small
road, like a private driveway. It curved round an avenue of trees, and
when I got around the last bend, I saw to my surprise a luxury villa. To the
front was a sunlit terrace, partly shaded by a creeper-covered trellis.
Below the house, terraced gardens fell away in planned and unplanned
disorder. There were fruit bushes, creepers and vegetables, tropical
flowers and flowering shrubs. I could see from the dusty soil and dried
pine needles that the summer heat had really parched everything. The
whole place was in dire need of attention.

As I approached the house, a woman came striding down the slope.
She was dressed in a long black skirt, blue blouse and boots. Her body
was so bony and flat you could have taken her for a man, but when she
lifted her head, and the broad-rimmed sunhat no longer hid her face,
there was no mistaking the fact that here was a beautiful, mature woman.

I decided right away to let her know who I was. What she did then
would be up to her.

'*Buon giorno, Signora. Mi scusa, sono inglese capitano ma non parlo bene
l'italiano*' – 'Good day, Madam. Excuse me, I am an English captain, but I
don't speak Italian well.'

She laughed. '*Ha ragione!*' – 'You're right!' she said and added, in
English, 'You look tired and thirsty. Come inside for a drink.'

She led me over a wooden dining-terrace and into a long, cool room
which had a kind of marble floor. The shutters were pulled over the
windows. What a relief it was to sit down in such cool comfort! The
woman took off her sun hat and I could see her properly for the first time.
She had thick, wavy black hair, naturally fine black eyebrows, long, dark
lashes and a simple air of half-suppressed gaiety. I liked what I saw.

'*Prego,*' she said, pointing to a chair. 'Wait here for a moment. I shall
bring something for you.'

In a few minutes she returned carrying a tray on which stood a bottle of
red, fizzy Lambrusco wine, a long, fat roll of bread cut into chunks, and a
small cake of creamy white goat cheese. She brought it to the side table,
smiling, her lips slightly parted as if she were enjoying some
long-forgotten pleasure. She poured the wine for us both and politely
nibbled a crusty chunk of bread to keep me company.

'I have already eaten,' she said.

A ray of sunlight coming through a partly open shutter lit up the
attractive outlines of her body. She was something different, a charmer
with such an engaging smile and a bewitching gleam in her dark eyes. I
really did like her. In fact, I was smitten.

We talked. She told me the latest war news. It was not good for the Allies. Severe setbacks with the landing at Salerno. She told me about her husband, who was away in the war. He had gone to Africa with General Alessandro Gloria's Bologna Infantry Division in June 1942 to join Rommel's Afrika Corps. She had heard nothing from him since November and the battle of El Alamein. Almost a year without any news at all.

'And you?' she asked, getting immediately to the point. 'You have a wife?'

I had been married only four months before going overseas, and lately I had found it increasingly difficult to conjure up a picture of my wife, no matter how hard I tried. She was just a face on a faded black-and-white snapshot. I told my hostess all this. And my name.

'Graziella is mine,' she said.

As I look back now on that day, it seems as though we both made decisions then which affected both our futures. But we did not tell each other then. That pleasure came later. In a way it was like a forty-minute interview for a job at which decisions are made which fling people together for the rest of their working lives. That's exactly how it was for Graziella and me.

A guest room had been prepared for me by Anna, an older woman with a wrinkled kindly face and smiling blue eyes. And I must have slept that night with a broad grin all over my face! I'd struck lucky again. My brother used to say to me that if I fell into a cess-pit I'd come up smelling of violets.

After a breakfast of hot, freshly baked rolls and coffee – real coffee, I started making myself useful about the garden and the pens of livestock, poultry, goats and pigs. I was happy to be doing something worthwhile again, and the time passed very quickly. I was surprised though when Graziella called me to come in. I did not think it was yet time to eat. As I reached the terrace steps, she ran down and pushed a saw, hammer and a bag of tools into my hands.

'Take them,' she said. She was excited but calm. 'Now listen carefully,' she said slowly. 'You are my brother-in-law from Turin. You have come to stay with me for a few weeks. At any time an officer of the Fascist militia, Signor Carpaccio, comes here. Someone must have seen you. No good hiding. You must deceive him and stop suspicion. When I see him coming in his old car, I shall start shouting at you. Say you are lazy. Tell you to go and mend the hen-house roof. You act the part.'

Quickly and quietly she talked me through the scene. She gave me a few useful phrases to throw in, as if I understood all she was saying – 'Subito', Si, si', 'Ma!' – and then, when she finished her harangue, I was to slouch off, bag over my shoulder and tools in hand.

We dared not sit down. We just waited, ready to launch straight into the act the moment the car appeared. Graziella was taking a great risk but now there was no other way. She was already committed, had harboured me overnight, fed me and not reported me to the authorities. A radio message that week had offered a reward of 3,000 lire for the capture of any British prisoners of war or information as to their whereabouts. The radio message repeated the penalty for sheltering prisoners of war – trial by court martial.

We heard the mayor's old car, clattering like a primitive sewing-machine, before it appeared round the bend of the drive. Graziella then launched straight into her attack on my 'bone-idleness', jabbing at my chest with her pointed index finger, flinging her arms about and almost spitting with anger. I would not have liked to have been the object of her real anger. Deliberately she had turned her back partly towards the driveway, so that she could carry on berating me as if she had not seen the arrival of the visitor. He was but a few yards away when she turned and saw him and stopped. Brusquely she told me to get off and finish mending the hen-house roof. 'And don't come back until you have finished!' she shouted after me as I slouched away, muttering, '*Subito*' and '*Si, si*' as if I'd understood every word. Then she was all smiles greeting the officer, offering hospitality, inviting him into the house out of the heat of the afternoon. She was indeed a charmer in every sense of the word.

For the best part of two hours the mayor and Graziella sat on the terrace sipping Vin Santo brought specially from the monastery at Urbino. The genuine article. They nibbled cheese, biscuits and olives and smoked black-market cigarettes bartered for eggs and Graziella's home-cured ham. They talked, each assessing the situation with only part of their mind on the topic. Yes, it was good news that General Rommel was going down to Naples to take command of the German troops. Yes, how terrible was the Allied bombing of Naples and Florence. Yes, soon General Graziani and Minister of the Interior Buffarini-Guidi would get things back to normal. '*Esperiamo!*' – 'Let's hope!'

And so the two of them droned on. Yes, the mayor would appreciate a little of the home-cured ham to take back to his family. 'You must have some eggs too.' The sun began to sink and the mosquitoes came out in force and began to bite viciously.

Mayor Carpaccio took his leave. 'Very pleased to know that all is well, Signora' – what a pleasant afternoon it had been ... so many routine visits he had to make ... usually such a tedious task ... such a lot of work these days ... he would be pleased to come again ...

He was still talking effusively as he placed the parcel of ham and eggs on the back seat of his car beneath his raincoat. He rattled off down the drive with a final wave, slowing only momentarily as he passed Ken Barker noisily hammering nails into the hen-house roof.

Now that Ken's cover was firmly established, there was little to fear from further visits. A few eggs and half a ham occasionally was a small price for Graziella to pay for having got what she had wanted for so long – a man about the house.

Ken now had two options open to him. He could try to make his way through German lines to the Allies or he could wait for the Allies to come to him. From his experience as an infantry officer in North Africa, he knew it was no easy matter passing through enemy defensive positions and equally hazardous at times coming back from patrols through your own. He could wait. In fact, he was beginning to enjoy waiting.

Autumn turned into a bitter winter, and Meldola was frequently cut off by heavy snows. Ken's fluency in Italian improved enormously. 'There is nothing quite as good as having a long-haired dictionary,' was the way he put it. As long as he spoke in short phrases, giving an edge to his words, he could pass for a north Italian from Turin. In that part of Italy men were supposed to be taller and often fair-haired, and so Ken's sun-bleached hair was not out of keeping with his role as brother-in-law from Turin.

Graziella's family owned several farms in the area, holding them in a semi-feudal system. Consequently she was generally held in some awe as a grand signora, greatly to be respected – greatly, sometimes, to be feared. She had few visitors. The servants were loyal and had learnt from experience over generations to be discreet and not to gossip. In any case, they too had taken to the man from Turin. He worked hard, always had a smile and a greeting for them. Far better than the signora's husband. For almost two years now there had been no news of him. And for very nearly a year it was obvious to the old retainers that the British captain was something more than the signora's temporary house guest. He was her lover. And they were pleased.

Towards the end of the hot summer of 1944 Ken Barker and Graziella's idyllic situation suddenly took a turn for the worse. At least, that was the way it seemed then. The rumbling of guns drew nearer, shells dropped on the road down the valley. A tragic procession of women and children with terrified faces hurried upwards from the town. All night there was continuous firing, and then at dawn two tremendous explosions shook the ground. The Germans had blown the bridges and roads.

It was shortly after midday that the moment of decision came for Captain Ken Barker, when a troop of seventy-two mules led by a motley collection of Arabs, some wearing the traditional red fez, others in helmets, bustled noisily down the driveway to the villa. At their head was a British officer riding a dapple-grey horse. He stopped and addressed Graziella and Ken, who had come out to see what was happening. He spoke in execrable Italian delivered in the supercilious accent cultivated at some time at the Cavalry Club in Piccadilly. The lines for his horses and mules were to be in the farmyards. He would sign an order for hay. Payment would come later. 'OK?' *Va bene?*' he concluded.

The reply he received pleased him. But it surprised Graziella. '*Va bene! S'accommoda*' – 'OK! Help yourself,' said Ken.

He had made his decision. No more soldiering for him. He was the *padrone*!

Graziella took his arm, smiled up at the boyish-faced officer with the fluffy moustache and said, '*Va bene!*'[6]

9 'Going My Way?'

You'll never know what we gave up for love!'
Lena McGaffey, a Yorkshire lass who married a GI

On the evening of 1 May 1944 Lena walked down the pretty, tree-lined village street of Welton with her two friends from the Land Army. There was but one thought in their minds.

It was not surprising. All day they had sweated in the fields of an east Yorkshire farm in a blazing heat never before experienced in May in the living memory of local villagers, and not to be equalled for another forty-five years. By sundown, all that those girls yearned for was a long, thirst-quenching drink in the cool inglenook of Welton's inn.

Conspicuous at one of the tables in the large room sat a group of six American soldiers. They had been sent up from Tidworth to test a new kind of radio, and their commanding officer had put a cross on a map which had brought them to a clover field up the Beverley road from Welton. Now all were sizing up that strange British institution, the public house. From the start they thought it a good thing, a great idea, both a social and democratic institution. They saw it as a poor man's club, a sanctuary and retreat. It filled a need for companionship in villages where there was little else. Now wartime had broken down traditional barriers about unaccompanied women's going up to the bar to order drinks, and Lena and her lithe Land Army companions were always made to feel welcome.

Towards the end of that evening in May, Lena became aware that a very tall American soldier was paying her a good deal of attention. He gazed at her over his pint pot, and each time he went to the bar he walked back with his eyes on her instead of on the brimming glasses, much to the detriment of the clothes of men he bumped into. Eventually their eyes met. They smiled at each other. Slowly the tall American levered himself up from his cramped position behind the heavy, iron-legged table. He advanced purposefully towards Lena.

'That was the way it was,' she recalled. 'He was really handsome. He did not use a well-practised line of small-talk, and I liked him right away. He said it was love at first sight, but I suddenly remembered what my mother had said about talking to Yanks. She didn't think it quite proper, because of what people had said about them. So I promptly left.'

Parents were naturally concerned for the well-being of their daughters, but their attitude to Americans was based upon preconceived ideas and impressions from films. Most British people generally thought Americans were big, noisy, not quite civilized, and boastful. And it took some time for local people to find, with some surprise, that the average American did not speak as if he had a Texan cowgirl for a mother, a Chicago, George Raft-style gangster for a father, or had been born in Brooklyn and raised in Dixie. Mutual understanding generally came slowly, but Lena's mother had to learn fast.

Two nights after their first meeting in the pub, Lena and her friend were leaving the village fish-and-chip shop hugging hot newspapers round their supper when they almost bumped into a US jeep parked by the doorway. A voice called to them: 'Going to the dance?' It was the same handsome six-footer who had spoken to her in the Green Dragon.

'I pleaded with my mother to let me go. She was not at all keen but at last she agreed. That was the start of it all.'

Going to a dance at a military camp was a novel experience for young women in wartime. The village buzzed with excited discussions among women about what they would wear. It took half a year's clothing coupons to buy a good dance-dress, but the alternative was cheap, drab, 'utility' clothing, so needle and thread came out to improvise on older, good-quality material from dresses belonging to parents and neighbours. (Clothes rationing was introduced in Britain in June 1941, with a basic ration of forty-eight coupons a year. A coat would need fourteen coupons and a dress eleven. 'Make do and mend' became a way of life for everybody.)

That night Lena brushed her hair until it shone before she came downstairs to wait for the transport that would pick her up, half-fearing that it might not come or that at the last minute she would be forbidden to go. But all went according to plan.

At the camp, girls were arriving by the truckload, laughing and chattering nervously. June Seaton remembers going to her first military dance at seventeen: there were British, American and French soldiers. 'In a way most of us dreaded being asked to dance, we dreaded not being asked, we dreaded dancing badly and stepping on our partner's toes. But we were always in such exuberant high spirits that it didn't matter.'

Any such fears that the Welton girls had that night quickly evaporated in the warmth of the welcome given by the soldiers waiting for them. They were part of General Le Clerc's 2nd French Armoured Division attached to the American Third Army, which would soon, under US General Patton, be marching as liberators into Paris.

Lena spotted Dave, her tall American friend, as soon as she entered the big, brightly lit hall. He waved excitedly, and his long legs carried him rapidly and easily to her through the crush of men hovering in the doorway. She was swept onto the dance floor.

Dave and Lena danced almost every dance together that evening. Finally they danced the last waltz, when traditionally the man would ask if he could walk his partner home – and Dave did ask. There was a roll on the drums, and they all stood to attention for the national anthems. Then, hand-in-hand, Lena and Dave plunged from the brightly lit hall into the blacked-out envelope of the night.

'After that beautiful walk home, our relationship never faltered. It was helped, ironically, by the fact that two weeks later I had to go into Beverley Hospital for surgery. In those days there was only one visiting day a week for civilians, but servicemen could visit every day. So Dave came daily, and then each evening he met my mother to tell her how I was getting on.'

By that time Dave McGaffey was convinced that young Lena was the nicest and most beautiful girl he had ever met. He knew also that he loved her, and though perhaps in those critical times he did not think of it in so many words, he knew that she was the girl with whom he wanted to share the rest of his life.

But there was no time left for courting: 'Suddenly, in the first week of June, all patients in our hospital were discharged. Every ward was cleared. The hospital had to be in a state of readiness for the opening of the long-awaited "Second Front". Dave drove with my mother to pick me up and take me home. Mother asked him in for dinner. A few days later he was gone.'

News came over the pear-shaped wireless in the Green Dragon that Allied troops had landed on the beaches of Normandy. There was a hushed silence as the voice of Prime Minister Winston Churchill told of the greatest amphibious landing in history. He did not tell his listeners that the German Army was fighting a ferocious defensive battle and that American troops were suffering terrible casualties as they pressed home the attack across open ground swept by a hail of machine-gun and mortar fire. He did not tell them that 2,000 Americans figured in the casualty lists. Reinforcements poured in.

There was no news of Dave during the next few weeks. Lena knew that his unit had gone to France. Now she was just another sweetheart waiting, hoping, praying. Never, though, could she have imagined how her prayers would be answered.

On August Bank Holiday Monday 1944 there was a knock on her door. Lena opened it to find a tall American standing on the mat. A soldier in combat kit. Dave. When they had stopped hugging each other and crying with delight and relief, he took a small box from his pocket and offered her an engagement ring. The visit was brief. Dave went back to his unit, for in that hot August 'Old Blood and Guts', General George Patton, was pushing on towards Paris.

Once again Lena waited. She began the tedious business of filling in forms and writing letters for permission to marry a US serviceman. And she worked hard too. The Women's Land Army was no easy option: they were not just milkmaids, they cared for livestock, drove tractors, blistered and gashed their hands hedging and ditching and even took part in rat-catching. In fair weather and foul these young women worked hard to grow food for the country. They were issued with a uniform (which suited some figures better than others) of sagging corduroy breeches, leggings, boots, green jumper, brown jacket and khaki, broad-brimmed hat. For an arduous fifty-hour week's work they were paid £2.8s. From these wages they forfeited 25 shillings if they were living in a hostel. These were run by martinets enforcing strict discipline.

Despite this well-known rigid control of the women, many farmers' wives became suspicious and jealous of them. They talked of them as 'tarts' who were after their husbands. The young, macho farmers were little better in their attitude. They parodied the WLA marching song 'Back to the land, we must lend a hand,' into a very much cruder version, beginning 'Backs to the land' and continuing with even coarser refrains. Unfortunately, the idea that Land Girls were an attractive bait for farmworkers was reinforced by official posters, which seemed to promise romance in the fields for servicemen on leave. The picture on the poster was of a smiling, full-bosomed Land Girl calling out to two soldiers running towards her, 'Come on, the Services! Lend a hand on the land!'

Jealousy, though, could work both ways. One *Woman's Own* reader wrote to the Agony Aunt: 'My husband is doing work on a farm at present and I can't help feeling a bit jealous of the Land Girls there. One in particular is most attractive and all the men admire her. We have only been married a short while and are so happy that I would hate anything to come between us.'[1]

And a soldier wrote to *Mother and Home*, 'My wife is working on a farm and I am in the Army. Each time I come home I see her being very friendly with the farm men, taking tea out to them and so on; and people tell me she always does this. Last time I came home unexpectedly she said she could not get off as they were harvesting, and I ordered her home. I feel angry and suspicious.'[2]

The reply which jealous wives and sweethearts invariably received from Agony Aunts was on the lines that, 'The right answer to your problem, my dear, is trust. If you love your husband/wife (as you do) you will trust him/her, and not allow any feelings of jealousy to cloud your feelings for each other. Above all do not permit any hint of suspicion to creep into your manner to your partner. Just be your usual sweet self. Next time someone tells tales, stop them and tell them to mind their own business.'

There was certainly enough work to keep the Land Girls busy that year, and just how successful they proved to be at their work can surely be witnessed by the number of ex-Land Girls who, when they did eventually marry farmers, did not drop into the traditional image of the farmwife who baked bread and scattered corn to the chickens in the backyard but made a real contribution to the day-to-day running of the whole farm, as indeed they do today.

The hot summer of 1944 was followed by a chilly autumn, and the bitterly cold, back-breaking job of potato-picking was over when Lena had an unexpected visitor from France. It was Dave. Absence had made his heart grow fonder, much fonder. He wanted to marry Lena straight away and saw no reason why he should not do so.

'I was thrilled,' said Lena. 'We had to get special permission from the archbishop of York. And we did get it! My brother, who had just got back from being a prisoner of war, helped a lot with the wedding arrangements. So it was that on 9 November 1944 we had a lovely wedding in the old parish church, with the Land Girls forming an archway with their shovels, rakes and spades.'

After the wedding everyone stuffed themselves with food and drink, toasted the couple, laughed and made the most of the day.

In the evening we took off for a two-day honeymoon in Scarborough before Dave went back to the war across the Channel.

Our first child was born in October 1945, but she was not to see her daddy for many years. At four months old she was taken seriously ill. Dave had already been shipped to the States, and I was left, torn between wanting to be with him and also with my sick daughter, who had to stay in Britain for treatment. Her recovery was very slow. When she was nine months old, after much soul-searching, I left her in the care of my parents and sailed across to the States and Dave. It was eighteen months then since we had seen each other. We had to start all over again.

It was not until 1950 that I went back to England to get daughter Jane, then, at last, a healthy 5-year-old. And by that time we also had another daughter, Peggy Ann. Family life then began properly for us all. Now we've had forty-five glorious years together and are looking forward to many more.

The other night we were watching the Miss America beauty competition, and I turned to Dave, saying, 'Who do you choose?' He just looked at me and said, 'I already have her.'

For all that happiness there was, it seems, a price to be paid. In one letter to this author Lena wrote: 'I was working outdoors with my flowers, and my neighbour said, "What are you singing?" I said, "I'll take you home again, Kathleen." It was a lovely morning, made me think of home. I turned to my neighbour and said: "You'll never know what we gave up for love." '

Like many of those thousands of GI brides, Lena gets homesick at times. She loves her pretty east Yorkshire village of Welton and the distinctive beauty of its countryside.

It was the sight of the English landscape seen through the windows of the express train rushing her from Cheshire to London as a GI bride that brought 22-year-old June Marsico to a decision not to join her husband in Ohio.

'I was too much in love with England and my home to face up to going to America. So when we reached London I took the labels off my hand luggage, avoided the US Reception Officer and caught the next train home,' she recalled. 'I was sorry for my husband but I felt more content and happy once I had come to a decision. My elder sister, also a GI bride was already in the USA but my only regret was that all my best clothes were in my heavy luggage previously despatched to America and I had no other clothing coupons.'[3]

On the other hand, the lure of Britain and the love for their homesick British brides brought many former GIs back to Britain. Buddy Weiner, who had met his future wife near the Selfridges store in London's Oxford Street in 1943, made the decision in 1946 to bring his wife Betty back to 'the land of the fog'. And it proved to be for him the land of opportunity and wealth. He opened a store in Bayswater which flourished so well that he eventually merged with the Tesco supermarket chain and now he sits on the board.[4]

For Buddy and Betty that wartime romance brought forty-five years of married bliss – and there was something more, an item of interest for sweethearts all over the world. If Buddy had not made that journey back to Britain, his daughter, Elizabeth Emanuel, might never have had the opportunity to design the wedding dress for the Princess of Wales!

Some GI brides had awful shocks when they arrived in the States. Dorothy Robbins of Saffron Walden, a former WAAF cook, arrived excitedly to meet her husband, Sergeant Harrison, only to find that he was already wedded to a woman he had married in 1935! He was charged with bigamy and sentenced in a Danbury court. Dorothy was given financial assistance for her passage home.[5]

Yvonne McIntosh had a shock of a different kind. She had been looking forward eagerly to living in America, saving for it even before she met her husband, in fact. But after they were married in Caxton Hall, Westminster, and he went back to the US Army base in Ireland, she began to feel the need to leave Britain and start her new life in America. Perhaps she could prepare some small home for his return? Her plans went well, and she was one of the lucky brides who managed to reach the United States before the end of the war. She sailed on the *Aquitania* and after a very long train journey arrived at her mother-in-law's house in Michigan. Her welcome was like a bucket of cold water dousing her from head to foot.

My mother-in-law's first words were not, 'Hello, I'm pleased to meet you', but 'Where's my son?' I told her he had been sent to Germany. Then she disappeared into another room and came back waving a bit of paper. It was my government allotment cheque. She had been opening all my mail! Most people would have reacted by telling the old lady off, right there and then, but I bit my tongue. I didn't want to get off on the wrong foot with my mother-in-law. But what happened next really taxed all the patience I had. She took me into the other room and showed me that my two boxes of luggage had arrived. They were lying there opened, picked over, things strewn about, and my wedding pictures had been removed from their covers and actually stuck into an old scrapbook! (I still have not got those photographs back.)

The next shock came at breakfast the following morning. Mother-in-law took a hard look at me and said, 'Well, when are you going to look for work?'

I had not really bargained for that sort of question, and side-stepped it then and for a few days afterwards, but at the end of the week she told me to pack my overnight bag and be prepared to leave in the morning in my father-in-law's car. He was going to take me to their daughter's house, and then I could apply for a job where she worked.

As we were leaving the next morning, mother-in-law shouted to me, 'Goodbye! We're moving house in a day or two!'

So that was my reception in America.

Mothers-in-law could be a problem for GI brides, especially those from Britain, who naturally expected their husbands to have come from families who spoke English – albeit with an American accent. These brides were often surprised at the foreignness of their newly acquired relations with their strong German, Italian or Polish accents. And they were all the more shocked to meet parental disapproval of the marriage expressed violently in a language they scarcely understood. To be confronted with such opposition at the beginning of a marriage took guts. But guts these women had in plenty. Had they not already faced the negative opinions of relatives and friends warning them: 'You'll regret it, going over there. Just you wait and see. You'll be back!' Had they not endured taunts at work, being greeted in the morning with: 'Haven't you gone yet?'

Sylvia Turner of Warrington recalled how articles in the local press made women feel like traitors marrying GIs. One letter in a national woman's magazine said, for example: 'I felt sad for the British troops sitting in the cheap seats at the cinema whilst GIs swaggered to the best seats accompanied by local girls. I felt like calling out to these women, "Your men have been fighting for you in Egypt, Greece and God knows where. Can you not give them some of your company?" '

Jibes they had endured. They had braved the emotional wrench finally of leaving home and assembling at the brides' transit camps at Perham Down and Tidworth, where many of them were greeted by a disgruntled officer (who thought he should have been repatriated), opening his address with the words: 'You may not like the way things are here, but remember no one asked you to come.'

There some had suffered – not always in silence – the discomfort of being packed together with a mixed bunch of over 600 women at a time, sleeping four to a hut, crawling through yet another jungle of red tape, completing endless forms which asked every imaginable question – from whether they had ever been in prison or an alms house to whether they intended 'by force or violence to try and overthrow the government of the United States'. Some had suffered the mortifying experience of stripping off all their clothes so that a medical officer could shine a flashlight between their legs to check for venereal disease, whilst rows of American officers looked on – an experience which Mary Coffman felt was nothing more than a peepshow.[6] Many had endured without complaint nine days of seasick misery crossing the Atlantic in slow 'rusty iron buckets' such as the old *Aquitania* and SS *Alexander*. Immediately following disembarkation many had travelled for two or three days by train.

After such an initiation, the brides could take a cantankerous and belligerent mother-in-law in their stride. They were not going to run back home to Britain with their tails between their legs. Not without a fight. Skirmishes were frequent, battles fought, but in the end compromises were made, and their endurance was well rewarded.

Typical of all this is the story of Winifred Vallese – one who won through.

When I was sixteen, I had to register for war work, and I was sent to a large country house near Salisbury where Saunders-Roe and the Air Ministry worked together designing planes. I was happy working there. Then the Americans arrived. I didn't really understand them at first. I wasn't too sure if I ever wanted to. Older people warned us that, 'Those Yanks are wild', and they told tales of what happened the last time they came over to Britain, in 1917.

Suddenly our world changed. They started coming to our dances. It was great. How they could dance! We learnt how to jitterbug, much to the disgust of the older women. At earlier dances it had been mainly girls dancing with girls. Now there were boys! Boys! And more boys! They smelt nice, and their uniforms were smashing, and they could charm. Oh how they could charm! A date meant a movie and a meal. We weren't used to all this attention. It was great.

The GIs had parties, with dancing to real American bands. And food, and ice-cream and colas ... so much food we had not seen for years, if ever. We had to have invitations to their dances. Not everyone could go. I discovered that the names of girls were submitted to the local police, so that no 'undesirables' were included. American trucks would pick us up (our parents were not too keen on this), but the US military police were strict: not one US soldier could ride in the trucks. Often boyfriends would try to hide, only to be found when MPs searched the trucks outside the camp. They would get hauled off, and we would get home safe and sound.

The first American we really got to know was a very quiet farm boy from Iowa. We had invited him to our home for Christmas dinner in 1942 and we have kept in touch with his family to this day.

My impression then of Americans was that they talked a lot – about themselves, about the United States, a land they would have us believe had plenty, bigger and better than anything anywhere. If you really believed it all, you were daft. They promised the world on a silver platter. They were a puzzle: friendly, yet at times arrogant, nice to children, polite to older people; they ate in a funny way, only used a knife to cut things with ...

I met my husband, Freddie, when he was stationed in Romsey, 1944. He told us about his family in Pennsylvania. He was one of seven children (I thought it must be great to have all those brothers and sisters, being an only child myself). He was planning to go to college after the war. My parents were impressed.

D-Day came. Convoys were going by day and night. We both knew he would be going over very soon. We became engaged, planning to get married after the war. I really thought he would go back to the States, see the girls he had left behind and forget about me.

May '45, victory in Europe. Freddie was trying to get back to England but found himself on a boat going to the Pacific. He fell ill and was flown to a hospital in Washington DC, where he stayed until he was discharged in January 1946. Then it was that we started making real plans for a wedding. Nothing definite, no actual dates, but what kind of a wedding we would like. Freddie was finding out that it would be a long time before he could get back to England. He decided it would be easier for me to go to the States. President Truman had signed a bill that fiancées of American servicemen could enter the United States on a special visa. And Freddie promised a bigger and better wedding because there was no rationing or restrictions as in England. Even my parents said that made sense.

There was a terrible amount of forms to be signed on both sides of the Atlantic. Freddie had to get affidavits to show he was single, had a home

Night

GI Bob Ames of Utica, New York and his English bride, 'Mickey' Norah McMullen gaze over the English Channel.

Sylvia Maycock, GI bride with a horror story.

Yvonne McIntosh, GI bride.

Daniel Militello – the GI who would not take 'NO' for an answer – with Katherina, his German wife.

GI bride Lena and Dave McGaffey leaving Welton parish church, East Yorkshire with a guard of honour of Women's Land Army bearing rakes and hayforks, November 1944.

For the girl he left behind. This brief message, scrawled across his tent, was left by one of the soldiers who took part in the D. Day invasion of France, 6 June 1944.

he American Rainbow club on the corner of Shaftesbury Avenue, London, where servicemen and women could relax.

GI brides embarking for the USA wave to their loved ones on the quay.

Claretta Petacci, Mussolini's sweetheart, sailing at Rimini.

The bodies of Mussolini and Claretta, with party members strung up high on the ruins o a petrol station roof, 1945.

Hitler's sweetheart, Eva Brau in Bavarian costume

Kay Summersby stands behind General Eisenhower as they celebrate the surrender of the German army. Her presence was removed in some official versions of the photograph.

Former Second Subaltern Elizabeth Alexandra Mary Windsor, the new Duchess of Edinburgh, leaving Westminster Abbey with her husband, former Lieutenant Philip Mountbatten, RN, now the Duke of Edinburgh.

Dora, in the farm garden at Schonau in the summer of 194 – the year that POW Stuart Brown met her.

Private Stuart Brown and Dora, his German bride, at Luneberg, 1945, waiting to enter Britain.

Fraternization was spontaneous, inevitable and could not be stopped.

diers of every nationality
e 'getting their feet under
e table' and being part of the
rmal world again. From
nple beginnings relationships
veloped.

Young wives eager to eke out meagre food rations for their families were often tempted to give sex for cans of milk and meat for their children. The practice was so rife that Deputy Chaplain General, Geoffrey Druitt of Montgomery's 21st Army Group declared: 'Soldiers are playing a shameful part in encouraging women and girls into prostitution by giving way to lust and temptation to exploit the needs of these women. Unless they pull themselves together the British Army will leave a shameful heritage behind them in Germany.'

Prisoners now, sweethearts soon! By 1948 800 German prisoners of war married British girls. Twenty thousand German prisoners of war chose to stay in Britain after the war and many, naturally married British women.

and a job; I had to fill in forms from the American embassy. It was hurry, hurry ... wait, wait.

In April 1946 we were still waiting. But Freddie made a record in Philadelphia telling me how much he loved me and missed me. That was all I needed to keep me going. (We still have this record.)

A chill breeze began to blow through Winifred's euphoria, however, when the next letter from Freddie arrived;

He wrote to say that when he had told his mother about me she was *furious*. She didn't want him to marry a foreign girl. She had already picked a nice Italian/American girl for him. But Freddie was not buying this one. I wasn't to get upset, everything was still 'GO'. Not to worry. I sensed that he was worried, but he insisted he wasn't. So we continued to get ready. Months rolled on.

In January 1947 Mum and I had to go the US consulate in London. (We got lost in the fog.) I spent the entire day filling in yet more forms, being interviewed, having another medical examination, more forms again, then over to the embassy to apply for priority transport. I had to agree to be ready at forty-eight hours' notice. My passport was stamped 'Valid for one year. Holder states she is travelling to USA for purpose of marriage.' I went home and waited. At last the letter came: I had a berth on the USS *Marine Falcon*, leaving Southampton on Wednesday 12 March 1947.

I was so excited to be going to America, but I was scared: I was leaving my parents, my country. I was nineteen years old, and I was going 3,000 miles away. I very nearly changed my mind. But I thought of Freddie and all the things he promised me. I loved him and I wanted to be with him. And I was fed up with wartime restrictions, the greyness of everything.

I'll never forget that day I left. Mother wore a red hat, and I stood on deck watching my mum and dad as we moved slowly down the South-ampton water. Even when the crowd had disappeared into a blur, I could still see my mum's red hat and I wondered if I would ever see her or England again.

The *Marine Falcon* was a Liberty ship, used to carry troops, nothing de luxe. It was filled with women and children, some already married to GIs, some like me going over to get married, and GIs returning to the US. The women and children were in 'cabins', actually holds with bunk beds about twenty to a cabin, very cramped. We lined up to get washed in the morning and to eat our meals. It was terrible.

The Atlantic was so rough that we took thirteen days for the crossing. As we inched our way into New York harbour, the city looked very large, skyscrapers reaching up into a grey mist. We all had to wait to be interviewed by US Customs, and we were all too excited even to think about breakfast.

At last I was allowed to leave the ship. Freddie was waiting for me at the gangplank. I had never seen him in civilian clothes – he still looked handsome. We left in a taxi with all my luggage and headed for the railway station. The taxi-driver welcomed me to America. I was touched. My eyes brimmed, and I was very excited. By the time we arrived at Freddie's home town, it was early evening.

As soon as I met Freddie's family, I realized I was in for a rough time. His family were Italian. I already knew that, but I had not realized it would be like living in Italy. They talked in Italian, his mother spoke only Italian. Their circle of friends was Italian, and Freddie's mother was still in shock that one of her sons would even think about marrying an '*inglese*'. She resented having anything at all to do with the arrangements for the wedding.

I asked if Freddie's niece and nephew could be in the wedding party. I got a categorical 'No'. I wanted to carry red roses. She went into an incomprehensible tirade. I didn't understand a word she was saying, but I knew it wasn't good. No bride carried coloured flowers. I would have white roses! I had brought my wedding gown over with me. It was wartime plain, and I was lucky enough to have a sympathetic sister-in-law who was a seamstress. She made it over into a beautiful gown.

Our wedding turned out to be a very small affair. To the church, back to the house, a chicken dinner with the family. No reception. No dancing. I wished I had stood my ground and got married at home, but I felt that I had made a bargain with Freddie. I loved him and thought that we could get past all the trouble.

I was never really accepted by the family. It was plain right from the beginning that I was an outsider. My mother-in-law always called me '*inglese*', even after I had given birth to a son and daughter. By this time I was so homesick I cried a lot. We lived with my in-laws for two years. The only happiness in my life was from my children. I wanted to take them back to England to meet their grandparents, but that was not possible. Years went by.

I met another English GI bride, and we became friends, talked about going back to England and formed a plan. We decided to book our passages a year ahead, so that we had time somehow to get the money together for the tickets. She was able to get an evening job with her husband's help, but I hit a snag. Freddie did not believe a wife should work. Her place was in the home. What could I do? I had an idea. I would mend or fix clothes. There were plenty of people always asking me how to do this or that, so why not charge for it? In one year we had enough money.

Yet another great day for departure came. We sailed on the SS *United States*. I was going home with my son, aged nine, and 4-year-old daughter. It was marvellous to be back in England. We stayed the whole summer. I didn't want to go back to America. I begged my father to let me stay. He couldn't believe it was as bad as I said, and he, being a wise man, explained that the children were American-born and that their father could take them back. So, because I could not bear to give them up, back we went.

Things did get better. I became busy with other matters, grew up with my children, and we did make other trips to England. Later on I did go out to work and was able to get some satisfaction from promotion in my new job. Now, forty-two years later, I still get homesick for England. I love English things and my children have the same love too.

Getting home to Britain when a marriage went wrong was not easy at the best of times, but when the custody of children was involved, it was almost impossible. The story of former WAAF Mary Maycock amply illustrates the problem.

I was the commanding officer's driver. I enjoyed my job and often drove important people who visited the station. Once I had the Duke of Kent as a passenger. I also liked the idea of visiting other RAF stations and meeting different people there. My horror story began really as a result of one such visit.

It all started pleasantly enough one evening when I attended a dance at a neighbouring RAF station, Halton. What made it such a memorable evening for me was the attention I was paid by the Polish contingent there. One in particular, a tall, tanned fellow called Karol, came time and time again to ask me to dance. We got on so well together that it seemed like the proverbial love at first sight. Added to this mutual attraction was the fact that I felt very much in sympathy with the Polish cause and with the Poles' hopes of returning to a free Poland after the war. For the next few weeks, Karol and I saw a lot of each other, and I even contributed articles to the Polish magazine, *Voice of Poland*.

During this time Karol told me things about his past life. Very interesting. He had left his *estancia* [farm] in Argentina to join the Free Polish Air Force and intended returning to his ranch after the war. It was all so very exciting, and our relationship developed quickly and soon we were engaged. Karol was a Catholic and had to get permission from his unit padre because I was a Church of England Protestant. I did not need to ask permission, nor did I get any real help or advice from WAAF officer.

The wedding arrangements all went smoothly, and I stayed in the WAAF until I was three months pregnant and then went home to my mother and grandmother for the birth of my daughter Vanda.

Then it was that things began to change for the worse. Karol was posted to South Wales. We were to join him, and after a very long and bitterly cold railway journey we arrived at a big, damp and draughty house. Vanda went down with pneumonia. She nearly died in hospital. I too fell very ill. Grandmother came to take charge of Vanda, Karol went to France, and I went into a convalescent home. Eventually, when I was feeling better, Vanda and I went to live in Portsmouth. We hardly saw Karol again until the war was over and he came home on leave.

The first surprise decision he made was that he was not going back to his *estancia* in Argentina but instead we would go to the United States. His aunt had a farm there. His sister lived in New York. It all still seemed exciting to me when he told me, but I did not realize then that we should have to wait two years to get on to 'the quota' giving a passage on a ship.

We sailed in April 1948. How wonderful the sight of the New York skyline seemed to me as I hugged Vanda by the ship's rail! At last we had arrived. I felt like shouting 'Hurray!'

Still excited, we bundled into a taxi which took us from the boat. Then slowly my spirits began to sink as I looked out of the window. We motored into the slums of the Lower East Side tenements.

That drive from the docks to the city centre of New York shocked many a GI bride. Novelist Monica Dickens recalled her horror:

Ameria was so ugly. That was upsetting at first. The introduction to England from Heathrow to London is not picturesque, but the drive south from New York docks, through the Lincoln tunnel, past the dumps of Secaucus to the New Jersey Turnpike is shocking.

Dismayed, terrified of marriage after so long an independence, I sat clenching the seat of the car and thinking, ugly, ugly, ugly as if the word could make any impression on that deliberately hideous landscape of dumps, oil tanks, scrap heaps and elevated roads conquering the sour marshes on stilted metal legs.

An ageing GI bride, I may have been the most insular English woman who ever ventured, for love, into the New World.[7]

Her loved-one, US naval officer Roy Stratton, was waiting to rescue her from her initial bout of terror. They were married the next day, and she began the task of settling down in one of Washington's intolerably clammy summers, in which she recalled, 'You are wet again with sweat before you can dry off after a cold shower.'

Though at first Monica Dickens wasted a lot of time and emotion being homesick, she had the support of relatives and friends to help her through those first few difficult days after the initial shock of the depressing entrance to New York. Mary Maycock had no such help. The taxi stopped in the slums.

There his family were waiting for us. It was a cheerful but very small apartment decorated in Polish style. That night seven of us slept in three small beds crowded together.

A few days later we rented an apartment of our own. He was not going to his aunt's farm (if ever there was one) but would find a job in New York. Our apartment had one window facing a brick wall two feet away. No fresh air. No daylight. To one side of the window were the windows of the flat opposite. At night we could hear people shouting, coughing, spitting. Outside, in the narrow street, washing hung on lines overhead, overflowing garbage bins stood on the sidewalk. Tramps scavenged in them. Karol became more and more short-tempered and abusive to me. There was nowhere for Vanda to play, except in a dirty concrete square full of rough kids. She fell ill. So did I.

I wanted to go home. But I was trapped. I could not leave the country with Vanda unless I had her father's consent. He flew into a rage when I mentioned this possibility and came at me with a kitchen knife, screaming, 'I'll see you in the soil first.'

I had no money. I needed a lawyer, a divorce and permission to leave the country with my daughter. I was in a mess.

To make matters worse, Karol had taken to drinking heavily. He began acting strangely too and started painting the furniture different colours and varnishing the floor so that we stuck to it.

I had an idea. By sheer good fortune, at that time the English actress Wendy Hiller was appearing on Broadway in *The Heiress*, and I had gone to school with her in Bexhill. I went to ask her for help. She was very concerned, lent me money and gave me clothes. Next I sought help from the British consul, who advised me to go to the Hotel Martha Washington, which was exclusively for women.

Then began the long haul to a court case for custody of Vanda and for a divorce. Whilst all this was going on, I supported myself and Vanda by working as housekeeper in various households. I was just beginning to feel secure when one day I answered the doorbell and found Karol standing there with a burly detective. They had come for Vanda. Apparently I had inadvertently moved over the state border and had no right to take Vanda with me. I nearly threw a fit. The press got involved. My employers did not like it; they said I had to go. I was now out of a job and had nowhere to live, but at least I moved back into the right state, and the law could not take Vanda from me. I found another place as housekeeper but still had only one aim in life: to get home to England.

At last my case came before the court in Brooklyn. I won. My marriage was over. And the nightmare too. Mother got a special dispensation from the Bank of England which allowed her to send money out of the country over the £50 limit of currency restrictions then in force. I bought my ticket for the trip.

Was it too good to be true? On 11 August 1949 I walked up the gangplank into my cabin, found it bedecked with flowers from my previous employers and a few friends. There was even a goodwill message from Karol's sister, saying she was disgusted with his behaviour. Oh, and she added a final bit of news: Karol had now painted the apartment gold! Ah well ...

Today Mary Maycock is happily settled in Essex, where currently she is busy helping her grandaughter with her examination syllabus for history of the Second World War. Is she ever asked the famous question: 'What did you do in the war, Granny?'

Naturally it is always the 'horror' stories that get talked about – such as that of the girl who got off the boat to find her husband with a barrowload of flowers. How lovely to be so extravagant, she thought, until he told her that she could now go on to the streets with him selling them! Happy marriages are rarely newsworthy. Nothing happens of note once the wedding celebrations are over. Most of the GI brides became inextricably involved with the lives of their husbands, their relatives and the culture of their newly adopted land.

Kathleen Parker Williams recalled how she found happiness through bending with the breeze and compromising where necessary.

She met her American husband, David, when she was eighteen. He was stationed at Aintree racecourse, home of the British Grand National steeplechase. They became engaged four months later and put in right away for permission to marry, at St Mary's parish church, Walton, on her twentieth birthday. That seemed to be allowing plenty of time for all the administrative red tape to be sorted out without any last-minute panic.

However, as poet Robert Burns remarked some 200 years ago, 'The best laid schemes of mice an' men gang aft agley', and so it was with Kathleen's plans. A short time before the wedding date she received a hurried note which put an end to all such possibilities. David was going back to the United States – not of his own free will: he was to be shipped home for medical treatment.

His message was urgent: 'Do all you can to get the paperwork for permission to marry all completed so that we can be married before my ship leaves.'

From then on it was hectic. I found out that permission was being held up by a deliberate US Army policy of purposeful delaying-procedures! Eisenhower had issued a specific memorandum to this effect.' But Kathleen was a match for the general and his tactics of procrastination. She went in person instead of writing letters.

I dashed down to Taunton, Somerset, to see David in hospital so that he could sign papers, then back to Liverpool for my mother to sign, as I was still under age, back to Taunton again on the Monday to wait for him to come out of the hospital for the afternoon so that we could get married by special licence in the local register office. Time passed. Every five minutes I was looking at my watch and wondering what could have happened. Two o'clock came and still no David. It was now visiting-time, so I went into the ward where he had been. He was still there, but this time sitting on the bed with his shoes on, threatening to go 'absent without leave' if they did not bring his pass. The ward nurse was begging him not to do anything rash. I stood anxiously by his side in my new blue suit and 'Deanna Durbin' hat.

Suddenly an orderly hurried into the ward with a bit of paper in his hand – the pass.

When we got to the register office, we needed a witness to 'stand' for David, so we asked a soldier outside the US canteen. The manager of the YWCA, where I was staying, came and 'stood' for me. We were married at four o'clock, ate a piece of cake at a Lyons' Corner House and walked back to the hospital for six o'clock. I was able to visit him just once more before he left for the boat to America.

The following day, from my home in Liverpool, I walked down to the Pier Head and gazed out at the ships berthed around the docks. One of them was a US hospital ship, *George Washington*. I didn't know that David was already aboard that very ship.

I began then a frustrating fifteen-month paperchase, running to London, the American embassy and so on, until I eventually had the right piece of paper in my hands which I had to sign saying that I would be available to travel at twenty-four hours' notice.

And that was all I did get. A telegraph boy brought the instructions: 'Come to Cunard Building tomorrow morning with "X" number of pounds. Sailing to US from Liverpool aboard Swedish ship *Axel Johnson*.'

Two weeks on the ocean were followed by train journeys to Columbia, South Carolina, and David.

Getting used to life in the country was quite hard for me, a city girl from Liverpool. The weather was very hot, my in-laws had a hard time understanding my English accent, but it was wonderful (now that I look back on it). I made some marvellous friends, and the little Episcopal church I belong to brought me yet more friends. Now we have two lovely adopted daughters, Patricia and Eve Lynne, and two wonderful grandchildren, David and Phoebe, twelve and ten respectively. I am the only English war-bride ever to have come to this small town of Blackville.

I caused quite a sensation on my first visit to the town for groceries, a few days after my arrival. I think everyone in town turned out that Saturday, and when I stepped out of the car, everybody stood and stared, and it was so quiet you could have heard a pin drop (or so it seemed to me then). It was such an odd feeling.

During the next few months there were some very funny incidents. One lady, upon introducing me to friends, said, 'Isn't she wonderful? She's only been here two months and doesn't she speak English well?' I wasn't a good cook – never had the chance at home to practise. People said that I treated David like a god – always giving him burnt offerings!

There have been many ups and downs in the marriage, many adjustments to make, both of us have had to compromise, but all worth it. God willing, David and I will have been married forty-five years on 17 April 1989.

South Carolina is a wonderful state, with very British roots. It's a good place to live.

Kathleen, like so many of the GI brides, had followed a flexible approach to her marriage and adopted country, and she had also heeded the stern advice in the booklet issued to women marrying US Army men, *A Bride's Guide to the USA*. One sentence from the booklet was never forgotten, and today it is just as relevant: '*Don't just sit around and die of homesickness!*' The brides were told to get involved with the family and work, and then they would have no time for homesickness.

'Americans, by "settling down", mean finding a line of work with prospects for higher pay and a future rather than security. Love of home is not necessarily connected with love of a house. Americans move often and may attach their home feeling almost entirely to their furniture and car. So get involved and you'll not be homesick!'

How far has that advice proved effective?

Forty-five years later many of those GI brides have found that homesickness is like malaria – a recurring malady for which there is no real cure. No doubt the occasional holiday in Britain has proved to be an effective antidote to recurring bouts of homesickness, but in fact, as the years roll by, many wartime brides, as well as their husbands, feel that it is the return flight to the USA that truly takes them home.

Netty and Ken Koch have made many such journeys, visiting relatives, friends and places which bring back happy memories. Amongst these places was the amusement pier in Southwold, where in May 1944 Ken Koch saw a pretty young Wren standing on the scales about to weigh herself. Quick on the draw, he put a penny in the coin slot before she got one out of her purse. Betty recalls:

When he offered to take me to a steak dinner, I could hardly say 'No'. Steak was so scarce in those days. After that, whenever he was off duty he cycled the eight miles from Halesworth to see me. It was only a little time after we had met that I told him that I was being transferred to London. He said straight away, 'You are the girl I am going to marry.' It was not a formal proposal, and I don't recall saying 'Yes'. But when he had visited my family and they had made him feel so welcome, it might have been that my family said 'Yes' for me. Whatever it was, I soon found myself preparing for my wedding.

We might have been married sooner, but the US 8th Air Force imposed a ninety-day delay on all applications. It was during this time that Ken had to bale out of his B24 Liberator bomber over Caen battlefield. A few days later he returned from France with the parachute which had saved his life. That parachute enabled me to have a white wedding – which would have been impossible with the clothes rationing then. My aunt Winn, a dressmaker, made all sixty-five yards into a beautiful wedding dress. We had a week's honeymoon in Halesworth.

One afternoon that week one of Ken's friends came to see me. On a mission to Munich he had seen Ken's aircraft going down with engines on fire. He was trying to break the bad news to me, but he delayed so long that Ken walked in before he got round to it! Again we'd been the lucky ones.

By 'Victory in Europe' day I was out of the Royal Navy and had flown to New York and set up home in Westbury, Long Island. Since then we have had two children. Ken served twenty-eight years in the Air Force reserve and retired as a lieutenant-colonel.

We often refer to the war as 'the good old days', forgetting those who suffered so much. But those were the days when so many people pulled together for such a good cause.

10 'Now Is The Hour'

There is love among the ruins, after strife,
There is life!'

Muriel Grainger, 'Love among the ruins
of London', in *Chaos in the Night*,
ed. Catherine Reilly (Virago, 1984)

Special Investigation Branch policeman C.V. Hearn bitterly recalled: 'A soldier could cover himself with glory on the battlefield, he could receive the highest award, but let him apply to marry a foreigner and he became an outcast immediately.'[1] Sergeant William Hammond found this to be true when he decided he wanted to marry the blonde 19-year-old Nella he had met months earlier in Cesena. He was posted, to cool his ardour. But instead it stiffened his resolve and made him all the more determined. He did marry Nella.

And why not? Everyone could now see that the war could not go on for much longer and that the hour had come when personal decisions about sweethearts and the future would have to be made – with or without War Office approval.

But as Hearn angrily wrote: 'Those fireside fusiliers back home considered that an ex-enemy Italian girl was only something that wore a skirt, was not made of flesh and blood and therefore had no feelings. Six months away from her in new surroundings would soon put an end to foolish attractions which had no place on their paper battlefields ... They invisibly but indelibly stamped on every application "THEY SHALL NOT PASS INTO MARRIAGE".'

It was not really surprising then that soldiers who had been through four years or even five years of active service abroad should at this stage cock a snook at those armchair warriors.

And many deserted. Some made alternative arrangements (as Ken Barker did with his signora), formed an association and cared not a jot whether they were legally bound in holy wedlock or not. 'What does it matter?' said Hearn. 'What do a few words mumbled by a disinterested priest matter provided husband and wife believe they are married in the eyes of God?' He remembered the fate that had befallen two of his colleagues, Jimmy Wardle (who one day would become a highly respected Metropolitan Police inspector) and his pal, who wanted to marry two beautiful Italian sisters, Rosa and Anna. They applied in the 'proper' manner, and in the 'proper' manner they were both posted away from their sweethearts.

Jimmy was lucky. For him love managed to survive despite all the opposition, military, religious and parental. (Even mothers were not entirely free from official brainwashing and therefore not always happy to see a daughter carried off to the promised land of a former enemy, even though Italy fought on the side of the Allies after 1943.) But Jimmy's story, like a good fairy tale, ended happily ever after. As Hearn recalled: 'Their love did not founder as those small-hearted bureaucrats prophesied, but blossomed in adversity.'

Jimmy's pal was less fortunate. He was posted to Greece, where he was killed.

As the American and British spring offensive in Italy pushed the Germans northwards across the River Po, the situation in the base areas behind the front lines became more static. Soldiers had time to relax and meet local girls as well as servicewomen. Said Ralph Buckingham:

> In places like Bologna's Giardina Margherita there were wonderful open-air dances every night. Coloured lights hung from the trees, a seven-piece band played and the girls were lovely. We'd been abroad for three or four years, and it was such a delight for us to have the companionship of a steady girlfriend again, even if it was only for a few months before we were posted home or to the Far East, where the war still looked as if it would never end. Somehow it was like getting back to a sane world to have a regular girl to take out after the mad world of war we'd taken as normal for so long ...
>
> What surprised me was the way the girls taught us their lingo and learnt to speak ours. There were no real barriers at all. Everything seemed so natural. They wanted to be with us, and we wanted to be with them, and nobody had any more right to dictate to us what we should do about our own futures. From then on it was *our* lives, and we made the decisions.

The hour had come too for drastic decisions to be made by sweethearts right at the top of the hierarchy controlling the war. A hundred and fifty miles from Bologna, to the north-west, Claretta Petacci, Mussolini's lover since 1931, stood by the window of her parents' apartment in Milan, staring vacantly over the morning traffic. Behind her stood a man, silent and patient, awaiting her command. Suddenly she reached a decision and turned to this man, Asvero Gravelli, one of the few Fascist Party officials who looked benignly on her relationship with Mussolini. She said, 'If you'd get me a Women's Auxiliary Force uniform, I'd be truly grateful.'[2]

She knew by now that, one way or another, Mussolini would not have long to live. The party official said he would do his best, but that was not enough for Claretta. 'Please, Asvero,' she urged, and then she added in an almost off-hand manner, 'I'm going to die with him.' But events moved too quickly for Asvero Gravelli to deliver the uniform.

Mussolini had sent his army into battle in 1940 'absolutely unprepared'. (Marshal Badoglio warned him not to declare war, because twenty of his divisions were only fifty per cent equipped, and twenty were only seventy per cent ready. 'It is suicide,' he said.) Now that army was on the run, from enemies within his own party, from Communist partisans and from the Allied armies. He sped north from Milan to Grandola, above Lake Como. There he wrote a last love-letter to Rachele, his wife – the shy girl he had married when he was a second-grade teacher at Tolmezzo and could keep chaos from the classroom only by bribing the children with sweets. In his farewell letter he wrote: 'I ask your forgiveness for all the harm I have unwittingly done you. But you know you are the only woman I have ever truly loved.'

Rachele was then only a mile away with her son Romano and daughter Anna Maria, in the charge of a Blackshirt bodyguard escorting them to safety in Switzerland. Mussolini urged her to make all haste. He would try to reach German troops in the Brenner, as soon as his own escort of ten armoured cars arrived. Only two reported. Abandoned now by so many of his old-guard Fascists – many of whom were hastily donning the red neckerchiefs of the Communist partisans, Mussolini and Claretta set off in the two armoured cars hoping to reach the German embassy in Merano. They did not get far for all the passes were blocked by partisan barricades. At one of these a small force led by Count Bellini stopped the convoy. The back door of Mussolini's armoured car was wrenched open. At gun-point he was forced out, a pathetic figure disguised in a Luftwaffe greatcoat so long that it brushed his shoes, and a helmet worn back to front. Emerging behind him was Claretta.

They were taken to a room in a peasant's house, as poor as the room in which Mussolini had been born, sixty-two years earlier. Count Bellini placed a guard outside his door and waited for further orders from partisan headquarters. He wondered what would become of the two lovers. He was not to know that this night would be the first whole night they had ever spent together.

At noon the next day the peasant woman served them a meal of maize porridge, *mortadella* and bread. It was dusk when she saw them being taken away in a slow-moving Fiat car, Claretta sitting in the back seat holding Mussolini's hand tightly. On one mudguard, cradling a machine-pistol, sat Walter Audisio, partisan leader. Five hundred yards down the road and round a hairpin bend, the car stopped at the big iron gates of the Villa Belmonte. Audisio prodded Mussolini and Claretta out and pushed them against a stone wall. He stepped back and squeezed the trigger of his machine-pistol. Nothing happened. He shouted to Comrade Moretti, 'Give me your gun.'

Moretti later remembered Mussolini's unbuttoning his grey-green jacket and saying in a clear voice to Audisio, 'Shoot me in the chest.' Audisio fired. It was Claretta who fell. He fired another burst, and Mussolini crumpled.

Faintly above the mountains came the rumble of guns – the American Fifth Army. They would arrive in time to witness an unforgettable spectacle in Milan's Piazzale Loreto. There, the next day, hanging upside down from the girders of a bombed-out petrol-filling station, was Benito Mussolini, his head but a yard above the ground. Alongside him hung Claretta Pettacci, her skirt lashed into pieces with a partisan belt. A crowd circled the bodies. United Press reporter James Roper witnessed the scene as a man from the crowd lolloped in like a goalkeeper taking a free kick, using Mussolini's head as the ball. It was the beginning of a sickening orgy of repressed hate being let out. Women ripped off his shirt, some spread their skirts and urinated on his upturned face. Then, just as quickly, the frenzied crowd quietened. Roper heard a woman murmur to her neighbour: 'Imagine. All that and not even a run in her stockings.'

Benito Mussolini was later buried beside his mistress in the paupers' plot of the Cimitero Maggiore in Milan.

On that same day, 29 April, in Berlin, dramatic decisions about the sweethearts of the Nazi hierarchy were being made too. At 1 a.m. Adolf Hitler, the Supreme Commander of the German Armed Forces, sent for Berlin municipal councillor Walter Wagner to perform a bizarre ceremony. 'Hitler, who had for so long lived in an impotent sexual no-man's land', as those who claimed to know told the writer, decided that the precise hour had come for him to marry his sweetheart, Eva Braun.[3]

Eva, the blonde who had been Hitler's close companion since 1933, had never been allowed to appear in public with him. For all those years she had endured his tyranny – she dared dance or smoke only in secret for fear of his wrath. She never liked to cross him. But she did defy his order that April when she arrived in Berlin and, like Claretta Petacci, announced her intention to stay with her lover to the end. She said she had no wish to survive him, and in those last few days she spent most of her time in the bunker, changing her clothes, doing her hair and making herself look pretty in order to keep up his spirits.

Now at last she was going to receive official recognition. Hitler explained why in his will: 'Although I did not consider I could take the responsibility during the years of struggle of contracting a marriage, I have now decided, before the end of my life, to take as my wife the woman, who, after many years of faithful friendship, of her own free will, entered this town when it was already besieged, in order to share my fate. At her own desire she goes to death with me as my wife. This will compensate us for what we have both lost through my work in the service of my people.'

It was a simple ceremony, performed in the map room of the bunker.

There, both bride and bridegroom swore in front of witnesses Goebbels and Bormann that they were of pure Aryan descent and then signed the register. In her nervous state Eva started to write her maiden name, Braun, but she crossed out the 'B' and put her correct signature – 'Eva Hitler née Braun'.

A short reception for the bridal party – one could hardly call them a 'happy couple' – was held in Hitler's private rooms in the bunker. His batman, Heinz Linge, served champagne to Bormann, Goebbels and his wife Magda, Hitler's two secretaries and his cook, whilst everyone talked nostalgically of the old days and of Goebbels' wedding, which Hitler had witnessed. A fantastic scenario!

The Soviet Army was but a mile away, and the German Army, which had once goose-stepped so proudly through every capital city of Europe bar London, was now reduced to a paltry few companies of weary, ragged soldiers, fighting desperately street by street. On the morning of 30 April all telephone communication between Berlin and the outside world ceased.

Hitler was preparing for the end. He sent for his favourite alsatian dog, Blondi, stroked its head affectionately for a few minutes and then sent it away to be destroyed by a lethal injection. His two other dogs were shot by the sergeant who looked after them.

That evening the SS Guard summoned all the women secretaries to Hitler's quarters, where they stood in one short line. Hitler came out of his room, his head slightly wobbling, flickering eyes glazed, left arm hanging slackly and twitching. He was exhibiting all the symptoms of a man suffering from the advanced stage of tertiary syphilis[4] as he walked along shaking hands with each woman, mumbling incomprehensibly. But they all knew now what to expect anyway. Hitler was about to kill himself. Immediately after they were dismissed, a strange wave of relief spread from room to room in the bunker, as realization hit all ranks that the tyrant, who had for so long dominated their lives, would soon be gone.

Incredibly, in the canteen of the chancellery that night a dance was in full swing! Suddenly there appeared an outbreak of back-slapping bon-homie as officers, NCOs and soldiers began greeting each other affably. They were really in a mood to enjoy themselves as the news quickly swept through their midst: 'Hitler has said goodbye!'

Meanwhile, Hitler had ordered that 200 litres of petrol be sent to the chancellery garden. Heinz Linge recalled how difficult it was for chauffeur Erich Kempka to find such a quantity all at once. All guards except those on essential duty were then sent away. Hitler was having a last lunch with his new wife, Eva. Eventually they emerged together to say yet another final 'goodbye' to the few who now remained. The 56-year-old Führer then walked slowly back, with Eva on his arm, to his green and white tiled study and for the last time closed the double doors.

In the passage outside, everyone waited. Minutes passed. Shells thudded around the chancellery, muffled by the thick concrete. Then came the single sharp crack of a pistol shot. No one moved. The group stood listening, wondering. Someone moved forward and opened the doors.

Hitler was sprawled on the sofa, the top of his head blown off. He had shot himself through the mouth.[5] On the same blood-soaked sofa lay Eva Braun, her head on the shoulder of the man she had idolized, an unused revolver by her side. She had swallowed poison.

In such a climax of macabre scenarios, the leader of the vaunted 'thousand-year Reich' – which had lasted but twelve, and his sweetheart, Eva, passed into history.[6]

It was half-past three on 30 April 1945.

Early the following evening, an even more bizarre and revolting scene was enacted. This time the protagonist was Hitler's fanatical and faithful follower Joseph Goebbels, the club-footed propaganda minister notorious for his great amours and philanderings with several women, over whom he mooned at the same time. Indeed, he had used his power to acquire a whole stable of starlet mistresses even when married to his wife Magda, by whom he had six children. Now, Goebbels was calling 'Time' on those children as well as on himself and his wife.

The children had just finished singing their bedtime story when they were visited by the physician – the same doctor who had attended to Hitler's alsatian Blondi. He gave each of the innocent mites a lethal injection. A few minutes later Joseph Goebbels and his wife walked arm-in-arm through the bunker, bidding goodnight and goodbye to those few they passed. They climbed the stairs to the dusk-shrouded garden and had walked only a few steps along the path when they were both dispatched to their deaths by a shot in the back of the head from the gun of an SS guard who had previously been given precise instructions by Goebbels. Their bodies, like those of Hitler and Eva, were doused in petrol and given a Viking funeral.

Seven days later, at exactly 2.41 a.m. on 7 May, the war in Europe was officially brought to an end with the signing of the surrender document at General Eisenhower's headquarters in Rheims.

There, taking care of the now tired and weary supreme commander, was Kay Summersby.[7] Now, though, she was no longer a 'Super Girl Friday' (as she once called herself for want of a better designation of the 'loving care' she provided for Ike) but a fully fledged first lieutenant of the American Women's Army Corps and appointed his 'official aide' – the first woman five-star aide in history.[8]

All this was very exciting for Kay. It gave her hope for the future. What other reason, she asked herself, could there be behind her transfer from the British FANY to the American Army, if not to be close to Ike? She recalled putting the question to him: 'Is this part of your master plan?' And he had replied: 'You bet it is!' Now she felt she could really think seriously of going to the States with Eisenhower after the war and perhaps marrying him. All indications pointed to that happy ending of their love-affair.

Shortly after 'Victory in Europe' day, Ike took her to London with his son John, General Bradley and one or two other close friends for a private victory celebration party. They went to a theatre, and Kay sat next to Ike, on his left. He appeared unconcerned at the publicity given to her presence. Afterwards they again sat together dining at Ciro's, and later, as Kay was to relate, she was in his arms for the first time in public when he invited her for the opening dance of the evening. 'It was heaven, that evening,' wrote Kay.

A week later, Allied Headquarters moved from Rheims to Frankfurt, where Eisenhower had one honour after another bestowed upon him. Kay was nearly always at his side for these ceremonies, and therefore it was not surprising that their relationship became a subject for speculation and gossip. Kay was heartened by the fact that Ike did not seem at all bothered by the talk.

The next encouraging development came when Eisenhower enlisted the help of President Truman for his British 'aide' to become an American citizen – only then could she possibly stay with him and enter that holy of holies for which he was now destined, the Pentagon.

By mid-October 1945 Eisenhower had some good news for her. Everything was now arranged for her to become an American citizen. She would just have to go to Washington first to take out her papers. Kay left for Washington. There, all went well.

But when she got back, a shock awaited her. Ike was packing. Later Kay claimed that that evening he reassured her that he would soon be back and that they would both leave for the States together early in January 1946. But Ike never came back. In the stark reality of peacetime Washington, he appears to have realized that the time had come to face the facts. He was a married man with a political future ahead of him. Not a time for a scandal.

At his instigation a letter was sent to Washington to his headquarters in Germany to say that his personal staff should be ready to leave for the United States in ten days. Hot on the heels of that letter came a telex saying that Lieutenant Summersby was dropped from the list of those scheduled to leave for Washington. There was no explanation, no reason given. Now the gossip ended. No more speculation. The war was over.

Kay summed it all up at the end of her book: 'We were two people caught up in cataclysm. Two people who shared one of the most tremendous experiences of our time. Two people who gave each other comfort, laughter and love.'

Why then did it all have to stop when it had looked so promising for

Kay? Eisenhower gave the answer in an official letter he had dictated for her. It would be impossible for him to keep her as a member of his 'personal official family' because there would be opposition to anyone who was not a completely *naturalized* American citizen working in the US War Department. The barrier against any further development or continuation of their relationship was 'naturalization'. Governments dug in their heels about naturalization when it came to people taking office in high places, and none was more obstinate than the British government in those days. It made no difference even if the request came from the king himself.

This was the problem, as is now well known, which two of Britain's best-known ex-service sweethearts had to face in 1946.[9]

Home from the wars came a 25-year-old, eagle-eyed, eagle-beaked, naval officer decorated for bravery in sea battles off Cape Matapan in the Peloponnese and those off the Greek mainland. He was a handsome young man with a shock of blond hair combed straight back from the forehead. Like many of his sailors, he had been writing letters for years to the young woman upon whom he had set his heart. She was shortly to become an ATS subaltern. The young woman in question was in love with him too.

What was it then that kept them apart? 'Naturalization.' And also the old business of 'What would people think?' For although the young naval officer had distinguished himself fighting for the Allied cause, people did not much like the idea that his four sisters had married Germans! And to make the matter worse, two of the German husbands had fought as officers in Hitler's forces.

The girl's father was, as the reader will have guessed, King George VI, and he told the ardent suitor, Prince Philip of Greece, to wait a while and that, if he was ever going to have any chance at all of marrying Princess Elizabeth, he must first win the approval of the people and present himself to them as an Englishman.

People were already asking: 'Who is this Greek?' and 'Why can't she marry a well-born Englishman?' And when the *Sunday Pictorial* put the question to its readers, 'Is Philip the right man for the Princess?' fifty-five per cent of those who answered said 'Yes' but forty per cent said 'Definitely not!' Public acceptance was clearly essential. So was naturalization. But that was easier said than done: naturalization procedures were still in a state of wartime suspension, and the Foreign Office was opposed to all attempts at naturalization because of the delicate situation in Greece, where, in the civil war currently raging, the royalist faction was accused of barbaric atrocities. Consequently, though Philip was prepared to renounce all rights to the Greek throne and to adopt the British-sounding name 'Mountbatten' instead of 'Oldenburg' (the name of the German dukes who had founded the Danish and later the Greek royal families), the possibility of early naturalization seemed remote.

All this rigmarole and red tape was a tedious irritation for a young man in love, and he, like many a returning ex-serviceman then, had stood more than enough of being pushed around at another's bidding. He wanted to be his own man, speaking his mind, doing his own thing. He wanted to be the one making decisions affecting his own future. He decided the time had come for him to take matters into his own hands, and he began to pursue the princess resolutely. He called frequently for her at home in the palace, driving his black green-upholstered MG sports car and accompanied her (usually in a foursome) to the theatre and to dine afterwards in fashionable restaurants. (It was oddly prophetic that the first play they saw together was *The First Gentleman*, a title Philip was later to be accorded as Elizabeth's husband.) Often they were seen together, driving in the MG, horse-riding. For years they had corresponded and exchanged photographs, and they had fallen in love with each other. Philip was determined to marry Elizabeth, and she was determined to marry him, whatever father or Foreign Office might say.

In the summer of 1946 Prince Philip was invited to spend his leave from the navy at Balmoral with the royal family. There (some say it was by a 'well-loved Loch with white clouds overhead and curlews crying'), he formally proposed marriage and, disregarding all the rules and conventions, Princess Elizabeth wholeheartedly accepted him.

Faced with a *fait accompli*, King George bowed to the inevitable but insisted that the engagement be kept private for a while. There was still the question of naturalization and what the public would say.

Eventually the time came for an announcement. In March 1947 Prince Philip was quietly granted naturalization, his name appearing in a list comprising mainly Jews and Poles, all swearing allegiance to the British Crown. Four months later, newspapers all over the world carried the following item of news: 'It is with the greatest pleasure that the King and Queen announce the betrothal of their dearly beloved daughter the Princess Elizabeth to Lieutenant Philip Mountbatten, RN, son of the late Prince Andrew of Greece …'

Prince Philip was at last rewarded. He had defied protocol and pursued his princess despite all the difficulties put in his path.

Rewarded too were all those of lowlier rank in the services who, when the moment of decision came, decided to take on the bureaucrats and law-makers in order to marry their sweethearts.

Barbara Collins was one who did just that. As we saw in Chapter 1, she had lost her husband in one of the first RAF raids on Germany just three weeks after they were married in 1939. For months she had waited, hoping and telling herself that 'missing' did not necessarily mean 'dead' and that Peter might turn up in a prisoner-of-war camp. One day she received a short letter 'regretting' that her husband, Flying Officer Peter Collins, must now be 'presumed killed'. It was hard to believe. Just a piece of paper saying that he was now dead. She could not bear the thought of never again seeing the man she loved so much, so she pushed all thoughts of him from her mind and took the edge off her grief by working longer hours than she needed and by being super-efficient at her job.

On forty-eight-hour leaves she would go over to RAF Scampton to see Peter's friend Stewart McCallum, but as she was still of non-commissioned rank in the ATS and he was an officer, they had to meet in a clandestine fashion. The station commander was very keen on discipline and had junior officers on the carpet in his office to reprimand them and give them extra duties for being seen in public with an 'other rank' servicewoman. 'This old-timer thought it was prejudicial to good order and military discipline for officers to be friendly with other ranks,' said Barbara, 'but we were not going to be put off by ridiculous red tape and petty regulations.'

Those regulations were already in question. In fact, the whole matter of officers consorting with other ranks of the women's services caused a flurry of letters and memoranda at the Air Ministry in 1943, as if there was nothing more important for the bureaucrats to do.[10] It all began with a letter from the public health committee chairman for Westmorland, Eric Crewsdon, which really put the cat among the pigeons. He expressed grave concern 'about the rule on some RAF stations that commissioned officers may not accompany other ranks in public places such as parks and cinemas'. He then posed a direct question which set the phones ringing in the War Office and Air Ministry: 'Would you please tell me whether this is an Air Ministry order or whether it depends upon the whim of the Station Commander?'

Mr Crewsdon reinforced his question with a matter of personal interest. Here was a man who would not easily be brushed off with a vaguely worded official reply. He instanced a particular case of a friend, 'a young Flying Officer training as a navigator, an exceptionally nice young man and a teetotaller', who had been up before his station commander because he had been seen in public with a WAAF 'other rank'.

He went on: 'Apart from my personal interest in the case quoted above, I have a general interest as Chairman of the Public Health Committee of this county. As such, the spread of venereal disease is continually being brought to my notice and I feel confident that one of the ways in which it is best combatted is by allowing young officers to make friends of decent Service girls. By forbidding such friendships, these officers are driven into the arms of diseased harlots.'

The question now before the war-lords was what ruling should be given to station commanders.

The Air Ministry drafted a letter in which there was a paragraph stating that, 'Association off the station between RAF officers and airwomen of the same station should be avoided particularly in the vicinity of the station.'

The Under-Secretary of State for Air immediately saw hazards ahead if such a letter should be sent. He wrote:

> It is just the kind of letter which, if circulated widely, as it would have to be, would invite criticism in the Press and in Parliament. Some people would say that the Air Council were seeking to uphold class distinctions, and others that the Council were adopting an old-fashioned attitude reminiscent of Mrs Grundy at her stuffiest.
>
> The Inspector General points out that it is desirable that we should, as far as practicable, march with the Army and Navy in matters of this kind.
>
> The War Office attitude is apparently to let sleeping dogs lie. The Admiralty apparently do not keep a dog at all.
>
> My own feeling is that we should be well advised to follow the War Office example.

The reply this elicited from the personnel department of the Air Ministry was to continue the canine imagery: 'But our dogs are stirring in their sleep; the Admiralty have no dogs since the WRNS are not under Naval discipline and get out of uniform when not on board. Our problem is different from that of the other Services in that our WAAF are so much more integrated with the RAF.'

And so the memos wittered on until they disappeared into the archives. Meanwhile sensible men and women took their own decisions.

For Barbara Collins, the problem disappeared when, as a result of her hard work, her merit was recognized and she was commissioned. Weekends with Stewart were all above board once she had a pip on her shoulder.

Once or twice a week Stewart mentioned the possibility of marriage, but Barbara was not keen on marrying a bomber pilot. She had met so many WAAF sweethearts who in the gathering dusk congregated at the end of runways when operations were on, to wish their loved-ones luck and wave them goodbye, knowing they might not be back for their breakfast. She had seen so many tragedies of women becoming emotionally involved and on the point of marriage when their men were killed. And then they would go through it all again with somebody else. The pain of Peter's death was still sharp, so she made no commitment.

When the war was over and before she was released from the ATS, Barbara took advantage of an offer to fly to Germany to visit a small churchyard on the outskirts of Wilhelmshaven. There she stood by the neatly tended grave of her husband, Peter.

'A cold wind was blowing in from the North Sea as I stood there in what had been an enemy country, now wrecked beyond description.

What was it all about, I wondered. Had it been worth it? I shed a few tears that almost froze on my cheeks as I turned and took one last look at the mound and a small posy of flowers some kind person had placed there. The picture of that bleak, windswept cemetery is with me still. I shall never forget that it is there that the body of my lovely young husband of three weeks now lies.'

For Barbara, that visit brought her to the reality of the situation. Peter Collins would never come back into her life, but life must go on. She was now twenty-six, she had her future to consider, and over the years she and Stewart had grown close together sharing a genuine care for each other. They had in fact the ideal basis for a happy marriage; not only did they love each other but were very good friends.

Stewart's release group number was fifteen, and it was coming up when he once again asked Barbara to be his wife. This time there was no hesitation. They were married in September 1946 and have forever blessed those days when they met so secretively – 'almost like foreign agents', as Barbara once put it – and ignored orders against 'consorting'. Their disobedience has brought over forty years of happiness together, two daughters and four grandchildren.

Although not all relationships between officers and servicewomen of other ranks flourished as well as that between Stewart and Barbara, most sweethearts found ways round the regulations, and 'sleeping dogs' were allowed to rest undisturbed. Occasionally, however, such liaisons produced rather comical situations. None more so than those of Airwoman Jean Edge and her husband, Officer Commanding Flying at RAF Grangemouth, as she recalled recently:

I was lucky in having a husband with a great sense of humour, who did not mind in the least that I was 'other ranks', and although I had been selected for officer training, it suited me better to be 'other ranks', because I was then more 'mobile' and could be more easily fitted into postings so that I could be nearer my husband wherever he was posted.

Once I remustered from my course as a radio-telegraphist to the trade of 'waitress', so that I could be posted for duties in the officers' mess at Drem, further along the Firth of Forth from Grangemouth, where Paul, my husband, was.

He was now a wing commander and frequently flew to Drem and dined with the station commander, Sir Archibald Hope, known as 'Sir Bald' because he was. It was fun serving them with their meals. On one occasion I could not resist putting a glass of Guinness in front of Paul. This puzzled Sir Bald, and Paul had to think quickly to explain its appearance without revealing that I was his wife and knew what he liked to drink.

On another occasion, when my parents were invited to a dinner and dance at the station, Paul was invited too. I was on mess duty that night. It was most amusing for me to be serving all the family alongside the commanding officer. But perhaps it was not quite so amusing to be watching Paul dance with the WAAF officers later on. Though I suppose I did not really mind so much, because I knew who he would be taking home that night.

In one way and another, Paul and Jean Edge coped with all the petty problems presented by the differences in their rank until the time came for it all to end.

In August 1946 Jean was released from service in the WAAF, and in September Paul was demobilized too. They had a happy return to civil life, Jean running the new home and Paul resuming his role as manager in textiles. The transition was eased too by their retention of Air Force contacts at Leuchers and other neighbouring RAF messes, and so they enjoyed the best of both service and civilian worlds.

The transition back to civil life was feared by many servicemen and women for, though there was much to grumble about, there was also much to like about service life.

Sheila McCall remembered those conflicting feelings: 'We all got "browned off" at times, but there was something about ATS life that I've never met anywhere else – a feeling of support. We all helped each other. If anyone was on leave, we'd take their shoes to be mended and their laundry to the quartermaster's stores. We shared each other's joys and sorrows. Yet how I longed for those forty-eight-hour passes so that I could get away from the chatter and noise! On the other hand, how I missed the good companionship once I left the Army. I know what good days they were when I look back on them now.'

Former ack-ack gunner Ruth Negus, too, found that as the hour drew near for her demobilization she was not looking forward at all to civil life: 'It was hard to realize that it would soon be over. Serving with Allied armies, we had mixed with men and women from many different countries and from all walks of life. Sometimes our days were hard and long, we knew what it was like to be cold, wet and weary, but we were all in it together. There was always a sympathetic ear and a friend in need. Yes, there was that indefinable something, a support that saw us through difficult times, comradeship, a kind of loving.'

There was more to women's anxiety about returning to civil life than the loss of affectionate friends, though. Wartime service had altered women's lives dramatically. They had been given challenging and satisfying jobs to do; they had acquired technical skills, self-confidence and a pride in duties well done. With many women, service had bred a new and fierce spirit of independence. Few now relished the prospect of relinquishing all the experience and skills they had gained, to be thrust back to the old order of the kitchen sink and hot stove. Furthermore, as women had settled into trades and careers previously dominated by men, they had also adopted the attitudes of, and the freedom expected by, men. Amongst all these liberties was sexual freedom in its broadest sense.

All things considered, it was plain that women were going to find that readjustment to their domestic role and civilian post-war society was not going to be easy.

This was brought home forcibly to Catherine Culbert in June 1945, when she came home on disembarkation leave after her long tour of duty in Egypt, Algiers and Italy. She had been looking forward eagerly to seeing her daughter, Jennifer, and her mother, and to just being home again. But things did not work out that way. Not at all. Jennifer was now thirteen and away at boarding school in Cumberland (a safe area); Catherine's home was empty, and her mother had a long story to tell about her husband, Martin.

'Well, I did write and say you should try to come home on leave ... but you were in Africa, you know ... And I thought things might work out all right anyway ... and I didn't want to worry you unnecessarily when you couldn't do anything about it ... and Jennifer was away from it all and happy at school ... so ... well ... now he's moved in with her ...'

Catherine gazed round her empty sitting-room as the story unfolded bit by bit. She still remembers the impression home made on her after all those years away: 'It looked so small, so shabby. Was it always so cramped, as if the sideboard was sticking right out, leaving scarcely enough room for a chair to be put at the table and still leave room to walk behind it? I just couldn't get used to it. It no longer seemed part of my life. I felt as if I was stepping into a different world altogether. And suddenly I felt awfully alone.'

Catherine caught the next morning's train back to her holding unit. She needed time to think. She needed advice.

'I felt more at home back in the ATS officers' mess. There, there were people I could talk to and get help from. I shuddered to think of going back to the home life I had known all those years ago. I'd simply grown away from it all. I wanted to stay in the ATS. And I knew I could not face the old life again.'

She signed on for another twenty-four years.

The home-coming of Catherine Culbert, fraught with emotional problems, was an experience common to servicemen and women returning to civil life after the war. When the shooting stopped, the social and personal problems seemed to multiply.

11 'It's Easy To Remember'

It was a great feeling to be out – there was no denying that; but I
was frightened. In fact I was very frightened indeed.

Ian Carmichael

Stuart Brown, the former Berwick newspaper reporter, and his German
sweetheart, Dora, had expected to face a few problems when the war
ended, but they could never have envisaged the absolute terror that
would come with them.[1]

The chain of events that led up to this began when Fusilier Brown
was captured with troops of the 51st Highland Division at
St-Valéry-en-Caux in June 1940. He was sent to Stalag XXB in
western Poland. There the utter boredom of camp life, with its
monotony of endless queues, the jostling and wrangling and the
mind-destroying fatigues, drove him to volunteer for farm work. It was a
decision which altered his whole life.

Under armed German guard, with several other prisoners, he went to
work for farmer Bruno Warkentin about a mile away from the camp. For
these prisoners, the war was now over. They could settle down to a
steady routine, each taking responsibility for particular aspects of farm
work as the younger German labourers were drafted away for military
service. Bob took charge of the stables, Paddy was the dairyman, whilst
Stuart and two other prisoners drove teams of horses. All the prisoners
got on well with farmer Bruno and his family, but they were still
surprised on 24 December 1941 to receive an invitation to join the
family for the traditional German Christmas Eve festivities.

There was, however, an even bigger surprise awaiting them all as they
assembled to sit down for dinner that evening. Another member of the
family had arrived, daughter Dora. They had all heard of this young
woman away at farm accountancy college, but none of the prisoners had
ever seen her. She was different – strikingly so, and one can well
imagine the effect she had upon those young British soldiers. It was a
long time since they had seen a girl like Dora. She was, as Stuart Brown
was later to write ' ... attractively dressed in purple velvet, pockets and
collar picked out in soft brown fur. Well-groomed and manicured, legs
clad in silk, neat feet in smart shoes, her appearance and impact was in

direct contrast to the girls of the fields with whom we had become friendly over the past few weeks.' During the meal the soldiers could not help glancing, under lowered eyelids, at this delightful creature now gracing their table.

Shortly after the festivities finished, the soldiers were settling down for a quiet hour in their own small room when there was a tentative tapping at the door. Dora stood there to ask, in hesitant English, if they would all like to hear some music on her portable gramophone. They would, indeed, and were delighted to listen to tunes they had all danced to in the days of their freedom, bringing back so many happy memories. And they talked together, excitedly. Dora had learnt a little English at school.

In that delightful, brief period of relaxation, something happened which Stuart did not notice. Bob did, though. Later, when Dora had gone, he turned to Stuart to give him the news: 'You've clicked there!' It was not long before that was evident to Stuart too, for that most wonderful and exciting of all human emotions washed over him. A revelation. He was in love, and Dora loved him too.

But that love was forbidden. There were rigid German laws against such fraternization between prisoners and German women. Punishment for all transgressors was severe. What future was there then in letting the relationship develop further? It would be particularly hazardous for Dora. All the eyes of the village were already upon her; she was an obvious target for attention and malicious gossip, for she was different from other women. She was beautiful, more refined and dressed in a city style. But more than that: she was the leader of the Bund Deutscher Mädchen, a youth movement for girls.

Dora was well aware of the risks she would be running. She showed Stuart a newspaper report on how a girl from a neighbouring village had flouted the fraternization law and suffered the penalty. Brown described what happened: 'Her head was shorn before she was paraded on her way to prison with a placard round her neck declaring: "I have been friendly with a prisoner of war." '

It therefore took a special kind of love for Dora to defy Nazi laws and run the risk of being thrown into a concentration camp. But it was also a love that gave her strength. It gave her the resolve to give up the prospect of marriage to a wealthy Luftwaffe pilot who was heir to a neighbouring farm, strength to fly in the face of her father's strong words of advice – 'You'll never be able to go with him ... He comes from quite a different world ... It's a complete waste of time to risk your reputation ... You'll never be able to marry him.'

And if all the warnings were not enough, the message was rammed home forcibly by the terrible experience of her sister, Nadja. She had run away with another prisoner of war, Paddy, whose child she was carrying. She had been caught and put in Stutthof concentration camp. After months of incarceration she returned, a shadow of her former self, so terrified by her experience and by the atrocities she had seen that she could not, dare not, speak of them. All she could do was to plead with Dora not to risk the same punishment by continuing her relationship with Stuart. 'It's terrible in there,' she cried. 'Don't have anything to do with prisoners.'

Despite all this, Dora and Stuart continued to meet secretly. At first the meetings were disguised as English lessons, although during these sessions the questions Dora asked were more about Stuart's background than English grammar. And there was, of course, the inevitable question, 'Do you have a girlfriend back home?' Stuart admitted he had but that in her case absence had not made the heart beat fonder, nor his. Her letters were now less frequent and considerably cooler. She was no rival for Dora. And Dora was there, with him.

One night, a memorable one, at the end of their lesson time, they parted with a kiss. (A loving kiss not a cursory thank-you one.)

Now the problem for Stuart, as he lay awake that night, was, 'Where do we go from here?' No decision was made. They continued to meet, and Stuart built a hide-away in the chicken shelter, so that they could just get out of sight behind it.

And so the clandestine love-affair drifted on for almost four years, until startling news came with soldiers from the Eastern Front. The Soviet Army was now pushing back the German divisions at a rapid rate. Any cheer which this might have brought to the prisoners was, however, quickly cancelled by the tales that came with it – horrendous reports of brutal atrocities perpetrated by Soviet troops, eye-witness accounts of murder, pillage and rape.

The day of decision came for Dora and Stuart early in January 1945, when the German guard came running into the farmhouse to tell Bruno to pack a cart with valuables and move west as quickly as he could. This caused a problem for sweethearts. Now there were others involved besides Stuart and Dora. Jimmy Pegg had his Olga, Bob had Fränz, and the other Jim had Luzi. Now all soldiers and sweethearts were faced with the stark reality of the situation that the war was ending in a way far different from all their previous imaginings. Stuart recalled: 'I had envisaged jubilant prisoners of war surrounding the British troops who would release us and would rush us home to a welcome, if not fit for heroes, that would at least be warm.' Instead, here they were, a thousand miles east of where they had been captured, and about to be overrun – it seemed – by drunken Soviet soldiers eager for loot and for women to rape.

This was no time for taking chances. The hour had come for decisive action. Stuart took it. He found a pair of scissors and cut off Dora's hair into a passable semblance of a soldier's style. He gave her his battledress jacket, an overcoat, an old pair of trousers, a forage cap and a pair of boots he had been given at the POW camp. They packed as much food and clothing as they could carry in two small satchels which Stuart had made from strong sacking and set off westwards with Dora's parents.

Soon, though, Soviet motorized units got ahead of them. Dora's feet were blistered raw; Stuart had developed dysentery pains and was passing blood. They took refuge in one cottage after another, all the time having to hide Dora from what Stuart later described as 'a stream of unshaven Russians in untidy, ill-fitting uniforms who no longer searched for valuables but women'. He told how ' ... two girls who were dragged into a bedroom with no more than a curt "come" returned later ashen faced, tearful and silent'.

On another occasion he and Dora had to hide under a single bed so short that their heads projected from the end, and they had to pile armfuls of litter on top of them and lie there, with one arm thrown over their noses to avoid suffocation. Whilst they were in this extremely precarious situation, a drunken Soviet soldier came into the room, pushed a girl on to the bed and threw himself on top of her. Then came the creaking of springs, the hard breathing of the man and the moans of the woman. After him came another, and then another and another. 'About a dozen used her before she was left alone,' wrote Brown.

When all was quiet and the soldiers had gone, Stuart and Dora left the house. Outside, Dora's mother and father were waiting anxiously. 'Are you all right?' asked the mother – meaning, had the Soviets raped her? Dora reassured her mother, who then revealed that she had not been so lucky. Though over seventy years old, she had been raped.

Such was the terror the lovers now faced on their long journey to the British lines in the west, as Soviet troops rampaged through villages. Their terrible lust for women and sex was evident on all fronts. The forward American troops found this too. The Soviets did not always have it their own way though: some paid the ultimate price for their bestiality.

US infantryman Daniel Militello, who also had a German sweetheart to look after, well remembers horrific scenes. This God-loving, born-again Christian is not a man given to embellishing stories for mere sensationalism, and this was obvious when he recently described to the writer what he, personally, had seen of the way in which some Soviet soldiers were treating women: 'It was right at the end of the war, the ugly side of the war, that no one knew anything about. I don't know exactly how many of my buddies shot Russian soldiers who were brutalizing German women, but they certainly did. I was almost involved myself on one occasion, for, you see, there was a bunch of them on to one woman. And we were armed and when we saw them doing that there was no question, yes, you shot 'em like you would a German enemy soldier. You shot 'em. It had really got down to animalistic life then. But it happened. That's the side of the war most people never see. Terrible.'

At last Stuart and Dora reached Berlin, where the British had only just arrived, and they took shelter in the Olympic Stadium. It was a revolting, filthy place where British troops had the unenviable job of clearing up the mess, including corpses, left by the Soviets. But for Dora and Stuart it was only for one night. The next day a British Army truck took them down the famous *autobahn* through the Soviet zone to Helmstadt and the British military zone.

'It's all over now,' Stuart told Dora.

It was not. The next day, when they both reported to the commanding officer of the displaced persons' camp at Luneberg, Fusilier Stuart Brown was brought back to the reality of British Army life.

On presenting himself at the office, he was greeted by a pompous armchair warrior with captain's pips on immaculate epaulettes, who disdainfully eyed Brown's crumpled uniform and brayed in the affected clipped speech of Sandhurst Military Academy, 'What's the idea of bringing that girl with you? She'll have to get out of that uniform, you know. She can't stay here. She'll have to go back where she came from.'

Although Fusilier Brown was forced to return to Britain and leave Dora behind, his battle now began to bring her to his side. It was long and metaphorically bloody. Brown had not been a journalist for nothing. Now he pulled out all the stops: he wrote to the War Office, enlisted the aid of his MP and applied pressure from all directions. So it was that in January 1946 an 'obedient servant' in the Aliens' Department wrote to say that the Secretary of State would grant permission for Dora to come to Britain, provided certain formalities were observed. They were.

Dora arrived, in gale-force winds on the Dover ferry, on 8 February 1946. Three days later, fittingly on 14 February – St Valentine's Day, she and Stuart were married in the Berwick register office. His mother was there, plus the village blacksmith and the taxi-owner who stood as witnesses.

Once again, as for Ronald Hankinson in Italy, love had prevailed over bureaucracy. Or, as Ken Barker also disovered there, '*Chi la dura, la vince*, – He who sticks it out wins.'

Not surprisingly, reports of prisoners of war returning with German brides occasionally featured in the tabloid press, and they stirred up a furore of protests from self-righteous 'patriots' who were outraged that this should ever be allowed. 'Not long ago these people were killing our young men! Are we going to forget so soon?' asked one woman, signing herself 'Disgusted'. Ironically, all those 'patriots' soon had cause to direct their wrath elsewhere. This time it was levelled against British women who in their hundreds were now having the audacity to apply for permission to marry German prisoners of war!

In Britain then there were quarter of a million German prisoners of war. Thousands worked away from their camps, on farms, on forestry work, on roads and in quarries. They were personable, fit young men. Many of them could speak a little English, and frequently they worked close to British women – young women suffering from the aftermath of a war which had robbed them of sweethearts, husbands and eligible young men for life-partners.

Gradually, as the war finished and the months passed, the restrictions governing the activity of German prisoners were relaxed. The British became kid-glove gaolers. All German prisoners, except those classified as ardent Nazis, were allowed to draw part of their pay in sterling and to use shops, cinemas, restaurants and public transport within a five-mile radius of the camp.

Theoretically, though, fraternization was not allowed. Indeed, 22-year-old Werner Vetter was sentenced to twelve months' imprisonment by a court martial in Droitwich for association with a British girl.[2] This provoked an outcry in the press and in Parliament. 'Would not the British Minister of War take steps to enable Vetter to marry the mother of his child?' a member of Parliament asked. And one of the few women MPs, Leah Manning, asked why the War Office was exercising sex discrimination in allowing British servicemen of the occupation forces in Germany to have German sweethearts yet preventing British women from having the same opportunities with German prisoners of war. Eventually the Minister of War, Bellinger, gave in gracefully. In a reply to a further question in the house, he retorted, 'I have never attempted to resist the inevitable course of nature.'

Resistance was, in fact, impracticable. In August 1947 the War Department reviewed the proceedings of twenty-seven military courts which had awarded sentences of imprisonment to prisoners of war for 'establishing relations of an amorous nature with members of the public', and where the prisoners were of good character, the sentences were remitted. In September Werner Vetter was joined in holy matrimony to Olive Reynolds in the quaint old Hampton Lovett church, Worcestershire, one hundred yards from his camp gates.

The national press was there in force. A *Daily Express* reporter wrote on 18 September:

To the singing of Schubert's Sanctus by a German prisoners' choir, they were married by the Rector, the Reverend Eric Bartlam.

As the couple signed the register, there was an "Ave Maria" duet. Outside there was more singing – a German song, "*Hoch, Hoch, Hoch*", and Vetter found some pennies to scatter to the crowd. Then they went off to spend the rest of the day at their reception, held in a Girl Guides' hut ...

They saw two wedding cakes cut. They heard speeches in German and English. Then came German folk songs, dancing and games, to the music of a prison camp orchestra.[3]

A marvellous day it was for Werner and Olive and the 150 German prisoners who were guests at the wedding. But what an anticlimax came when the evening ended! *Everyone* then went home, including Werner to his camp at Hampton Lovett, Olive to Droitwich, 1½ miles away.

Though marriages were now possible, they were not without certain implications. Any British woman marrying a German would automatically lose her British nationality. Furthermore, no promise could be given that the husband would be allowed to stay in Britain when his turn for repatriation came round. But perhaps most daunting of all was the fact that the wife would not be allowed to live with her husband after the wedding. He would have to return to his camp each night and still be restricted by all the rules governing POW life then.

Daunting? Off-putting? Not a bit. Eight hundred marriages quickly followed between British women and prisoners of war. By July 1948 all POWs had been repatriated, but an astonishing 20,000 chose to stay and make their home in Britain. Harm Cremer, who was one of the first prisoners in the camp at Malton, North Yorkshire, married a local woman and settled in York, working as an engineer. 'Our treatment was first class. We worked hard but the people were very good to us. When we were out on the farms they would often slip us a packet of cigarettes. Later when things relaxed we got invited out to Sunday lunch and Christmas parties.'[4]

The hand of friendship was often offered to those young prisoners of war far from home, the British and Americans in Germany, the Germans and Italians in Britain. Yes, they were men who had been killing one another for the past six years, but what a crazy waste it now seemed to many of them. Romance was transcending the enemy fronts, and a new life was opening for them all, the victoriously free and the defeated prisoners alike.

No story exemplifies this better than that of a former German paratrooper who had fought on the Russian Steppes and at Arnhem. He is Bernhard Carl Trautmann, son of a Bremen eletrician, who was taken prisoner by the British at Emmerich, put in a POW camp in Northwich, Cheshire, in April 1945 and very soon was the idol of all the local young men, and many women too.

He had been playing football for his POW camp team when a league club football scout spotted his remarkable talent as a goalkeeper. Too good to waste on a camp team, Trautmann was invited to play for league club Wigan Athletic. The crowd, who could not pronounce his name, loved him. The team manager invited him home to tea after the match. And thereafter events moved rapidly.

Soon 'Bert' Trautmann, as the fans came to call him, had attracted the admiration not only of the bigger league clubs but also that of the manager's daughter, with whom he had fallen in love. As soon as permission became available, they were married. Trautmann was then captured in another way – by First Division football club Manchester City. He became their regular goalkeeper for years. The home crowd loved him and took him to their hearts. He was not to fail them when the big day in any footballer's life came, the FA Cup Final at Wembley in April 1957. *The Times* reporter wrote: 'The final memory was of the great goal-keeping of Trautmann the German, for Manchester City, a man with wrists of iron swooping on shots high and low like a predatory eagle. It was an exhibition of grace and power to remember.'

He was undoubtedly the hero of the day – and more so the next, when the full story was known that midway through the second half he had emerged from a dive at the Birmingham centre forward's feet with a broken neck! The pain was excruciating, but in those days, substitutes were not allowed, so he played to the final whistle. He was just able to climb those steep stairs to the royal box to receive his cup-winner's medal from Her Majesty The Queen. It was just ten years to the day since he had been let out of the POW camp to play football for the local club and had fallen in love with the manager's daughter.

In retrospect, how stupid those non-fraternization orders now seem. But they were promulgated in 1945, in the context of war.

In 1945 the government was beginning the task of bringing the troops home and demobilizing them gradually on the basis of points calculated according to a formula of 'first in, first out'. The last thing they wanted was the procedure to be complicated with foreign brides and families.

Demobilization was a slow process, and consequently many troops were left in Germany with no war to fight. A change began to come over them, a change which had been accelerated by the astonishing result of the general election of June 1945, when the servicemen's vote removed Prime Minister Churchill from office and let Labour in. After this, Labour MP Denis Winston Healey, who had served as a major in North Africa and Italy, said: 'Among servicemen there was the feeling that they were as good as anybody else, and they wanted the right to tell their officers off once the war was over.'[5]

Those who had fought in Germany and were left there waiting for their release number to come up were consequently in no mood to be told which sweethearts they could have and which they could not. Thus when the non-fraternization order came out, forbidding American and British troops from having German girlfriends, it was blatantly ignored.

Military historian and writer Charles Whiting, then a 16-year-old soldier with the reconnaissance regiment of 52nd Infantry Division in Germany, remembers how it really was then:

> Despite all the warnings, the threats of punishments and monetary penalties of being caught fratting, very few of the troops took any notice. They wanted women – and they were going to get them. To the victor belongs the spoils.
>
> 'Fratting' had its consequences of course. In the six months from May to December 1945, twenty-two thousand illegitimate children were born in the American zone of Occupation alone. Today there are thousands and thousands of middle-aged Germans whose real fathers were British, American, Canadian, French, Russian and so on.
>
> The warnings about fraternization had no effect whatsoever, they were almost universally ignored. The fine of seventy-five dollars that the GI had to pay if he were caught with a German Fräulein was meaningless, for with a pack of Lucky Strikes going for ten dollars on the Black Market the GI could easily pay for any fine levelled.
>
> It is not easy to imagine the situation German women were in then. For years they had been deprived of the warmth of a man's love. Most German young men were either dead, crippled, missing or prisoners of war. 'Fratting', as it was called in defiance of Eisenhower's non-fraternization edict, was in fact the rage.[6]

Margaret Bouchard of Berlin, who married an American, said: 'No one could enforce the no-fratting order. There was too much of it going on.'[7]

And indeed there was, from generals and top administrators downwards. As early as November 1944 General Eisenhower realized this and stressed the need for British and American servicewomen to be posted for duties in north-west Europe, so that the orders about non-fraternization would stand a better chance of being obeyed. But drafts of women were too few and too late.

'You couldn't expect the GIs, whatever their rank, to behave any differently,' said one former American infantry captain. 'Those men had been in the thick of the fighting for months. They were ready for a rest and for the comfort of a woman's company. For heaven's sake, it's only natural in peacetime after a bad day at work; it was even more natural after what those guys had been through. The no-frat policy was unworkable from the start. I was a happily married man but I too felt the need for a woman by my side, even if only to drink with. Men were lonely, they needed to love for a change and be loved.'[8]

The truth of those words was evident in the streets and houses and villages and towns wherever troops were billeted. Love knew no frontiers, respected no creeds, brushed aside political doctrines. Love

Now he thought he would follow the correct procedure for a civilian without a passport. He registered as a displaced person. No one raised any objections to this. They were married by German civil authorities on 13 June 1946, and six weeks later their son, Robert, was born.

Sure now that everything had been done properly, according to current regulations, Daniel went confidently to the American consulate in Frankfurt to register his son as an American citizen born abroad. He also asked for transportation to the States to be arranged for his wife and child. Then, as Danny today recalls, 'All hell broke loose.' He was arrested, charged with being a seaman absent without leave, sentenced to a month in gaol and told that when he came out he would have to return to the States *without his wife and child.*

The simple matter of getting married was now involving more twists and tedium than a second-rate soap opera. And the former soldier Daniel Militello was really incensed. But not beaten. He brought in the big guns that soldiers always relied on when all else failed – the press. For the British soldier this was usually in the form of a letter to their champion, the *Daily Mirror* (where Barbara Castle was then 'forces adviser'); Daniel Militello smuggled his letters out of gaol to the American national press, to the American forces newspaper the *Stars and Stripes* and to German newspapers. They all reacted indignantly, with headlines such as, 'IS IT A CRIME TO MARRY?'

Danny did not stop with the press. Once he had found a way of getting his letters out of prison, he wrote to the heads of all the relevant government departments and also to the Roman Catholic Cardinal Spellman. Still the US War Department dug in its heels and refused to budge. It even vociferously defended its attitude as being in the best interests of everyone concerned. General Joseph McNarney, commanding general of US Forces in Europe, argued that young men needed protection: 'There are many reasons for this,' he said, 'but one of the principal ones is the extreme youth and susceptibility of a high percentage of our enlisted personnel, combined with a surplus of German women who are in straitened circumstances, to put it mildly, and who will take calculated advantage of these young soldiers. This may be a paternalistic attitude but I consider it a serious problem and that it is our responsibility to protect our own people.'

Fortunately for Daniel Militello, there were others in high places who did not hold the same opinion, and they took up the cudgels on his behalf. Congressman Elsaesser of New York interceded, and in October 1946 General McNarney approved an exit permit for Katharina and Robert to fly to the United States – much against his wishes. 'He hated having to back down,' recalled Daniel. 'He said to me, "You've made me look an absolute fool in front of the whole state department. I could hang you for that!" '

Daniel Militello did not linger to be hanged! His house was besieged by lines of GIs wanting advice on how they too could get their wives home to the States, for Daniel had opened the floodgates. By the end of December 1946, 2,500 GIs had filed applications for permission to marry their German sweethearts. And on 27 March 1947 the *New York Times* announced the first officially approved wedding, between Sergeant Peter Rupeka and Erika Schaefer of Frankfurt. Military government officials said they now expected 6,000 weddings a year.

By then, Daniel was home: 'I was escorted by two jeeps of military police to the Frankfurt airport to board an American Overseas Airline flight back to New York city. In November 1946 my wife and son arrived. I had made a promise to God, long before praying for his help and accepting his blessings, that my child upon arrival would be presented to him in church as thanks before continuing on home. This I did, and my marriage was blessed.'

Daniel and Katharina's son Robert, is now forty-three, with four children of his own. He trained as a journalist and is a preacher and pastor. Daniel also has a daughter of forty-one with three children, and one of thirty-six with four children. They have all brought great happiness to Katharina and Daniel.

'It was one heck of a fight getting Katharina back to the States as my wife but it was surely worth it. Recently, when the German magazine *Stern* asked me if I would do it all again, there was only one answer: "*You betcha!*" '

What about the other sweethearts? Would they do it all again? What would they say now – Jean Edge, Kathleen Williams, Ken Barker, Joyce Rowland, Margaret Dippnall, Margaret Carmada, Mabel Smyth, Barbara Collins and the host of others with whom we have reminisced?

Barbara smiled reflectively when the question was put to her, as if it had been in her thoughts many times before. She could look back on nearly fifty years of happy married life with former bomber pilot Stewart McCallum, and perhaps she spoke for many a sweetheart when she said:

'We are the lucky ones. We've had a good life together. We have lovely children, and I would not have missed a minute of it all, not one in all those years, yet … well … they say time is a great healer, but I wonder if you ever do get over your first love – especially when he is snatched away from you so suddenly, as Peter was. However, he is still with me in a way. You see, there are times when I sit here on the garden seat in the dusky grey quiet of a summer's evening, and in those silent moments when the wind rustles through the leaves, some chance sound or smell triggers off an odd association of thoughts, mental pictures and sounds from the past. And then quietly they are all back with me, just as they were long ago, laughing and talking excitedly, Peter, his friends and mine … crowding into my mind ... so real ... so young. And I know that my lips are lifting in the suggestion of a smile, and I wonder where all the years have gone ...

They were great years, despite all the horrors of war, marvellous years to be young and in love. Years when out of the sadness of all the conflict, so many of us, servicemen and women, found a simple and constant love that lingers untarnished over the years ...

Indeed, there seems to be something special about those wartime sweethearts that makes them shine brightly in the memory. Periodically they flash on to the screen of the mind's eye into such sharp focus that people are moved into action.

Such was the experience of a former US marine, now retired.[9] He could never forget a girl he met in Hawaii just before Pearl Harbor, and though he had seen her only twice and exchanged barely a few words of conversation, her picture refused to fade. On one of those occasions when his thoughts turned to her, he made a decision. He would seek help from Lloyd Shulman, who specialized in tracing lost loves, a service for people who wonder what life would have been like if they had stayed with their first love. Shulman found the 'girl'. The marine telephoned her and within the hour he was aboard a flight from Miami to Fort Lauderdale, where she was waiting. Now, living together, they are finding out for themselves what life might have been like had they got together earlier and proving too that it's never too late to fall in love again.

Maureen Cope recently had a similar experience. A former American Air Force bombardier, John Marmonowski, who had seen Maureen's name in an Air Force journal, wrote to ask if she could locate an old girlfriend he had been fond of while stationed at Shipdham. All he had was her name, Cathie Field, and a rough idea of where she lived. He had lost touch with her when he was posted on completion of his missions. His wife had now died, and memories of his old flame of wartime days returned frequently to his mind.

Maureen wrote back, saying that she would try to find Cathie. She set off with friends, first to Shipdham, where they quizzed the postmistress. They then asked several older men and women they met in the village. They were led to Yaxham, then to Eddie Nelson's pub, the Cross Keys. There they talked to the locals and were pointed in the direction of Higham, and from there to a woman who used to work for the US Red Cross. And so the search went on until, at last, they located Cathie's sister at Garvestone.

It was then that Maureen began to have doubts. Should she pass on to John the location of Cathie's sister? Perhaps she should let sleeping dogs lie? But Maureen was already hooked. She picked up the telephone and rang the sister. Gingerly she introduced herself and explained the reason for her call.

There was a long silence at the other end, then a whoop of disbelief: 'Not Chad? You really mean Chad?' – that was their fond name for him.

Now Cathie and John 'Chad' Marmonowski are getting to know each other again.

Thoughts of a wartime sweetheart can so easily be stirred by a tune, a song heard on the radio or even a smell which pulls back curtain after curtain to reveal people and places vibrantly alive again.

'Rarely do I enter a fish-and-chip shop today without thinking of Iris Williams, the beautiful fair-haired girl I always wanted to take to the Saturday night dance at Stretford town hall. Her father kept a fish-and-chip shop. Just as I had plucked up courage to ask her, I was posted away,' recalled Stanley Palmer of the Royal Fusiliers.

But he has never gone back. Yet.

GI bride Catherine Roberts Swauger has, though. She went back to the old haunts in which she was happy and in love. And though she found, as we do all too often, that such places are subject to the ravages of time and redevelopment, something of the past still remains, the spirits of people. Catherine recorded her experience:

I am back in the RAF base at Old Sarum ... the grass is so high ... I hear faint echoes of the Air Force march and voices ... I come upon an old grey house, dark and melancholy ... its pillars of marble standing on guard. I open the creaky door ... the sunlight has long faded and the shadows have cast their purple hue upon the panes ... but there is the sound of laughter, music and dancing ... the doughboys from 'over there' and the girls in WAAF blue are dancing to the strains of 'I'll be with you in apple blossom time', which wafts through the old house ... And I am looking for someone ... I search the four corners ... why, yes ... there he is, coming towards me, a tall, Nordic boy with his hand outstretched and calling my name ... and he waltzes me around and around ... and the air is filled with laughter ... and we are happy. Oh, so very happy ... And as I leave the airfield, I think how very lucky I am to have these memories ...

Indeed, they were memorable years. And for thousands of young men and women they were glorious years. They were the years of the sweethearts!

And now for that question again: If you asked them – the Kens and the Kathleens, the Margarets and the Mabels, the Joyces and Jeans – would they do it all again? What would they say? They would, no doubt, echo the words of former US infantryman Daniel Militello: 'YOU BETCHA LIFE WE WOULD!'

York
26 November 1989

Appendix: What Happened To Them All?

Did they all live happily ever after? Who knows what goes on when curtains are drawn and doors closed? We have seen already how happily events turned out for some sweethearts. Readers might like to learn what happened to others whose experiences are featured in the book. Briefly they are listed in alphabetical order for ease of reference.

Baguley, Mabel
Mabel and Bill Smyth were married in St Mary's Church, East Parade, Bradford, on 16 June 1945. They had the reception in the room above the Co-op and went for a week's honeymoon to Coombe Dingle, Bristol.

Whilst Bill was waiting to be demobilized, Mabel and her mother bought a house in Turner Lane, Bradford, for £275 (about a year's pay for a good joiner in those days), bought lino on the black market and furnished the house with money from Bill's gratuity from the Army.

And they lived happily ever after.

The author was pleased to be invited to a buffet dance to celebrate Bill's seventieth birthday on 30 November 1989.

Beeston, Brenda
Brenda's sailor husband, Phil, did not in fact go to the Far East after the wedding in 1943 but was posted to the Home Fleet instead. For the rest of the war he was tearing up and down the Channel beating up German E-boats.

They have now been together for forty-six years and have four beautiful daughters, two grandsons and seven granddaughters, for whom they are eternally grateful. Brenda is also mindful of the debt she owes her sister Eileen, who wrote to Phil after the damp parcel of letters had arrived and she had written to say that there was no point in carrying on the relationship.

Brenda now says: 'I nearly lost Phil eighteen months ago, when he had a heart attack, but he recovered and is with me still, and still looking after me – as he did all those years ago when he snatched me back from under the wheels of a double-decker bus.'

Brown, Stuart and Dora

They started their married life in a small Northumberland village and then, as Stuart's career in journalism progressed, moved to Edinburgh. He became news editor of *The Scotsman* and later its managing editor.

Stuart and Dora returned to the farm at Schönau exactly twenty-five years to the week after leaving it. They found it to be a drab, unhappy place, with nothing much recognizable of the old family homestead.

They still keep in touch with Jimmy Pegg, who married Olga when the pair of them reached Warsaw. For a short while they lived in Northumberland and then they went to Canada. In 1978 Stuart's fascinating account of his captivity in Poland and of his exciting journey home with Dora was published by Paul Harris of Edinburgh under the title *Forbidden Paths*.

Bygraves, Max

Max married Blossom, his lovely, slim WAAF, despite strong opposition from her mother, who thought Blossom deserved more than a mere airman with no trade or future when the war was over.

After the war Max went back to working on a building site. But not for long. An RAF officer, who was a famous London impresario and had directed some of the wartime shows that Max had appeared in, gave him the chance of a job with the BBC. From there he went to bandleader Jack Payne, who had turned impresario, and then Max never looked back.

How wrong mothers can be! Max and Blossom stayed together, despite being in a business not famed for happy wedlock.

The ups and downs of Max Bygrave's successful and colourful life can be read in his autobiography, '*I Wanna Tell You a Story*', published by W.H. Allen in Star Books, 1973.

Carmichael, Major Ian

Ian enjoyed his last few months in the Army working at 30 Corps Headquarters in Germany, where he was responsible for organizing entertainment for troops in the British Zone. In April 1946 his wife gave him a daughter, and in July the Army gave him a plain cardboard box tied with string in which were his demob suit, a mackintosh, a pair of shoes, one shirt and three matching collars.

So it was that at the age of twenty-six he had to start making his way again in the theatre. It was hard. He and Pym never had a holiday in fifteen years. They had no car, no fridge, no TV and only a hired radio. Soon Pym was pregnant again, and although Ian worked hard and steadily on the stage, money was always scarce.

His big chance came in 1955 with two films for the Boulting Brothers, *Private's Progress* and *Brothers in Law*. From then on, one success followed another. His name was nationally known. He played Jim Dixon in Kingsley Amis's best-seller *Lucky Jim*, and by this time money flowed freely enough for him to drive to the studios in his own Mercedes 300, feeling 'like a belted earl'. Actor Ian Carmichael had arrived. In style.

He is well remembered for a later film, *I'm All Right Jack* and for playing Bertie Wooster in Wodehouse's *The World of Wooster* in the TV series.

And of his marriage to the woman he had met only once before declaring he would marry her, he says, 'I have been incredibly lucky. I have had the most tolerant, steadfast and loving of wives, two most beautiful daughters and four enchanting grandchildren. Indeed Ian and Pym enjoyed more than forty years of happy married life before she died.

Today he lives quietly and contentedly in his Yorkshire Shangri-la.

Chappell, Min
Former ATS telephone-operator Min Chappell was sincere when she said goodbye to leading Aircraftsman Peter Jeffrey in Egypt that September 1945, promising to keep in touch. Peter had to serve for another five months before he got a boat home. By the end of March, he and Min were engaged; he started working for Cable & Wireless on the Embankment in London, and three weeks later they were married.

For close on forty years they enjoyed life together and, having no children, were free to travel extensively. Peter retired from work in 1982, and shortly afterwards Min was taken ill and died. He now looks back nostalgically on those days when they were young and in love, but also he is happy to reflect that, as they grew older, life was good too. His latest postcard to the writer came from Australia.

Collins, Barbara
As we have already seen in Chapter 10, Barbara married Stewart McCallum. They had two daughters and have four grandchildren. They went to live closer to Stewart's parents in the Perth area of Scotland, where they now enjoy quiet retirement and good health, apart from Stewart's recurring ear trouble which he attributes to his service in RAF Bomber Command.

Churchill, Randolph
He returned to civil life after the war with an OBE for his activities with the Special Air Service behind the lines with partisans in Yugoslavia.

Pamela and he were divorced on the grounds of his desertion beyond a period of three years. Pamela was awarded custody of their 5-year-old son Winston, now Conservative member of Parliament for Stretford, Manchester. Randolph then married the vivacious June Osborne: they quarrelled violently from the start but stayed together for the sake of their daughter.

He fell ill, had an operation on his lung and died nine days after his fifty-seventh birthday.

Culbert, Catherine

Finding that her marriage had broken up whilst she was in the ATS, Catherine signed on for further commissioned service with the WRAC. After a total of twenty-four years she left the corps and took on the management of a charitable home for the aged. There she met and married a man from the Forestry Commission. Both are now happily retired and enjoying an active life – as far as arthritis allows.

Dippnall, Margaret

The boy born to Margaret and Jim in Egypt is now forty-five years old. After leaving school he joined the junior leaders' course of the Royal Army Ordnance Corps and then at the age of eighteen went into the regular army. He served for twenty-two years and came out as a warrant officer 1.

Margaret and Jim now live in Heywood, near Manchester, where they have many friends, keep up with their ballroom dancing and have recently celebrated forty-seven years of happy marriage. As Margaret works about the house today, one of her favourite songs is still 'Love is all' – her reveille song in Egypt.

Edge, Jean and Paul

Paul, released from the RAF in September 1946, became manager of a textile firm at Alloa, not far from his old RAF station of Grangemouth. He and Jean had almost forty-five years of happy married life before he died just three days before their forty-fifth wedding anniversary. Jean still keeps in touch with many of her Fighter Command friends and lives now in the south of England.

She recently went back to her former Fighter Command station at Drem but found that it had reverted to being a turkey farm. Little remained to remind her of the exciting days of the early forties.

Ellison, Edna

Edna married and moved to another village in the neighbourhood of Ightfield where the two Czech paratroopers, Jan Kubis and Josef Gabchik, had visited her and her family before setting off to assassinate Reinhard Heydrich, former Gestapo chief and Reich Protector of Czechoslovakia. Though alone now, she still treasures the memory of all those happy days the two young lads spent with her and her sister Lorna and mother.

Hankinson, Ronald
Ronald Hankinson married Rosina Constantini, daughter of the family
who had sheltered him as an escaped prisoner of war in Italy, and their
daughter Maria was born in Italy in 1946. Ronald reported to the British
consul in Rome to register his daughter as a British subject but received
no co-operation whatsoever. It was not until 1952 that the British
authorities recognized the marriage.

From 1946 until 1952, Rosina suffered terribly in Italy at the hands of
the returning anti-British Fascists.

Eventually, when all other efforts failed, Hankinson wrote a personal
letter to Churchill and then another to the new prime minister, Attlee,
asking for their help in bringing Rosina and daughter to Britain. As a
result of these letters, the British consul in Rome was instructed to verify
the particulars of the case and to arrange necessary documentation. At
last all was settled, and Ronald and Rosina began to make their home
life in Liverpool. But all was not plain sailing there. His family, staunch
members of the Orange Lodge, ostracized him for having married a
Catholic, and his mother never spoke to him again until the day she
died, in 1984.

Ronald, formerly a senior male nurse, and Rosina live an active
retired life helping the mentally handicapped. They have their daughter
and two granddaughters to keep them busy too.

Hersey, Bill
Bill Hersey married Augusta, the French inn-keeper's daughter,
brought her mother over too from France and settled down to work on
the watercress farm at Addlestone. It seemed that a happy life now lay
ahead for them, but one disaster followed another. When Augusta gave
birth to a son in September 1941, he was mentally retarded. The
watercress farm was ruined by the excessive use of pesticide by a
neighbouring farmer. Augusta contracted cancer and died. The son is
now in a home for the mentally retarded. Bill died in his early sixties.

Kennedy, Kathleen
Kathleen's husband, Bill Cavendish, Lord Hartington, was killed in the
heavy fighting before Arnhem. Kathleen carried on with her work for
the American Red Cross and in time became once again a popular figure
in the London Social Season. In the spring of 1948 she took a holiday
on the Riviera with friends and was returning to Paris on the unlucky 13
May with her new friend, Earl Fitzwilliam, in his private plane when it
crashed into a mountainside. All on board died. Kathleen's father
hurried to the scene and was just in time to see the body of his daughter
being brought down. She was buried at Chatsworth, Derbyshire.

Kingdon, Jean

Jean married her Czechoslovakian sweetheart, went to live with him in Moravia and then was advised to leave as soon as possible because of the worsening political situation and the immient arrival of the Iron Curtain. John was to follow as soon as he gained his release from the Army. He was not given his release. Now Jean, in Britain, was a displaced person and had to report regularly to the police station. She applied for her British nationality and eventually went through the whole process of swearing allegiance to the king in front of a magistrate who said to her afterwards: 'You speak beautiful English, my dear.' Now Jean is herself a magistrate.

Three years after leaving Czechoslovakia she received a letter from John asking for a divorce. This went through, and she was given custody of the child. After twenty-one years bringing up the child and living on her own, Jean married again. Her new husband, Ewan, made a surprising suggestion after he retired. He asked if Jean would like to go to Czechoslovakia to meet her former husband. They went, met John and his family and talked of what they had done during the last twenty-odd years.

Recently, as part of their twenty-first wedding anniversary celebrations, Jean and Ewan made a round tour of Britain, and the writer was pleased to join them for part of their tour of Yorkshire in February 1989.

Lynn, Dame Vera, DBE

At the end of the war Vera Lynn returned from Burma very tired. Her husband, Harry, had been invalided out of the RAF, their home had been badly damaged by bombs. They bought a twenty-two-bedroomed house on the Southern Downs with 108 acres of land. Their baby was born in 1946.

Vera realized that she could not go on singing wartime songs and decided to retire. Harry needed a healthy outdoor job so they decided to begin a new career in market gardening. They soon found that raising food to sell at a pittance offered no future security at all. 'A lettuce we'd grown and packed would earn us a farthing,' wrote Vera. Consequently she went back to work on the stage, with Harry as her manager. Since then she has toured the United States, New Zealand and Australia. Though her appearances are now far fewer, they are always much appreciated. She readily supports ex-service charities.

The thrill of her life came with the accolade of Dame of the British Empire. But for all those who went to the war of 1939–45 she will always be remembered with so much affection as simply 'the forces' sweetheart'.

Niven, David

David Niven returned to California soon after the war ended, and began making films for Goldwyn and Universal. His wife Primmie joined him, with sons David and Jamie, in the charge of former ATS gunner Pinkie. 'I never could have imagined how happy I could be,' wrote Primmie some time after settling into the film-world routine.

One day David returned from a week's golfing with Clark Gable, Rex Harrison, Nigel Bruce and Ida Lupino to find that he and Primmie had been invited to a barbecue party at the home of Tyrone Power. After an early meal around the swimming pool they all went into the house. Someone suggested a game of sardines – an old children's game in which all the lights in the house are put out and a form of hide-and-seek is played. David was upstairs hiding under a bed when he heard Tyrone Power shouting, 'Come down quick! Primmie's had a fall.' In the dark she had opened a door in the hall thinking it was a coat closet. It was the door to the cellar. She had fallen down the steps and was lying unconscious on the floor. Though rushed to hospital immediately, she never really recovered and died a few days later.

Not long after Primmie's death, David met the top Swedish model Hjördis. Ten days later they were married. Apart from a six-week period of 'trial separation', when Hjördis left Niven to discover if she was still an 'individual', the marriage was a very happy one.

David made many more successful movies, although there were fewer demands for the part of the refined English gentleman he played so well. Later in life he achieved great success as a writer. His number one bestseller *The Moon's a Balloon* sold over 4 million copies.

David Niven died in 1988 of motor neurone disease.

Summersby Morgan, Kay

In 1973 Kay Summersby Morgan's doctors gave her six months to live. She stretched it into more than a year and wrote *Past Forgetting – My Love Affair with Dwight D. Eisenhower*. In it she told how in 1946 she went to Washington and saw Ike again. He wrote her a glowing testimonial for employment in the US Women's Army Corps. She was assigned to a small public relations unit in California – as far as one could get from Washington and still be in the United States.

When she left the Women's Army Corps, she went to live in New York, where she met Reginald Morgan. They married. She died in hospital in New York, and her ashes are scattered over the Irish acres on which she was born and grew up.

Townsend, Group Captain Peter

The former fighter pilot was sent to Buckingham Palace as equerry to King George VI in February 1946. On the afternoon of his arrival he was walking down a corridor of the palace when he met 'two adorable-looking girls, all smiles'. They were 17-year-old Princess Elizabeth, shortly to join the ATS, and 14-year-old Princess Margaret.

Townsend's marriage to Rosemary (after a whirlwind courtship) had broken up, and he had been awarded custody of the children. He remained at the palace for eight years and by 1952 Princess Margaret and he had 'found increasing solace in one another' – as he was later to write. They were very much in love, but the Establishment was opposed to the idea of marriage. Prime Minister Churchill advised the Queen that it would be disastrous for her to consent to the marriage of her sister with a divorced man. Furthermore, the Queen could hardly assent to Princess Margaret's marriage to a divorced man after the crisis caused by Edward VIII's abdication to marry divorcée Wallis Simpson.

Eventually, after much speculation in the national press, Peter Townsend left London on 15 July 1953 for duties with the embassy in Brussels. The fairy-tale love-affair was over.

Another then began. Peter Townsend met Marie-Luce Jamagne. She fell senseless at his feet when her horse crashed into a fence at a Belgian show-jumping competition. Townsend rushed to her aid and was invited to her house afterwards. He became a regular visitor. At forty-four, twice the age of Marie-Luce, he married her quietly at Boitsfort, Brussels. The happy marriage has produced three children, Marie Françoise, Marie Isabelle and Pierre.

Young, Jimmy

After the war the romantic life of the former RAF physical training instructor was not without its problems.

His professional career took off well. He starred as a singer and soon he was topping the charts – especially with the all-time hit 'Too Young'. In the sixties he established himself as a top disc jockey, and today his is one of the most popular voices on the air.

At first he would bear in mind the one line of advice given to him by his father: 'If they're good enough to sleep with, they're good enough to marry.' But then he found ' … that experience showed what nonsense it was'. Sweethearts came and sweethearts went. What was wrong with his love life? Philosophically he says: 'I frequently ask myself why I have never found real emotional happiness and the basic answer that recurs is that I have never had an anchor. There was my parents' broken marriage, and my leaving home, the war and the shunting around one lived as a serviceman, my own two marriages that crumbled, the continual touring with its frustrations and temptations!'

What he wanted is something we all want when it comes to the crunch. As he was to write: 'What in my heart I really wanted to do is settle down, but so far it has never been my fortune to find the right person to settle down with. I have been lucky, however, that the people in my life have been wonderful people.'

He must surely have the satisfaction also of knowing that he is loved by millions of listeners. He tells the remarkable story of his fascinating life in a book which surprises and sometimes shocks his radio listeners, called *J.Y.* (W.H. Allen, 1973).

References

1 'Wish Me Luck As You Wave Me Goodbye ...'

The following have contributed to this chapter in letters and/or interviews: Jean Kingdon, Margaret Dippnall, Joan Dunhill, Catherine and Martin Culbert, Jean Edge, Stuart Brown, Barbara Collins, Stewart McCallum and Audrey Brownlow.

1. Rose Fitzgerald Kennedy, *Times Remembered* (Collins, 1974)
2. Anita Leslie, *Cousin Randolph* (Macmillan, 1985)
3. Brian Roberts, *Randolph* (Hamish Hamilton, 1984)
4. Peter Townsend, *Time and Chance* (Collins, 1978)
5. The BBC programme *Portrait*, 16 October 1989
6. Vera Lynn, *Vocal Refrain* (John Murray, 1975)
7. Robert Dougall, *In and Out of the Box* (Collins, 1973)
8. Max Bygraves, *I Wanna Tell You A Story* (Star, W.H. Allen, 1977)
9. Jimmy Young, *J.Y.* (Star Books, 1974)

2 'After You've Gone ...'

Major Reginald Cooke, once the author's company commander, contributed information for this chapter.

1. Rose F. Kennedy, op. cit.
2. Field Marshal Montgomery, *Memoirs* (Odhams, 1956)
3. Ewan Butler and Selby Bradford, *Keep the Memory Green* (Hutchinson, 1950)
4. Intelligence officer's report in Basil Bartlett, *An Army Officer's Journal* (Chatto & Windus, 1941)
5. Walter Lord, *The Miracle of Dunkirk* (Allen Lane, 1983)
6. Charles Whiting, *The Poor Bloody Infantry* (Stanley Paul, 1987)
7. The author is grateful for detail of the story from Mr Terry Hersey, Bill's nephew, and from Bill's adopted sister, Mrs Ann Kinmond, and also from Richard Collier's excellent account, *The Sands of Dunkirk* (Dell Publishing, 1961).

3 'As Time Goes By'

Letters and conversations with the following: Jean Edge, Steve Guinell, Vera Cole, Pat Bridger, Ruth Nixon, Brenda Beeston, Diana Lee, Jenny MacKenzie, Catherine Culbert.

1. John Pudney, *Beyond This Disregard* (John Lane, The Bodley Head, 1943)
2. Peter Townsend, op. cit.
3. Chris Martin, in Vern Haughland, *The Eagle Squadrons* (David & Charles, 1979)
4. Ibid.

5. Margaret Sherman, *No Time For Tears* (George Harrap, 1944)
6. Chris Martin, op. cit.
7. Ibid.
8. W.E. (Johnnie) Johnson, *Wing Leader* (Chatto & Windus, 1956)
9. W. Simpson, *The Way of Recovery* (Hamish Hamilton, 1944)
10. Ibid.
11. Rose F. Kennedy, op. cit.
12. *Roberta Cowell's Story, An Autobiography* (Heinemann, 1954). Robert Cowell (once a Spitfire pilot, racing motorist, husband and father of two discovered after the war, when a violent emotional shock upset his glandular system, that his feminine characteristics became more marked. He sought advice from a Harley Street sexologist, accepted his femininity and underwent treatment. In 1951 his birth was re-registered, and Robert Cowell became legally a woman – Roberta Cowell.

4 *'Dancing in the Dark'*

Letters and conversations with the following: Joan Dunhill, Peter Johnson, Jean Kingdon, Catherine (Roberts) Swauger, Margaret Carmada, Joyce Rowland.

1. Ian Carmichael, *Will the Real Ian Carmichael ...* (Macmillan, 1979)
2. Lord Carrington, *Reflect on Things Past* (Collins, 1988)
3. Charles Whiting, *The Battle of Hurtgenforest* (Orion Books, New York, 1989)
4. David Niven, *The Moon's a Balloon* (Hamish Hamilton, 1971)
5. Sheridan Morley, *The Other Side of the Moon* (Weidenfeld & Nicolson, 1985)
6. Jane Waller and Michael Vaughan, eds., *Women in Wartime – The Role of Women's Magazines* (Rees Macdonald, Optima, 1987)

5 *'Yours'*

Letters and conversations: Edna Wilison, Mabel (Baguley) Smyth and Bill Smyth, Winifred Beaumont, Mary Osborne, Colin McGregor, Violet O'Brien.

1. Alan Burgess, *Seven Men at Daybreak* (Evans Brothers, 1960). Frau Heydrich confirmed this information in an interview with the author at Burg, and after the war Labour MP R.T. Paget said that the provocation of reprisals was the main aim of the Heydrich assassination operation.
2. *Woman's Own*, 10 December 1943
3. Stephen Francis, quoted by Jane Waller and Michael Vaughan, op. cit.
4. Betty Wason, *Miracle in Hellas* (Museum Press, 1943)
5. William Shirer, *The Rise and Fall of the Third Reich* (Simon & Schuster, New York, 1960)
6. Vera Lynn, op. cit.
7. Jill Allgood, *Bebe and Ben* (Robert Hale, 1975)

6 *'Love Is All'*

Letters and conversation: Margaret Dippnall, Catherine Culbert, Peter Jeffrey, Harry Claring.

1. Winston S. Churchill, *Memories and Adventures* (Weidenfeld & Nicolson, 1989)
2. Mary Soames, *Clementine Churchill*, (Cassell, 1979)
3. Sarah Churchill, *Carry On Dancing* (Weidenfeld & Nicolson, 1981)
4. Richard Collier, *Duce* (Collins, 1971)

5. Michael Denison, *Overture and Beginners* (Gollancz, 1973)
6. John le Mesurier, *A Jobbing Actor* (Elm Tree Books, 1984)
7. Jimmy Young, op. cit.
8. Maud Diver, *The Englishwoman in India* (1909) and Alexander Walker, *Vivien* (Weidenfeld & Nicolson, 1987)

7 'Let's Do It, Let's Fall In Love'

1. Leslie Frewin, *Dietrich* (Leslie Frewin, 1967)
2. J.M. Cowper, *The Auxiliary Territorial Service* (War Office, 1949)
3. C.V. Hearn, *Desert Assignment* (The Adventurers' Club, 1963)
4. Kay Summersby Morgan, *Past Forgetting* (Collins, 1977) and *Eisenhower Was My Boss* (Prentice Hall, 1948)
5. David Irving, *The War Between the Generals* (Allen Lane, 1981)
6. David Irving, op. cit.
7. Ibid.
8. Charles Whiting, *Patton's Last Battle* (Stein & Day, New York, 1987)
9. Roderick Owen, *Tedder* (Collins, 1953) and David Irving, op. cit.
10. David Irving, op. cit.
11. Ibid.
12. Ibid.
13. Harold Macmillan, *War Diaries* (Macmillan, 1984)
14. Alistair Horne, *Macmillan*, Volume 1 (Macmillan, 1988)
15. Ibid.
16. Ibid.
17. Harold Macmillan, op. cit.

8 'Che Sará, Sará!'

Letters and conversations: Nancy (Walley) Adams, Ken Barker, Ronald Hankinson.

1. Eric Newby, *Love and War in the Appenines* (Hodder & Stoughton, 1971). The story continues in Newby's *A Traveller's Life* (Picador, 1982)
2. Anthony Deane Drummond, *Return Ticket* (Odhams, 1952)
3. Charles Whiting, *Patton's Last Battle*, op. cit.
4. John Costello, *Love, Sex and War* (Collins, 1985)
5. John Verney, *Going to the Wars* (Collins, 1955)
6. With this spur-of-the-moment decision they avoided the 'vetting' process carried out by British Field Security, the Italian Pubblica Sicurezza and the *carabinieri* to which Allied personnel wishing to marry Italians were subject. At the same time, Ken avoided being sent back to his unit and into battle again. He had had enough of all that. Today, from time to time, the Ministry of Defence still puts out calls for deserters to report in, without incurring punishment, in order to 'clear the books', but few respond.

Like thousands of others in the Italian Army, Graziella's husband never came back.

9 'Going My Way?'

Letters and conversations: Lena McGaffey, June Seaton, Yvonne McIntosh, Sylvia Turner, Winifred Vallese, Mary Maycock, Kathleen (Parker) Williams, Betty Koch.

The author is indebted to Pat Morgan, editor of *Together Again*, the GI brides' magazine, for her great help in contacting so many of the GI brides mentioned in this book.

1. Jane Waller and Michael Vaughan, op. cit.
2. Ibid.
3. *News of the World*, June 1946
4. *Daily Mirror*, 16 August 1989
5. *News of the World*, June 1946
6. Elfrieda Shukert and Barbara Scibetta, *War Brides* (Presidio, New York, 1988)
7. Monica Dickens, *An Open Book* (Heinemann, 1978)

10 'Now Is The Hour'

Letters and conversations: Barbara Collins, Jean Edge, Sheila McCall, Ruth Negus, Catherine Culbert.

1. C.V. Hearn, op. cit.
2. Richard Collier, op. cit.
3. Interviews with Reichminister Albert Speer in Heidelberg, Foreign Press Officer Ernst (Putzi) Hanfstängl in Munich, and Hitler's personal servant Heinz Linge in Munich. Otto Strasser, one of Hitler's enemies and consequently not an unbiased witness, told the author how Geli Rabaul, one of Hitler's girlfriends, had wept when repeating to Strasser the perverse demands Hitler made of her. She was found dead later, in mysterious circumstances.
4. According to reports which the former Nazi chief of the foreign press department, Ernst (Putzi) Hanfastängl, repeated to the author in Munich, Hitler contracted syphilis as a young man in Vienna. See also Alan Bullock, *Study in Tyranny* (1952), p.392.
5. Subsequent research suggests that Hitler clenched his teeth on a glass cyanide phial the second before he squeezed the trigger of his 7.65 Walther pistol.
6. The Führer's evil dream of a Thousand-Year Reich which should stretch from Strasbourg to Riga and from Rostov to Trieste.
7. Eisenhower's naval aide, Captain Harry Butcher, said of Ike's condition then: 'The last four days of negotiations had taken more out of him than the past eleven months of the campaign' (*Three Years with Eisenhower*, William Heinemann, 1946).
8. Kay Summersby Morgan, both books previously cited
9. Details of the courtship and marriage of the royal couple can be found in the following: Elizabeth Longford, *Elizabeth* (Weidenfeld & Nicolson, 1983); Unity Hall, *Philip* (Michael O'Mara Books, 1987); Graham and Heather Fisher, *Consort* (W.H. Allen, 1980); Robert Lacey, *Majesty* (Hutchinson, 1977)
10. P.R.O. File Air 2/10919

11 'It's Easy To Remember'

Letters and conversations: Daniel Militello, Barbara Collins, Maureen Cope, Stanley Palmer, Catherine (Roberts) Swauger.

1. Stuart Brown, *Forbidden Paths* (Paul Harris Publishing, 1978), and in conversation with the author
2. *The Times*, February 1946
3. *Daily Express*, 18 September 1947
4. *Yorkshire Evening Press*, July 1985
5. BBC Television interview, 1989
6. Charles Whiting, *The Last Battle* (Crowood Press, 1989) and *The Poor Bloody Infantry*, op. cit.
7. Elfrieda Shukert and Barbara Scibetta, op. cit.
8. Personal interview with the author.
9. *Sunday Times* colour supplement, 1 October 1989

Bibliography

It would not be practicable to list all the books, files and documents I have read and referred to in my research; consequently only the main ones are given below.

Absalom, Roger, *Il Mondo Contadino Toscano e La Guerra 43–45, Passato e Presente* (Instituto Nazionale per la storia del Movimento di Liberazione in Italia, 1978)
Allgood, Jill, *Bebe and Ben* (Robert Hale, 1975)
Arbib, Robert, *Here We Are Together* (Longmans, Green & Co, 1946)
Bartlett, Captain Sir Basil, *My First War* (Chatto & Windus, 1941)
Beaumont, Winifred, *Detail on the Burma Front* (BBC, 1977)
Burgess, Alan, *Seven Men at Dawn* (Evans Bros, 1960)
Burns, John Horne, *The Gallery* (Secker & Warburg, 1948)
Butcher, Captain Harry, *Three Years with Eisenhower* (Heinemann, 1946)
Carmichael, Ian, *Will The Real Ian Carmichael ...* (MacMillan, 1979)
Carrington, Lord, *Reflect on Things Past* (Collins, 1988)
Churchill, Winston, *Memories and Adventures* (Weidenfeld & Nicolson, 1989)
Costello, John, *Love, Sex and War* (Collins, 1985)
Cowell, Roberta, *Roberta Cowell's Story* (Heinemann, 1954)
Cowper, J.M., *The Auxiliary Territorial Service* (War Office, 1949)
Crawford, Robert, *I Was an Eighth Army Soldier* (Gollancz, 1944)
David, Lester and Irene, *Bobby Kennedy* (Sigwick & Jackson, 1986)
Dennison, Michael, *Overtures and Beginners* (Gollancz, 1973)
Dougall, Robert, *In and Out of the Box* (Collins, 1973)
Eisenhower, Dwight, *Crusade in Europe* (Heinemann, 1948)
Fisher, Graham and Heather, *Consort* (W.H. Allen, 1980)
Frewin, Leslie, *Dietrich* (Leslie Frewin, 1967)
Hall, Unity, *Philip* (Michael O'Mara Books, 1987)
Harman, Nicholas, *Dunkirk – The Necessary Myth* (Hodder & Stoughton, 1969)
Haughland, Vern, *The Eagle Squadrons* (David & Charles, 1979)
Hohne, Heinz, *The Order of the Death's Head* (Secker & Warburg, 1969)
Horne, Alistair, *Macmillan*, Vols 1 and 2 (Macmillan, 1988)
Johnson, Derek, *East Anglia at War* (Jarrold, 1978)
Kennedy, Rose Fitzgerald, *Times to Remember* (Collins, 1974)
Lamb, Richard, *Montgomery in Europe 1943–45* (Buchan & Enright, 1983)
Lejeune, C.A., *Thank You For Having Me* (Tom Stacey, 1964)
Le Mesurier, John, *A Jobbing Actor* (Elm Tree Books, 1984)

Leslie, Anita, *Cousin Randolph* (Hutchinson, 1985)
Lewis, Norman, *Naples '44* (Eland Books, 1978)
Lewis, Peter, *A People's War* (Thames Methuen, 1986)
Longford, Elizabeth, *Elizabeth* (Weidenfeld & Nicolson, 1980)
Longmate, Norman, *The GIs* (Charles Scribner's Sons, New York, 1975)
Lord, Waler, *Miracle of Dunkirk* (Allen Lane, 1982)
Lynn, Vera, *Vocal Refrain* (W.H. Allen, 1975)
Macmillan, Harold, *War Diaries – The Mediterranean, 43–45* (Macmillan, 1984)
Masters, Anthony, *The Man Who Was M* (Grafton, 1986)
Miller, Joan, *One Girl's War* (Brandon, 1986)
Morgan, Kay Summersby, *Past Forgetting* (Collins, 1977)
Niven, David, *The Moon's a Balloon* (Hamish Hamilton, 1971)
Origo, Iris, *War in the Val d'Orcia* (Cape, 1947)
Reid, Ian, *A Game Called Survival* (Evans Bros, 1980)
Roberts, Brian, *Randolph* (Hamish Hamilton, 1984)
Selwyn, Victor, ed. *Poems of the Second World War* (Everyman, 1985)
Sherman, Margaret, *No Time For Tears* (George Harrap, 1944)
Simpson, William, *The Way of Recovery* (Hamish Hamilton, 1944)
Terry, Roy, *Women in Khaki* (Columbus, 1988)
Walker, Alexander, *Vivien* (Weidenfeld & Nicolson, 1987)
Waller J. and Vaughan, M. *Women in Wartime – The Role of Women's Magazines* (Macdonald, 1987)
Warren, John, *Airborne Operations in World War Two* (US Air Force Historical Division, 1956)
Wheeler-Bennett, John, *King George the Sixth, His Life and Reign* (Macmillan, 1958)
Whiting, Charles, *Poor Bloody Infantry* (Stanley Paul, 1987)
                     Patton's Last Battle (Stein & Day, 1987)
Winfield, Roland, *The Sky Belongs to Them* (William Kimber, 1976)
Wyatt, Woodrow, *Confessions of an Optimist* (Collins, 1985)
Young, Jimmy, *J.Y.* (W.H. Allen, 1973)

Index